PLANTING SEEDS OF THE DIVINE

The Jewish Publication Society expresses its gratitude for the generosity of the sponsors of this book:

The Pardes Institute of Jewish Studies, in honor of our cherished faculty member, Yiscah Smith, whose passion for teaching, love for Torah, authenticity, and deep sensitivity inspire us all; and whose esteemed work embodies our commitment to expanding access to deep Torah learning.

University of Nebraska Press | Lincoln

Planting Seeds
of the Divine

Torah Commentaries to Cultivate

Your Spiritual Practice

YISCAH SMITH

The Jewish Publication Society | Philadelphia

For customers in the EU with
safety/GPSR concerns, contact:
gpsr@mare-nostrum.co.uk
Mare Nostrum Group BV
Mauritskade 21D
1091 GC Amsterdam
The Netherlands

Library of Congress Cataloging-in-
Publication Data
Names: Smith, Yiscah, 1951– author.
Title: Planting seeds of the divine: Torah
commentaries to cultivate your spiritual
practice / Yiscah Smith.
Description: Philadelphia: Jewish
Publication Society; Lincoln: University
of Nebraska Press, [2025] | Includes
bibliographical references.
Identifiers: LCCN 2024054309
ISBN 9780827615717 (paperback)
ISBN 9780827619319 (epub)
ISBN 9780827619326 (pdf)
Subjects: LCSH: Bible.
Pentateuch—Commentaries.
Classification: LCC BS1225.53 .S5953 2025 |
DDC 222/.107—dc23/eng/20250219
LC record available at
https://lccn.loc.gov/2024054309

Set in Merope by A. Shahan.

A time is coming—declares the Sovereign GOD—when I will send a famine upon the land: not a hunger for bread or a thirst for water, but for hearing the words of GOD.

—*Amos 8:11*

The teachings of the Piaseczner Rebbe, Rabbi Kalonymus Kalmish Shapira (twentieth c., Poland), guide me along the sweet path that satiates my spiritual hunger and thirst to hear the words of GOD. His radical, refreshing, and redemptive teachings provide me with the spiritual bread and water I need in order to holistically sense the Divine Presence within me and around me. As I reflect on his sacred and encouraging words, I dedicate this volume to his memory. May the memory of the righteous be for a blessing.

Eternal our God, make the words of Your Torah sweet in our mouths and in the mouths of our descendants and the descendants of Your people.

—*Berachot 11b*

As I gaze into the future, I also dedicate this book to my wonderful and amazing children and grandchildren. Many times, visualizing them someday in the future discussing portions of my book, with each other and their friends, gave me the encouragement I needed to keep writing. This is my spiritual legacy to them, as I pray that the words of Torah remain sweet in their mouths.

CONTENTS

ACKNOWLEDGMENTS

I am forever grateful to my Blessed Creator for instilling within me the Divine Calling to write this book, and for giving me the capability to hear the calling and heed it. The Divine held me, inspired me, and guided me to bring this to fruition.

The call to write this volume began when, in January 2022, under the leadership of David Bernstein, dean emeritus at the Pardes Institute of Jewish Studies, I participated in Pardes's Jewish heritage trip to Poland. While standing at the gravesites of the Piaseczner Rebbe's mother, wife, and son at the Warsaw Jewish cemetery, in the bitter cold, wobbling on the frozen snowy ground, and paying homage to the Piaseczner Rebbe, Rabbi Kalonymus Kalmish Shapira, I sensed a seminal idea manifesting in my consciousness: God is asking me to write a book. The Piaseczner's radical, redemptive, and refreshing spiritual ideas came to salt and pepper the work. To David Bernstein I extend my deep gratitude for leading me to this momentous sacred moment in my life.

I remain especially grateful to Jonah Gelfand, my research and editorial assistant. His belief both in me and the book's vision, his commitment to see this project through to completion, and his devotion to never compromising his high work ethic have played a significant role in bringing this book to The Jewish Publication Society and the University of Nebraska Press. It has been a source of great joy and blessing to collaborate with such a talented, skilled, and kind person.

Each of the following individuals, in their unique way, helped me manifest my calling, as I moved from developing my ideas to writing the manuscript: Rabbi Levi Cooper, Rabbi Meesh Hammer-Kossoy, Rabbi Ariel Evan Mayse, Rabbi Leon A. Morris, and Joel Weiss. Thank you for supporting me, believing in me, and encouraging me.

I extend my gratitude to the Pardes Institute of Jewish Studies for supporting and encouraging me to heed the call to write this book, and for their generous donation to the volume.

To my friends, who from the generosity and kindness of their hearts, financially helped support my writing project. You were there for me when I needed you, and your support and belief in me is part of the reason I was able to bring my manuscript to completion. Thank you: the Arvai family, Christopher Carnrick, Yisrael and Marsha Donshik, Francine McMahon, the Nebenzahl family, the Röder family, Stephanie Rosekind, Rona Shaffran Tannenbaum and Dov Tannenbaum, Peter and Aviva Turner, Drs. Leslie and Michael Windman. Thank you also to John, Solomon, and those who wish to remain fully anonymous.

To two incredibly talented and special people, Elias Sacks, then director of The Jewish Publication Society, and Joy Weinberg, managing editor. Your patience, encouragement, wise guidance, insights, feedback, and your belief in my project have been invaluable to me—and will continue to be so. Thank you both for pushing me and challenging me with compassion and care. You both saw and expressed to me more than once how the world today needs to hear my Torah.

Eli, you worked with me from the very beginning, and generously shared your time with me, coaching, guiding, and suggesting your ideas, until the manuscript became ready for peer review.

And, Joy, a double thank you. As part of the behind-the-scenes process you diligently and patiently worked with me to bring out my creative best, helping me to appreciate how adding or changing one sentence, or even one word, can transform good writing into exceptional writing. But even beyond changing a word or phrase, you asked penetrating and challenging questions that helped me actually access and channel the Divine Presence, guiding me along this birthing process actualizing sacred potentials. And further, you provided suggestions and ideas to bring the practice section to a much wider audience of readers, extending far beyond people already engaged in spiritual practice. This can now reach many more seekers. I remain eternally grateful to you for believing in me.

I enjoyed every interaction with the both of you, and not only for the deep wisdom each of you possesses and so freely shared with me. You are two of the nicest and kindest people I have been blessed to meet and work with.

And thank you to the University of Nebraska Press staff for copublishing this volume. From the inception of this book, I prayed that a university press would see enough value to want to publish it. With the combined efforts of The Jewish Publication Society and the University of Nebraska Press, my prayer has come true.

Over the past several years, I have been leading monthly Shabbat morning spiritual gatherings in my ever-blossoming garden for people seeking a direct and personal encounter with the Divine. A rainbow of Jews—and, occasionally, non-Jews, who are always invited to join us—enjoy an alternative sacred space to celebrate Shabbat with like-minded souls.

As all of us, locals and visitors to Israel alike, settle in, I share a spiritual teaching on the weekly Torah portion, followed by a guided contemplative spiritual practice that leads into quietude, and, from there, a chanting of sacred melodies, a sharing of insights, and a concluding Kiddush lunch. Energies of connection, compassion, and community grow.

Through the years, a great number of participants have asked me essentially the same question: "Yiscah, can you recommend a book modeled after your Shabbat sacred gatherings?" "Is there a book of spiritual practices anchored in biblical texts and possibly even in the weekly Torah portion?" "Is there a book that will teach me hands-on techniques to encounter the Divine within me and beyond?"

For years, I replied, "Not to my knowledge."

But in January 2022, as I visited the family gravesites of the Piasec-zner Rebbe (Kalonymus Kalmish Shapira, twentieth century, Poland) in the Warsaw Jewish cemetery, I received the Divine Call to write this volume. It became clear that my own next step and a way for me to leave the world with my own legacy was to move from "Not to my knowledge" to "Yes, in fact, I am writing a book on this right now."

Our Dual Human Needs

We live in a consumer-based world that defines success, fulfillment, and happiness through the acquisition of physical goods, the assignment of titles to our names in recognition of specific accomplishments, and the accumulation of wealth and power. While these attainments can lead to an easier life, an easier life does not always equate with feeling successful, fulfilled, happy, and sustained.

On the contrary, I have found that feeling successful, fulfilled, happy, and sustained comes from different attainments: feeling connected to our authentic selves, and building an ongoing relationship with the Divine Presence deep within us. Just as we need to sustain our bodies—to ingest, chew, swallow, and digest healthy food and water—I am convinced that all of us need to sustain our souls in the same ways.

If we understand Judaism as a spiritual practice, then Judaism's sacred texts can provide the foundation for the "end destination" of experiencing uniquely intimate encounters with our Creator as manifested through the Divine Presence within each of us. This is why some of the Hasidic masters refer to Torah as *lechem and mazon* (bread and food) and *mayim* (water). We need to ingest, chew, swallow, and digest the Torah we intellectually acquire. Then, and only then, can the text move into the heart, allowing for our emotional and visceral encounter with the Divine. Internalized, heartfelt Torah knowledge vivifies and enlivens us spiritually, as healthy food and water vivify and enliven the body.

During the interwar period in Warsaw, a Hasidic leader, the Piaseczner Rebbe, observed that many of Warsaw's Jews believed in God, practiced Jewish observance with devotion, dedicated time to learning Torah, and attended prayer services in synagogue—and yet, seemed to lack awareness of the Divine Spirit within themselves. The sense of vitality he knew each of us has the capacity to experience within Judaism appeared absent. It was as if the Jews he knew were moving about without souls, as if they had stopped breathing.

Believing in the existence of the Divine was in itself insufficient because, he understood, our *emotional landscape* provides the pathway for each of us to experience the Divine Force both within and beyond us. While external acts of observance, study, and prayer play major roles in sustaining the Jewish people, the *internal experience* of a personal and unique encounter with the Divine is a Jew's spiritual umbilical cord with one's Creator.

Thirty years after the Piaseczner Rebbe's observation and across an ocean, the renowned artist Leonard Cohen similarly noticed: "We no longer believe we are holy. . . . There is an absence of God in our midst."[1]

The biblical narratives in Genesis portray the patriarchs and matriarchs as people who directly encounter God in their midst. In fact, Abraham's call to leave a culture steeped in idol worship is often understood as a call to leave the familiar for a yet-to-be discovered new and radical way of living with God, which he would teach to future generations: "For I [God] have loved him [Abraham], because he commands his children and his household after him that they keep the way of the ETERNAL, being righteous and just" (Gen. 18:19).

The Piaseczner Rebbe compares the painful experience of sensing distance from God to that of a child who yearns for a missing parent.[2] Spiritually, one may feel estranged and exiled from the deeper parts of oneself, without even knowing why.

By contrast, an encounter with the Divine may bring a sense of closeness and connection, and an open heart to experience the diverse and fluid feelings produced by the human condition. Quite organically, without force or manipulation, one may then begin sensing the Divine Presence in one's interactions with other people, too. Becoming sensitive to this Presence in human beings may enable this sense in our engagement with birds, fish, vegetation, trees, herbs, flowers, and plants as well—and eventually evolve into an awareness of the Divine Spark in soil, water, metals, gems, and other inanimate creations.

This can happen because the Divine Creator's presence within the individual is the same presence around and beyond the individual. The more I encounter this energy within myself, the more I sense the same externally. My essence, as a creation by God, is God. This perception of my essential being helps me foster connections with the same Divine Energy around me. Essence connects with essence as the God beyond becomes synonymous with the God within. The Zohar refers to the Divine Creator as a reality of both immanence and transcendence with the teaching, "The greatness of God . . . fills all worlds and encompasses all worlds."[3] Likewise, the prophet Jeremiah proclaims, "For I fill both heaven and earth—declares GOD" (Jer. 23:24).

This way of internally "being Jewish" can significantly affect how we externally "do Jewish." The behavioral expressions of Jewish tradition may now transform from seemingly robotic, stagnant, and lifeless actions to heartfelt and emotional experiences imbued with aliveness and fluidity. Observance of Jewish practices, prayer, and study may now be energized and permeated with soul and spirit.

Into the Soul

Becoming increasingly aware of the internal dimension to our lives brings us to our deeper selves—the domain of the soul.

Every human being is a duality. "The ETERNAL God formed a Human from the soil's humus, blowing into his nostrils the breath of life: the Human became a living being" (Gen. 2:7). The "soil's humus" creates the human being's physical body; "blowing into his nostrils the breath of life" gives the human being a spiritual dimension, a soul. Only after both exist together does the verse conclude that this creation is now "a living being."

The Hebrew words for soul and for breath are *neshama* and *neshima*, teaching us that we can experience our soul through the energy in our breath. Each time we inhale, the giving of the life force that was originally breathed into Adam and Eve repeats itself. Our own breathing cycle—receiving and returning breath as we inhale and exhale—invites us to become aware of the Creator's presence within us. We may also understand the nonphysical spiritual breath as the life force of our soul keeping our physical body alive—another awareness that can bring us closer to sensing the Divine Presence within us.

"What Is God?"

It is also true that those of us who strongly believe in God may still find it difficult to articulate what it is we believe in. Adding to this uncertainty, the Jewish tradition employs several names for God (or GOD): the Creator, the Eternal (or the ETERNAL), the Divine, and the Omnipotent, to name a few. How can a person cultivate an intentional awareness of God without some sort of understanding of what God means?

As someone who dedicates time daily to furthering my awareness of the Divine, I have long felt the urgency to answer the challenging "What is God?" question for myself. After grappling with this over decades, my conclusion is that there is no answer. The infinite Creator of all life cannot be defined within the parameters of limited language. God's infinitude transcends all attempts to pin God down through a human definition.

In this volume, I invite you the reader to consider, instead, "What is God for me?" I invite you to know God through your own lens, hopefully one of a curious explorer.

All the while, when I myself speak of "the Divine," or use another name, I am often specifically referring to my own understanding and experience of God. If the internal dimension is indispensable, I cannot do otherwise. I experience God as energy flowing within me—my mind, body, heart, and soul. Cultivating various practices of breath awareness sharpens my experience of the energy of life moving through me. My intuition speaks to me through the "still small voice" (1 Kings 19:12) of the Divine Presence. The voice invites my limited self to become more Godly and part of the Infinite. Without any supporting empirical evidence, I simply know the voice to be true—without doubt, without question, and even if I do not like the message.

This voice invites me to explore the deeper part of myself, where pristine truth dwells. This voice reveals clarity, direction on the path of my life journey, and the most creative energies in my being. This voice speaks spontaneously, without any advance notice—any attempt on my part to manipulate or force it to communicate with me fails. This voice opens the gate to my internal dimension: the dimension that includes inner serenity, trust, compassion, connection, wonder, closeness—and also total nakedness, defenselessness, and raw vulnerability. I trust this part of me—that regardless of how low the lows in my life may bring me to, somehow the internal dimension of my life will work out to the benefit of my spiritual well-being. I cannot overemphasize that this is purely subjective and may be unique to my experience, rather than an absolute dogmatic conclusion.

The voice I hear does not need me to recognize it. However, *I* need to develop the sensitivity to become aware of what is already occurring within me for my relationship with the Divine to be a real force in my life. As I do this, I begin to naturally sense the Creator's presence around me in all of Creation. For me, this voice that softly speaks from my deepest marrow captures what I mean by the word God and all the other names the Jewish tradition uses to refer to God.

Some readers may feel a resonance with other names, such as "the Force," "the Universe," "the Infinite Energy," or "_____." What I am strongly arguing for has less to do with identifying a name and more to do with cultivating an awareness of a nonphysical "something" within ourselves and the world—a "larger than me" mindset that the Jewish tradition refers to as God consciousness.

I invite you to replace the word "God" with whatever resonates with you. What is it you believe beckons you to be in service to advancing your own inner being and that of all other beings? What requires you to become a producer, rather than a consumer, to better the world?

Potential Readers of This Book

This book is addressed to all those who wish to explore their spiritual side, both Jews and non-Jews, both traditionally practicing Jews as well as Jews committed to nontraditional modes of Jewish practice. In casting a wide net, this book may prove useful to clergy and teachers who wish to address spiritual practices through a Jewish lens by delving deeply into the weekly Torah portions. Just as importantly, this book is meant to offer unaffiliated, spiritually seeking Jews who are unaware that the Jewish tradition contains a wealth of mystically infused texts and practices what I believe many of them hope to find in other people's traditions.

At the same time, since I myself have been inspired by other spiritual traditions (Tibetan Buddhism, First Nation North American spirituality, Christian mysticism), I know how valuable learning from other cultures can be. This book shares how the Jewish tradition can "be a light unto the nations" (Isa. 42:6, 49:6) by teaching all people how to be in relationship with the Divine and with the world at large. For non-Jewish theologians and clergy, this book addresses how awareness of a person's soul affects people's engagement with others and with the greater world. For non-Jewish laypeople, this book offers a spiritually informed way to live in the world and combat the growing crisis of separateness.

At its essence, this book is for people searching for other ways to live—with compassion, love, humility, and gratitude. It teaches how to live a more heart-driven and less power-driven life that approaches each human being as a creation in the image of the Creator.

Starting Your Inner Garden

Imagine yourself in the role of the gardener. The gardener is in service to care for all the trees, plants, bushes, and flowers, one at a time. The gardener diligently tends to the garden, ensuring that each plant receives the proper hydration, combination of sun exposure and shade, and type of soil conducive to its unique needs to blossom.

You, the reader—as a gardener—are invited to plant and cultivate your own unique inner garden with forty-seven assorted seeds that correspond to forty-seven weekly Torah portions.[4] Each seed contributes to the garden's beauty: the beauty of a higher God consciousness.

For each of these Torah portions, the volume offers you a "chewable," multitextured teaching that supports the prophet Amos's vision twenty-eight hundred years ago: "A time is coming—declares the Sovereign GOD—when I will send a famine upon the land: but not a hunger for bread or a thirst for water, but for hearing the words of GOD" (Amos 8:11). As you digest each week's nuggets, a process of internalization may begin to manifest in you, affecting you in positive and profound ways.

Middot as the Cultivator

As someone who spends significant time nurturing my physical garden, I diligently seek ways to refine and improve this physical work. Each of us can also continuously work on our inner, spiritual gardens, improving the ways we serve them best.

Jewish tradition prioritizes the refinement of one's behavioral traits and dispositions as essential to living an authentic Jewish life. In 200 CE, Rabbi Judah haNasi, the leading rabbinical authority in Israel at the time, codified in writing a guide for ethical and moral behavior, *Pirkei*

Avot (Ethics of the Fathers). Many centuries later, in nineteenth-century Lithuania, Rabbi Yisrael Lipkin Salanter founded Musar, a movement aimed at developing ethical and moral character, built upon ideas in classical rabbinical literature focusing on the refinement of *middot* (*middah* in the singular), one's emotional dispositions and character traits. *Middot* also describe the active behavior that infuse seemingly otherwise passive dispositions. For example, I may be naturally inclined to receive guests in my home. However, when I cultivate this inborn *middah* as a mindful way to connect with other people, then my behavior reflects the *middah* of hospitality, an important practice in the Jewish tradition. In our day, new streams of Musar are building upon Salanter's innovations.

This book considers *middot* primarily as resources in a person's spiritual toolbox—seeds to plant in our inner garden. Through this consciousness, *middot* extend far beyond becoming a good person or a good Jew. Refinements of our *middot* enable us to perceive God's world through God's lens, transforming us into Godly beings. As the Designer of all the *middot*, the Creator imbues the human being with the potential to reveal diverse ways of becoming Godly. Each *middah* teaches us how to "show up" in the world with more sensitivity and intention. Continued refinements become the means for strengthening inner awareness of and encounter with our souls. External ethical and moral behaviors can draw inspiration from our spiritual DNA—the inherent potential to not only be a good person, but to be a Godly one—hopefully bringing forth the blossoming of a magnificent garden of the soul.

As one example of how this works, we might consider the *middah* of forgiveness. All of us hurt each other, even unintentionally. Where hurt can compromise the integrity of a relationship, forgiveness can heal the ensuing pain. And forgiveness can be even more restorative on a larger scale, strengthening the fabric of any society that values healthy human relationships. Certainly the Jewish tradition places significant value on both seeking and granting forgiveness. In the daily morning prayer service, a section dedicated to confessing one's sins and then asking the Eternal to forgive plays an important role. On Yom Kippur, the Day of Atonement, forgiveness reigns as the paramount mood, and the tradition recognizes its seriousness by calling this holiday the holiest day of the year. For any and all of these reasons, the *middah* of forgiveness might be seen as contributing to each of us becoming a better human being.

Even more, this volume reveals spiritual and Divine manifestations in this *middah*. Forgiveness may enable us to manifest the Divine Presence in our lives (see "Va-yiggash: Seeking and Granting Forgiveness" in chapter 1, "Genesis"). As the Eternal forgives us, we can reflect this healing process by forgiving others. Forgiveness may now become a sacred act nourishing our intimate connection with our Creator.

Thus it is that each *middah*, as a planted seed that blossoms, may anchor our spiritual work in nurturing a sense of the Divine Presence in the world. All our gardening can be rooted in the delight of sensing the Divine Presence. The Jewish mystics call this the spiritual dimension of *Gan Eden* (the Garden of Eden)—in essence, the garden of spiritual delights.

Structure of This Volume

The volume is organized into five chapters: Genesis (Bere'shit—twelve commentaries), Exodus (Shemot—ten commentaries), Leviticus (Va-yikra'—seven commentaries), Numbers (Be-midbar—eight commentaries), and Deuteronomy (Devarim—ten commentaries).

Each of the forty-seven commentaries includes six components:

1. The name of the weekly Torah portion, followed by the *middah* of the week. For example: "Bere'shit—The Need to Connect with Others."
2. Selected verse(s) from the weekly Torah portion containing the week's *middah*.
3. "Where We Are": a brief summary of the biblical text as it unfolds from the prior Torah portion to the one under discussion, to familiarize readers with biblical narratives and traditions and contextualize the selected verse(s).
4. "At First Glance": traditional commentaries and Rabbinic narratives on the selected Torah verse(s), such as from the Babylonian Talmud (legal discussions and interpretations of biblical narratives by leading Rabbinical scholars in ancient Babylon, third–sixth centuries); the midrash (additional expansive Rabbinical exegesis interpreting biblical narratives, compiled primarily in the Middle East and northern Africa,

fifth–thirteenth centuries); renowned biblical commentators, including Rashi (Shlomo Yitzhaki, eleventh c., France), Ibn Ezra (Abraham ibn Ezra, eleven–twelfth c., Spain), Nachmanides (Moses ben Nachman, thirteenth c., Spain and Jerusalem), and Sforno (Obadiah ben Jacob Sforno, fifteenth–sixteenth c., Italy); and other thinkers, among them Rabbeinu Bahya (Bahya ben Asher ibn Halawa, thirteenth–fourteenth c., Spain), the Bekhor Shor (Joseph ben Isaac Bekhor Shor, twelfth c., France), the Hizkuni (Hezekiah ben Manoah, thirteenth c., France), the Me'am Lo'ez (Yitzchak ben Moshe Magriso, eighteenth c., Turkey), the Netziv (Naftali Zvi Yehuda Berlin, nineteenth c., Poland).

5. "A Deeper Dive": spiritually infused teachings primarily by the Hasidic and Neo-Hasidic masters that address each text's deeper spiritual dimension, opening pathways to encounter the Divine Presence (more on this below), as well as my own insights on advancing spiritual awareness and God consciousness.

6. "The Practice": emotional, experiential, and heart-centered spiritual practices involving visualization and breath work to help cultivate and nourish the spiritual teachings in "A Deeper Dive" (see meditative preparations for this weekly practice further below).

Annotations and the bibliography will hopefully give you a clear path to planting new seeds in your garden.

I would add that I see the volume as part of an expansive paradigm shift in which Judaism recognizes the legitimacy of each of our individual voices. As I share my own commentaries, understandings, and resources, may you the reader honor and elevate your voices and resources as well. In this way, week by week, may you begin to cultivate your own spiritual garden.

The Hasidic Masters and Their Spiritual Descendants

The radical stream known as Hasidic thought began in eighteenth-century Eastern Europe with the Ba'al Shem Tov (Israel ben Eliezer), who emphasized and encouraged the cultivation of spiritual closeness with the Divine Presence, regardless of a Jew's knowledge of Torah or level of observance. His innovative approach has been understood as the deeply needed spiritual resuscitation of a people in Europe who were barely surviving, both physically and spiritually, because of poverty, disease, pogroms, and antisemitic policies. The hope was that this novel way of being Jewish would begin to move the spiritual needle from barely surviving to thriving.

The close-knit circle of disciples of the Ba'al Shem Tov's teachings became the first generation of the Hasidic masters, known as the Hasidic rebbes. Their disciples are referred to as Hasidim, literally meaning "the pious ones."

In the interwar period, a new or Neo-Hasidic approach to both commentary and practice began to gain traction. The contemporary Israeli scholar Moshe Idel explains: "Neo-Hasidism and its reverberations are more concerned with a community that shares ideas, attitudes, and a richer and more variegated intellectual and spiritual life, while the older forms of Hasidism represent a community that is more interested in producing what I call 'performing bodies', with a lesser emphasis on belief and striving for an intense spiritual life."[5]

Ironically, the Ba'al Shem Tov's efforts to push back on the dry status quo Judaism in his time eventually became another dry status quo nearly two centuries later. This new void was then filled by the likes of Neo-Hasidic thought leaders such as Martin Buber, Hillel Zeitlin, Abraham Joshua Heschel, Zalman Schachter-Shalomi, Shlomo Carlebach, and Arthur Green, and, more recently, by thinkers (including women) such as Nancy Flam, Estelle Frankel, Shaul Magid, DovBer Pinson, Josh Feigelson, and Or N. Rose.[6] Insights by Buber, Green, Heschel, and Schachter-Shalomi, among others, enhance this volume. Sadly, I was unable to provide additional commentaries written by Hasidic women prior to the Holocaust for no other reason than that none were available.

Although the Piaseczner Rebbe himself was addressing traditional Hasidim, I understand his teachings as also imbued with Neo-Hasidism's emphasis on cultivating a spiritual life. He clearly challenged the status quo of "performing bodies" as an effective way to honor one's spirit.

My first teacher of Jewish meditation and contemplative practice, Rabbi Dr. James Jacobson-Maisels, suggests that the best way to understand Hasidism is through what he calls "a methodology of practice."[7]

He argues that the Hasidic rebbes, especially the Piaseczner, assumed you would be trying out their teachings in your own life, and so, to truly understand them, you have to implement them.[8]

Institute for Jewish Spirituality Executive Director Rabbi Josh Feigelson furthers this insight: "These great teachers of Torah were not only masters of the Jewish textual tradition, but, critically, interpreted Torah as a spiritual practice grounded in mindfulness. In this, they made Torah come alive: it is more than simply a set of interesting or provocative ideas; it is an eternal conversation and set of practices through which we reveal the Divine Presence that resides within and amongst us."[9]

"A Methodology of Practice"

I believe such "a methodology of practice" can respond deeply to the anxiety, depression, confusion, and sense of being overwhelmed so prevalent, if not accelerating, in our times. Rav Avraham Yitzchak HaKohen Kook (nineteenth–twentieth century, Jerusalem) says, "When we stop paying attention to the inner life of a person, everything becomes confusing and unclear."[10]

The objective of this book's practice, commonly referred to as the "sit," is to reclaim, restore, and renew a God consciousness through a personal and intimate experience with oneself. While the term "sit" itself derives from Western Buddhist communities, both Jewish and non-Jewish meditation modalities have come to integrate the practice of staying in a seated position for a dedicated time.

Our "sit" objective of exploring and discovering our deeper, Godly selves takes on added importance when we consider that the biblical narratives in Genesis describe leaders who dedicated time in seclusion to commune with the Divine. In particular, from the birth of Moses in Exodus until his death 120 years later at the end of Deuteronomy, we see a leader who appears to have spent more time in private solitude with God than with the public. Consequently, when we dedicate time for a "sit," we are not only opening ourselves up to experience God consciousness (as if that weren't enough!). We are simultaneously reclaiming an important part of the Jewish tradition that dates back four thousand years, even before the actual Giving of the Torah at Mount Sinai.

I have been reclaiming this ever-evolving practice for more than a decade, with unexpectedly amazing results. My daily "sits" have opened me up to deep religious experiences, times when I excavate precious gems of awareness of what always existed but was hitherto concealed, many moments when I too hear the "still small voice" of the Divine Presence, within and beyond.

I would suggest that readers approach each chapter's "sit" practice as a partnership with the text. It contains four steps:

1. *The practice of breath awareness.* This gently brings us into the present by directing our attention to our inner breathing cycle. As you inhale, imagine that God is breathing the breath of life into you. Try to experience that more than breathing yourself, you are being breathed into. In this sense the Supernal exhalation transforms into the earthling's inhalation.

Then pause for a moment to take in this moment of being alive, of receiving the gift of life through the breath. Try to open yourself to the idea that all of us are reliving Adam and Eve's original experience when they received the first breath at Creation.

Then, with gratitude for living, gently return this gift to God, understanding that it is not ours to keep. We do not own it; it is on loan. The earthling's exhalation now transforms into the Supernal inhalation.

As you empty your body of all its breath, pause for a moment to gaze at the absence of breath—observing how you experience this short moment of "death"—before beginning the breath cycle anew.

During these cycles, direct your awareness to the life-giving energy moving through you. Try to sense its movement, as it descends from the universe above, entering through the crown of your head and palms of your hands, moving through your body, into the core below the navel and further down your legs and out through the soles of your feet into the earth. Likewise, direct your attention to the life-giving energy moving from the core of the earth, entering your body through the soles of your feet, moving up through your core, ascending further as it leaves through the palms of your hands and crown of your head into the universe.

As contemporary meditation teacher Rav Dovber Pinson remarks:

> The process of simple, conscious breathing can teach us more about ourselves, about life and about the Divine creative process than all of the intellectual philosophies. . . . Breath meditation helps us to "unlearn" and awaken from the dream that we exist as an independent entity. Breath in the most overt way shows that we "need" the outside world for oxygen. Accordingly, we are thus able to see ourselves as one with the universe and the Ultimate Beingness that continues to give rise to the universe.[11]

Try to enter fully into your being-breathed-into cycles to enhance this opportunity. If you become distracted, as all of us do from time to time, consider using an anchor to bring your attention back to your breathing. An anchor is a physical experience that helps the practitioner remain centered and aware. For instance, you may place your hands below your navel with your fingers facing and touching each other. As you receive breath, your belly expands, and your fingers will naturally move apart from each other. As you return breath, the belly contracts and the fingers resume touching. Some find placing their hands on their heart helps them stay focused, as they feel their heart beating. Others focus attention on the subtle sounds of inhaling and exhaling through the nostrils. These anchors can sensitize us to the embodied experience in the "sit." Step 3 is also likely to be useful.

2. *The contemplative practice of text review.* Immerse your consciousness into the ideas in the text as you review and reflect on the week's *middah*. Dedicate time to contemplating how these teachings inform your personal self—mind, body, heart, and soul. Be encouraged to see your individual self in the text, and then to find the text within you.

3. *The practice of quieting down the mind.* While immersed in your breathing cycle and thoughts, integrate the "quieting down the mind" method designed and taught by the Piaseczner Rebbe, a technique

to help the practitioner gain spiritual control over one's never-ending onslaught of diverse thoughts, each competing for attention.[12]

First, direct your awareness to whatever thought is most strongly moving through your mind at this moment. With nonjudgmental curiosity, ask yourself, "What am I thinking?"

Now, explore and expand this one thought in both breadth and depth. This should naturally begin to slow down the torrent of many other thoughts anxiously vying for your recognition.

From here, you can move into a more relaxed, reflective, and responsive (rather than reactive) state.

As you become aware of a quiet emptying out, fill the new empty space in the mind with a thought expressing spiritual awareness, such as by gently repeating a phrase from the Torah. The Piaseczner Rebbe suggests you choose a verse that helps you connect with the spiritual part of yourself, such as "The ETERNAL alone is God; there is none else" (Deut. 4:35). Recite your chosen verse (the Jewish version of a mantra) repeatedly until you sense it is filling up your consciousness. The experience may feel sacred. As the American writer and translator Stephen Mitchell puts it, "The point of all spiritual practice is to wake up from the dream of a separate self."[13]

Now,—as an experiential practice to help you plant, cultivate, and nurture the *middah* of the week—seek guidance from God to help you refine those parts of your personality touched upon in the week's *middah* that need more attention. Reaching out to the Divine now may also help you become more aware of and present for a relationship with the Divine.

The Piaseczner would bring the practice to a close by repeatedly chanting Psalms 86:11, "Teach me Your way, O ETERNAL One; I will walk in Your truth; let my heart be undivided in reverence for Your Name," set to a beautiful melody. You might adopt this or another verse in song, or conclude by chanting a deeply resonant melody without words.

These first three steps apply to all of the commentaries. You may wish to bookmark their pages now, since, as you will later see, within each practice section of the forty-seven commentaries, you will be encouraged to reference these pages to begin the initial three phases of the practice.

4. *The middah practice.* The fourth step is the central focal point in each portion's practice, intended to cultivate the specific *middah* of that portion and awaken one's inner being and connectedness to the Divine in ways that academic review of the selected verse and *middah* cannot. Imaginative visualizations invite you to express yourself creatively and fully, in the past, present, and future, without externally imposed boundaries.

Throughout the *middah* practice, invite yourself to gently move away from what may sometimes feel like a dulled and closed heart to sense open-heartedness and vulnerability. The practice becomes the path to connect with the weekly teachings in your own subjective, emotional, and spiritual way, one that requires less judgment and more openness to possibilities.

To maximize the effect of each week's practice, visit this daily for at least five minutes during the week of the Torah portion, like a gardener paying day-to-day attention to the garden. Since more than five minutes are needed to practice all the steps, choose the step that seems to resonate with you most each day. Or, perhaps, depending on your mood or schedule, you may wish to "sit" for more than five minutes some days and combine a few steps. Feel free to customize your daily practice as it feels meaningful and possible.

As you become acclimated to daily practice, the door opens to many variations. Consider bookending your day by visiting your inner home for five minutes soon after waking up and for five minutes before going to bed. Perhaps on Shabbat or days when you have more free time, spend a little more time (many meditation guides suggest twenty minutes) on your practice.

Guidance for the Gardener

Just as my work in my physical garden never really ceases—requiring daily intention and attention—likewise the spiritual garden I cultivate through my practice requires ongoing care. A midrash suggests this ongoing engagement between the gardener and the garden: "When the Holy Blessed One created Adam, He gave him all the trees in the Garden of Eden and said, 'See how beautiful and praiseworthy My deeds are. Everything that I have created, for you I have created, take care not to spoil and destroy the world.'"[14]

Rav Ya'akov HaLevi Filber, a contemporary Israeli rabbi, comments on this midrash: "The role of the human being is not merely to abstain from spoiling and destroying the Blessed Holy One's world, because the human being was not created in order to be a passive creation who does not make nor create anything. Rather the fundamental role of the human being is to enhance and complete the world."[15]

The prophet Isaiah compares a person's soul to that of a plant in a garden, proclaiming in reference to the people of Israel, "They are the shoot that I planted, the work of My handiwork in which I glory" (Isa. 60:21). Commenting on this verse, Moshe Alshich, the Alshich HaKadosh (sixteenth century, Turkey and Safed, the Holy Land), sees God as saying, "The soul in each person's body is the shoot that I have planted with My own hands, the spirit that I drew from under My Throne of glory."[16]

Expanding upon these teachings in light of this volume, I encourage readers to see the Divine Creator as having gifted each of us with a "starter garden" of basic *middot* that we can plant and cultivate. As we do, we may increasingly sense the Presence of the Divine, similar to the physical garden that reveals the Presence of the One in nature.

Rebbe Nachman of Breslov (eighteenth century, Ukraine) even compares conversing with the Omnipotent to making a bouquet out of the beautiful plants we have gathered in our garden.[17] Planting seeds of the Divine can blossom into beautiful bouquets. And, as with my own garden, we not only add; we prune, we weed—we pay attention to cultivating and gently letting go in ways that become a mindful practice in of itself.

A Blessing for You

I hope you will view this book as an infusion of spiritual oxygen of sorts: a hands-on how-to guide for cultivating your spiritual practice—one

Torah portion at a time, one *middah* at a time, one week at a time, one day at a time, one minute and even one moment—this moment—at a time.

Ve-zo't ha-berakhah—and this is the blessing: You, the reader, now have before you a packet of assorted *middot* to plant in your own spiritual garden. The Torah commentaries that follow are your guide to uniquely plant the seeds of the Divine. May the Gardener of all gardeners bless your garden with all the beauty that you hope and dream for, and as it takes root, may your higher consciousness of the Divine blossom.

NOTES ON TRANSLATIONS

1. Unless otherwise noted, all biblical verses follow THE JPS TANAKH: Gender-Sensitive Edition (otherwise known as RJPS, the Revised Jewish Publication Society translation of the Hebrew Bible), issued in print and on Sefaria in 2023.

2. Generally speaking, RJPS adopts the following approach to divine names: The tetragrammaton (YHVH) is typically rendered as "GOD" (in small caps). Other words for God (such as Elohim) are typically rendered as "God." When these terms appear together (e.g. as YHVH Elohim), they are typically rendered as "the ETERNAL God" or "the ETERNAL your God" (with " ETERNAL" in small caps). For further details, see the "Preface to the Gender-Sensitive Edition," xvi–xviii (also available at purl.org/jps/rjps-preface).

3. Unless otherwise indicated, either in the notes or the bibliography, almost all of the other quotations in the commentaries and in the introduction have been translated by this author from the original Hebrew.

4. This volume adheres to the policy of maintaining the original Hasidic masters' God terminology in quotations, to be faithful to how they themselves saw the world. Elsewhere, the commentaries do not gender God, so that readers can experience God however they themselves experience God.

PLANTING SEEDS OF THE DIVINE

1

Genesis (Bere'shit)

Bere'shit

The Need to Connect with Others

> And God created humankind in the divine image, creating it in the image of God—creating them male and female. . . . The ETERNAL God said, It is not good for the Human to be alone.
>
> Gen. 1:27, 2:18

Where We Are

The six days of Creation bring us to the formation of the human being. Every physical entity—from light to animals—precedes this moment.

The formation of the world comes to completion on the seventh day with the introduction of Shabbat—the appointed day of rest.

At First Glance

God creates the human being in the singular, but all other creations (e.g., schools of fish, blades of grass, granules of sand) in the plural. Why?

In the Mishnah, the Rabbis discuss why the human being was created in the singular:

> It was for these reasons that the human being was created as one person: (1) Scripture teaches that anyone who destroys a life is considered to have destroyed an entire world; and anyone who saves a life is considered to have saved an entire world. (2) And also to promote peace among the creations, so that no person would say to their friend, "My ancestors are greater than yours." (3) And also, to express the grandeur of the Holy One blessed be He: For a human being strikes many coins from the same mold, and all the coins are alike. But the King, the King of Kings, the Holy One blessed be He, strikes every person from the mold of the First Person, and yet no

person is quite like the other. Therefore, every person must say, *bishveli nivrah ha'olam* — "For my sake the world was created."[1]

On the above teaching that each person is obligated to say that "for my sake the world was created," Rashi (Shlomo Yitzhaki, eleventh c., France) comments: "That is to say that I am as important as an entire world, and therefore I would not diminish the world through sin; rather, I will enhance the world through good deeds."[2]

And yet, might this teaching foster arrogance and a sense of inflated self-importance? There must be another way to understand this.

A Deeper Dive

By unpacking the letters of the word *bishveli*, the Ba'al Shem Tov (Israel ben Eliezer, eighteenth c., Ukraine) teaches that it does not only mean "for my sake," but also can be read as *b'shvil sheli*, "in my path."[3] In other words, the human being had to be created in the singular to highlight that each one of us has our own unique path. Hence, as the Mishnah teaches, each of us is obligated to say, "For in my path, the world was created."

With a mix of relief and gratitude, I view this as the Creator's expression of a world that leaves no one out. There is more than enough room for each of the world's inhabitants to follow a unique calling and customized path.

This may be the ultimate proclamation of the all-inclusive space that many of us desire. God's world contains space for every human being. God's world does not exclude anyone.

Several generations after the Ba'al Shem Tov, Reb Simcha Bunim of Pryscha (eighteenth–nineteenth c., Poland) expands this idea through a comment on the following Mishnah: "Rebbe said, 'What is the *derech* — "path" — of integrity that a person should choose for oneself? Whatever brings beauty to the doer and invites beauty from the world around them.'"[4]

"That is to say," Reb Simcha Bunim comments,

that the soul of each individual has its own style in the service of God, in the performance of Torah and commandments, which he should not change [due to societal expectation]. Therefore, he should not take a path that is not special or unique to him, even though he greatly admires the way of service of another individual; he must hold fast to his path. And that is the proof that his path is true. And this is the sense of the above Mishnah that he has a path for himself that is correct for him by which he holds. Nevertheless, he can praise and admire the path of his fellow.[5]

Rav Kook (Avraham Yitzchak HaKohen Kook, nineteenth–twentieth c., Jerusalem) suggests that "everyone should greatly cherish one's own unique path."[6] Elsewhere he points out that "true *shalom* — peace — is impossible without appreciating the value of pluralism intrinsic to *shalom*. The various pieces of peace come from a variety of approaches and methods that make it clear how much each one has a place that complements another. Even those methods that appear superfluous or contradictory possess an element of truth that contributes to the mosaic of *shalom*."[7]

Returning to Reb Simcha Bunim: "Thus, for a person to embark on a path of truthfulness requires not only the analytical demand for self-awareness, but the spiritual acumen to recognize that there is a spark of the Divine within each person."[8]

While these teachings may help diminish the above concern that focusing on one's own uniqueness may lead to arrogance and an inflated sense of self, other concerns may arise. For one, even if a person intellectually agrees that it is good to cultivate an awareness of the Divine Spark in other people, might that person ultimately choose to focus solely on cultivating oneself instead?

In Genesis 2:18 we learn: "It is not good for a person to be alone." In light of the previous verse, we might ask: Why is this so? Why is it not good for a person to be alone, especially since this is how God created each of us? Aside from the utilitarian biological, economic, and psychological reasons, we might contemplate the answer to this through a spiritual lens.

Biblical scholar and linguist Nechama Leibowitz (twentieth c., Israel) observes that not only is it not good for an individual human being to be alone; it is also not good for all of humankind. An essential word in this verse, *he'yot*, is usually translated as "to be"—hence, "It is not good for a person *to be* alone"—but, she says, "to be" is not the most precise translation. *He'yot* is more accurately translated as "existence"—and as such, the teaching is better understood as "It is not good for existence for a person to be alone."

From this, a teaching often attributed to Leibowitz explains that God created each of us as an individual with the inherent *need* to be in relationship with another, to connect with another and to share with another.[9] This simultaneously benefits both the individual and all of humankind.

In bringing these two verses together, where each one complements the other, we may come to realize that each of us is created to explore, discover, encounter, honor, and express our unique inner selves by walking our unique path. Each of our lives possesses inherent value with its own God-bestowed life journey. And this very sense of our individual unique self becomes the most precious gift we can offer another human being.

In fact, through a spiritual lens, the purpose of all of Creation was, and continues, to bring and reveal relationship, closeness, and connection—with oneself, with God, with other human beings, and with all of God's creations. Each time one enters into a relationship with another, one is actually advancing Creation to its next stage, by bringing healing and purpose to the world as a cocreator with our one Creator.

The Practice

1. Begin with breath awareness.
2. Then, reflect on the text.
3. Move to quieting down your mind.

These three steps are explained in detail in the introduction.

4. Visualize what your ideal path in life would look like. Consider your options. What are your thoughts? What feelings awaken for you?

Seeing it as a physical path, visualize yourself as a curious hiker. You've received the opportunity to explore any landscape of your choice. What would be your dream scenario? What would awaken your passion? What do you believe is worth your dedication? Climbing up a challenging, winding mountain trail in a thick, wooded forest? Walking far along a quiet beach hearing the crashing waves as they meet the shore? Or . . . ?

As you begin to venture out on your chosen path, how do you imagine you will feel? How would you like to feel? And as you meet fellow travelers moving along their own paths, envision that at any intersecting point, the sense of connection enhances your own joy—as if the two of you are excited to share your stories of your individual path with each other. This intersecting, encountering, and sharing with each other brings you closer to each other. And you then realize it was only because you were on the path that is your ideal path, the path that the Divine calls you to embark on, the path that brings inner joy, that you are able to share your inner joy with others who are on their unique paths as well.

Reflect on this, examining it as a curious observer. What are you thinking? How are you feeling?

How does it feel not to connect—and then to connect?

Noaḥ

Talking to the Divine

Make an opening for daylight in the ark.

Gen. 6:16

Then GOD said to Noah, "Go into the ark,
with all your household."

Gen. 7:1

Where We Are

The six days of Creation bring us to the formation of the human being.
Every physical entity—from light to animals—precedes this moment.
The formation of the world comes to completion on the seventh day
with the introduction of Shabbat—the appointed day of rest.

Adam and Eve are expelled from the Garden of Eden for having eaten
from the forbidden Tree of Knowledge of Good and Evil. Eve gives birth
to two sons, Cain and Abel, and when they are grown Cain kills Abel.
Ten generations after Adam, humanity's evils abound. God decides that
the depravity must be destroyed so that a new world can emerge in its
place. He calls Noah, the righteous one, to build an ark and populate it
with pairs of all living creatures. Noah, his family, and their menagerie
will act as progenitors of this new world.

At First Glance

In his commentary, Rashi (Shlomo Yitzhaki, eleventh c., France) wonders
why God commanded Noah to build an ark when there were so many
less painstaking ways to save him. Rashi offers a talmudic explanation:
"so that the people around him had time during the 120 years it took

Noah to build the ark to ask 'What do you need this for?' and so that he might answer them, 'The Blessed Holy One is about to bring a flood upon the world'—perhaps this may cause people to reconsider their mean-spirited behavior."[1] Even in this ultimate judgment, God leaves space for a turning toward good.

As this first section of this parashah (Torah portion) continues, we read a detailed description of how Noah is meant to build the ark. In the midst of these instructions, Noah is told to make a *tzohar*. What exactly is a *tzohar*? Its root denotes some form of light, and that makes sense: while living inside the ark for a prolonged period of time, Noah's family and all the animals would need to be able to see. But what kind of light was it? Rashi observes: "Some say this was a window; others say that it was a precious stone that gave light to them."[2] Ibn Ezra (Abraham ibn Ezra, eleventh–twelfth c., Spain) holds that *tzohar* specifically "means an opening through which light would enter."[3]

And yet how could one window, or precious stone, or opening illuminate the entire ark, three hundred cubits long, fifty cubits wide, and thirty cubits high (even if a cubit's exact measurement remains unclear)?

This apparent disconnect may drive us to search for an additional understanding—one that may lead us to uncover the hidden *middah* of talking to God.

A Deeper Dive

The Ba'al Shem Tov (Israel ben Eliezer, eighteenth c., Ukraine) teaches that the word *teivah*, normally translated as "ark," can also mean "word." By reversing the order of the first verse quoted above ("Make an opening for daylight in the ark"), he understands the verse to also mean, "Let the *teivah*—word [of Torah and prayer]—*matzhir*—radiate light."[4]

This type of light would seem to convey a depth of understanding: a sense of clarity, spiritual illumination, and awareness, as in the phrase, "Oh, I see. . . ." In other words, the words of Torah, and the words of prayer, will guide us, nourish us, and heal us.

Through the Ba'al Shem Tov's teaching, we can understand the Creator's invitation to "come into the *teivah*" as "come into the word of prayer." There, we will find tranquility. There, nothing will extinguish our eternal flame—our love for the Divine. And there, too, we will be safe—from the waters of the flood.

We might arrive at this spiritual teaching by another pathway. Song of Songs (8:7) exhorts, "Vast floods cannot quench love, Nor rivers drown it." Rabbi Shneur Zalman of Liadi (eighteenth–nineteenth c., Belarus) explains: the vast floods refer to our preoccupation with earthly matters—financial sustainability, health-related issues, family, and other relationship issues.[5] The love that cannot be quenched is understood as the love for the Divine embedded in each of us.

But how do we go about "entering the ark" to survive the flood and experience this love? The great-grandson of the Ba'al Shem Tov, Rebbe Nachman of Breslov (eighteenth–nineteenth c., Ukraine), teaches the spiritual practice of *hitbodedut*. The word itself means "to cause oneself to be alone." Rebbe Nachman would stress to his followers the importance of dedicating a significant time each morning to talking to God alone.

Ideally, he and his followers would enter a forest alone or otherwise seclude themselves wherever they could speak from the heart, opening themselves to uninhibited, unfiltered, pure connection to God. Yet *hitbodedut* was not intended to replace traditional participation in the daily communal morning prayer service. Rather, Rebbe Nachman intended for *hitbodedut* practice to precede the codified morning service in synagogue.

However, the Piaseczner Rebbe (Kalonymus Kalmish Shapira, twentieth c., Poland) pointed out that holiness could not necessarily be summoned by set schedule. "Quite commonly, when we pray there is no inner motion to holiness, as one may not be ready to awaken spiritually," he lamented. "[Similarly,] the times when we do feel moved and alert we do not pray, as it may not be the set time for prayer."[6] Taking this understanding to heart, many modern Jews have come to engage in *hitbodedut* practice at any time during the day when they feel inspired.

Zev Wolf of Zhitomir (eighteenth c., Ukraine) teaches as well that there is no one way to come into your *teivah*. When, he says, God tells Noah to "take of everything that is eaten and store it away, to serve as food for you and for them" (Gen. 6:21–22), this "is hinting at the varied possibilities of awakening within this service of prayer."[7] Some Jews may experience spiritual awakening from a prayer established in the prayer book. Others may hike in the woods or walk on the beach or sit at home. Likewise, some will awaken in community and others may awaken in solitude. Most importantly, the Divine invites each one of us to be in conversation, and in a way that speaks from the heart.

The Practice

1. Begin with breath awareness.
2. Then, reflect on the text.
3. Move to quieting down your mind.

These three steps are explained in detail in the introduction.

4. Visualize this scenario: You arrive at synagogue (or any other venue for communal prayer) one morning to pray, feeling more obligated than eager. You pronounce every prayer in the prayer book somewhat robotically while keeping pace with the community. From time to time, you notice your mind wandering to home concerns, business concerns, health concerns, family concerns, on and on. When the service ends, you close the prayer book, wish everyone a nice day, and leave. *How do you feel?*

Now, visualize the next scenario: You move through your day, maybe as robotically as you prayed in synagogue that morning, when suddenly, unexpectedly, you become aware of feeling deeply broken-hearted and overwhelmed. You seek out a moment to be with yourself. The call to pray surfaces. It feels as if the Divine is inviting you to honor this moment—to enter into your own ark, your own *teivah*, with your own words. Suddenly, you find yourself speaking to the Creator, your words rising spontaneously within you. *How do you feel?*

And now visualize the concluding scenario: Over the past weeks, you have been cultivating a "speaking to God on my own when troubled" practice. Now, you enter a synagogue or other communal prayer venue for morning prayers and hear yourself whisper the Piaseczner's teaching, "When you undertake this practice, you won't ignore even a sigh, because even with a simple, slight sigh about this-worldly matters, a sigh that comes from within your *heart*, the heart of the Israelite, you can attain a great revelation of your soul and bring her closer to God."[8]

How do you feel?

Lekh Lekha

Taking Our Next Step

> GOD said to Abram, "Go forth from your native land and
> from your father's house to the land that I will show you."
>
> Gen. 12:1

Where We Are

God promises Noah that a flood will never destroy the earth again. As the world begins to rebuild, people (who all speak one language) build the tower of Babel, intending it to reach the heavens. God disperses them all over the world with different languages, halting the project. Ten generations from Noah to Abraham are recorded. Abraham marries Sarah.

Abraham hears God's call to leave his country, home, and family. God guides him to go to Canaan and promises to give the land to his offspring. Abraham and Sarah then go to Egypt and return to Canaan. God now promises that Abraham's offspring will be as numerous, indeed uncountable, as the dust of the earth.

At First Glance

Abraham's willingness to follow God's word is often thought to exemplify how to be in service without thought of reward. The most common translation of *lekh lekha* is an adamant "go!" or sometimes "get thee out!" Yet Rashi (Shlomo Yitzhaki, eleventh c., France) comments that, grammatically, the command *lekh lekha* is literally "go on behalf of yourself" and adds the clause, "for your own benefit and for your own good."[1] He asserts that the call continues, "There I will make from you a great nation while if you stay here you will not merit the privilege of having children. Furthermore, I shall make known your character throughout the world."[2] In other words, Abraham's service did involve a reward. By honoring the command, he would gain wealth and fame, and become a blessing.

The Netivot Shalom (Sholom Noach Berezovsky, twentieth c., Israel) resolves this apparent contradiction by teaching that from Abraham's vantage point, receiving a reward was not a consideration. Out of his strong love for God, Abraham felt compelled to obey whatever God commanded him to do, and he did not even consider that by responding to God's command the very next verse ("And I will make of you a great nation; I will bless you and make your name great and you shall be a blessing") would be fulfilled.[3]

Complicating the matter, Pirkei Avot tells us that "Our father Abraham was tried with ten tests and he withstood them all."[4] Maimonides (Moses ben Maimon, twelfth c., Spain and Egypt) lists *lekh lekha* as the first test.[5] It is reasonable to imagine Abraham feeling challenged in leaving everything familiar behind in order to set out for an unknown destination of God's choosing. Still, how could this be considered a test, if Abraham is following God's command out of sheer love for the Divine?

Perhaps Abraham's test is not so much about his obeying God's call for action, but something else.

A Deeper Dive

The midrash hints at what that might be with a beautiful analogy: "What did Abraham resemble? A vial of perfume closed with a tight-fitting lid and lying in a corner, so that its fragrance was not disseminated; however, as soon as it was shaken up and the lid removed, the beautiful fragrance spread out into the world."[6]

This midrash understands Abraham's calling in Lekh Lekha as invitation to encounter his deeper self, his inner truth. Employing the metaphor of a sealed vial of perfume, the midrash surmises that as long as Abraham remains in his familiar environment, he will never venture to discover his beautiful internal fragrance — his inner essence waiting to be released. And, continuing with this metaphor, his inner essence involves opening up himself to himself, and then disseminating his newly discovered truth of the One Eternal Being to other human beings. The midrash frames this by stating, "Similarly, the Blessed Holy One said to Avraham, 'Travel from place to place and your name will become great in the world' [for spreading your "fragrance," awareness of the One God]."[7] Could it be that since Abraham is our progenitor, we might also possess an "inner fragrance" and beauty yet to be discovered and revealed?

Indeed, the Lubavitcher Rebbe (Menachem Mendel Schneerson, twentieth c., United States) believes so, and he speaks of both Abraham's and our own inner essence:

By conventional standards the development of one's natural instincts [to survive] . . . constitutes the ultimate in human achievement. However, there is a higher self to the human being. This is the "spark of Godliness" that is the core of one's soul—the divine essence that God breathes into each one of us, the "image of God" in which each one of us was, and continues to be, created. This is *ha'aretz*—"the land"—that God promised to show Abraham.[8]

In other words, the "land" promised to Abraham was an internal realization of his true authentic self.

Similarly, each one of us has our own unique inner fragrance—our soul. And we ourselves have to be willing to travel inward, shake ourselves up, and open that vial—to transform ourselves from merely surviving to thriving. Otherwise, like Abraham before he left everything familiar behind for an unknown destination, we too may be limited in how much beauty we can bring to the world.

What drives a person to shake up and open that vial? The Rebbe answers: something is *already* driving us to do it. We human beings have a propensity to go beyond the familiar and comfortable—a disposition that is innate to our human condition. Could it be that we humans likewise have a yen to search for our deeper and less apparent identity?

When we gaze into the mirror of our identity, what do we see? A body? A soul? Both? Ego? Beyond ego? For the Rebbe, our essential ingredient is our soul—our spiritual center, the image of God within each of us. And this is Abraham's deeper test in Pirkei Avot: to gaze into this mirror.

As part of this, Abraham might have considered his calling to be a leader. He may have wondered what leadership means. And we may wonder the same, especially if we sense our own call to rise to leadership. "Leaders lead," writes Rabbi Jonathan Sacks (twentieth c., England) about what happens when people claim a piece of themselves that now characterizes them as different from the status quo. "That does not mean to say that they don't follow," he continues. "But what they follow is different from what most people follow. They don't conform for the sake of conforming. They don't do what others do merely because others are doing it. They follow an inner voice, a calling."[9] This, too, seems to speak deeply to how Abraham passed the test.

Like perfume, the inner voice impelling each of us is unique to each of us. Abraham's *lekh lekha* is different from mine and different from yours. And yet heeding this inner voice to lead—and, in so doing, to reveal our own unique perfumes—may define all of us leaders.

A story Reb Simcha Bunim of Przysucha (eighteenth-nineteenth c., Poland) is said to have told every one of his students speaks to this idea:

> R Isaac from Cracow dreamt that he would find treasure under a certain bridge in Prague, and went to Prague to find it. Upon his arrival, he discovered soldiers were guarding the bridge day and night. Still, he hung around, hoping he would eventually be able to dig.
>
> After several days, a soldier asked him why he was there, and R Isaac proceeded to reveal his dream. Dismissing him mockingly, the soldier responded, "Who believes in dreams? I had a dream that I should travel to Cracow and dig in a R Isaac's house and find treasure there."
>
> Hearing the soldier's dream, R Isaac understood that the treasure was actually in his own home—and discovered it upon his return.[10]

Scholar Michael Rosen understands the story to mean "that a person must know that the truth lies within one's own self. A person must not search for it by imitating another, however pious, but rather by going inside [one's] inner being."[11]

In the history of Hasidism, no figure embodies this teaching more than Reb Zusya of Annipol (eighteenth c., Ukraine), who is often quoted as saying, "In the coming world they will not ask me, 'Why were you not [more like] Moses?' They will ask me: 'Why were you not [more like] what Zusya was meant to be?'"[12] We are to live fully as ourselves—the only standard against which we can be judged. And the pathway to that authenticity can be revealed by listening to our inner *lekh lekha*.

But how are we supposed to know if the path we are taking is actually our own *lekh lekha*? I have learned over decades, the hard way, that if my path does not lead to me sensing my inner beauty, then I've taken a wrong turn. On the other hand, when I "shake myself up" and then "spray my special fragrance" into the world, I then sense the Divine Presence all around me.

Attending faithfully and lovingly to our unique *lekh lekha*, we may discover our own special vial of spiritual perfume. Embarking on the journey that beckons may lead us to break the seal of our concealed selves and encounter the special fragrance of our soul.

The Practice

1. Begin with breath awareness.
2. Then, reflect on the text.
3. Move to quieting down your mind.

These three steps are explained in detail in the introduction.

4. Visualize the following scenario: You're going about your day as you usually do. With your eyes closed, visualize what that looks like. From when you woke up until the moment you began this practice, replay your own "script." Suddenly, without warning, and quite unexpectedly, you begin to hear a "still small voice" within you. This voice suggests that you need to take a new, significant step in your life—deepening a relationship with someone, or choosing a new career, or moving to a new city, or refining an emotional disposition that might need more tending to . . . or something else relevant for you.

This "still small voice" is the inward *lekh lekha* that spoke to Abraham and continues to speak to each of us. And now, shockingly, it beckons you to leave much of what is familiar to you in order to pursue a next step. Not only are you beginning a new part of your life journey; to succeed, you're now enjoined to move out of your acquired and familiar comfort zone too.

As you play out this new script in your mind, observe with curiosity and without judgment: What feelings arise from this? Is there a range of feelings? If so, which feelings are strongest, and why?

You might also consider gathering a few like-minded, spiritually sensitive souls to engage this practice together. Give everyone the opportunity to share their *lekh lekha* calling if they wish to do so.

The practice of intentional, compassionate listening to one's inner being opens up innumerable possibilities that await our discovery. And this is the time and space where we encounter the Divine.

Va-yera'

Cultivating the Spiritual Practice of Hospitality

> GOD appeared to him [Abraham] by the terebinths of Mamre; he was
> sitting at the entrance of the tent as the day grew hot. Looking up,
> he saw three figures standing near him. As soon as he saw them, he ran
> from the entrance of the tent to greet them and, bowing to the ground,
> he said, "My L/lord! If it please you, do not go on past your servant."
> Gen. 18:3[1]

Where We Are

A deep sleep falls upon Abraham. He dreams of the future exile in Egypt
with its enslavement of his descendants, followed by redemption and
then the return to Israel.

After ten years in Canaan with Sarah unable to conceive, Abraham
takes Hagar, Sarah's handmaid, as a second wife and she births Ishmael.
God commands Abraham to circumcise himself as a sign of the covenant
with the Divine, and he does. Going forward, all boys at eight days old
will enter the brit—covenant—through this rite. God promises that
Sarah will also conceive a son, whose name will be Isaac.

Now we witness one of the most famous scenes in the Bible. As Abraham sits at the entrance to his tent in the heat of the day, healing from
his circumcision, "God appeared to him." In the midst of this spiritual
experience, Abraham notices three strangers standing by him. What
happens next is both complex and ambiguous, depending on how you
interpret it. Abraham says, "My L/lord! If it please you, do not go on
past your servant."

The tradition is unclear about whom "my L/lord" refers to. Rashi (Shlomo Yitzhaki, eleventh c., France) offers two ways this can be understood. One interpretation suggests that Abraham is addressing the three strangers, in keeping with the ancient use of the term "my lord" as a traditional way of showing respect to other people.[2] The second interpretation suggests that Abraham is speaking to the Blessed Holy One. In this case "my L/lord" actually means "my Eternal One."[3]

In the first scenario, even in the midst of his own spiritual encounter with the Divine, Abraham notices the three strangers, runs toward them, bows down to the ground before them, addresses them as "my L/lord," and graciously urges them to stay. Abraham and Sarah then make haste to receive their guests in their home, lavishing on them food and drink.

In the second scenario, as with the first, Abraham becomes aware of three strangers passing by in the midst of his encountering God; he hurries from his tent door to meet them and bows down to the guests; and then—this time turning to God—asks God to wait ("My L/lord! If it please You, do not go on past Your servant") while he provides the strangers with the necessary hospitality.

This is an extraordinary interpretation: in the midst of his own Divine Revelation, Abraham asks God to wait while he attends to the needs of his guests! Yet this is how most commentators agree the passage should be read.

All the more, this radical and daring interpretation became the basis for a major talmudic principle: "Greater is hospitality than receiving the Divine Presence."[4] Faced with a choice between extending a personal encounter with the Divine and offering hospitality to human beings, Abraham chooses the humans. The Divine accedes to his request, waiting until Abraham and Sarah have brought the visitors food and drink before engaging Abraham in dialogue about the fate of Sodom. Only then does Abraham realize that what he thought were human beings were actually angels, divine messengers (Gen. 18:9–16).

Referring to Abraham's asking God to wait, Rabbi Jonathan Sacks (twenty–twenty-first c., England) asks: How can this be so?

Is it not disrespectful at best — and heretical at worst — to put the needs of human beings before attending to the presence of the Divine? Rabbi Sacks answers clearly, no! The passage is telling us something of immense profundity.

Some additional context will help us to understand the text. In Abraham's time, idolaters worshiped idols rather than the Divine, as this verse in Psalms proclaims: "Their idols are silver and gold, made by human hands. They have mouths, but cannot speak; eyes but cannot see; they have ears, but cannot hear; nostrils, but cannot smell. . . . Their makers become like them, and so do all who put their trust in them" (Ps. 115:4–8).

Rabbi Sacks explains:

> You cannot worship impersonal forces and remain . . . compassionate, humane, generous, and forgiving. Precisely because we believe that God is indeed personal — a deity to whom we can say "You" — we honor human dignity as sacrosanct. Abraham knew the paradoxical truth that to live the life of faith is to see the trace of God in the face of the stranger. It is easy to encounter the Divine Presence when God appears as God to the individual. What is difficult is to sense the Divine Presence when He comes disguised as three anonymous passersby. That was Abraham's greatness. He knew that attending to God and offering hospitality to the strangers were not two things but One.[5]

To this point, the Lubavitcher Rebbe (Menachem Mendel Schneerson, twentieth c., United States) suggests that we might understand Abraham's plea, "Please do not go on past Your servant," in two senses — first, that the Divine should not depart from him, and second, that God should accompany him in the mitzvah of *hakhnasat orchim* (hospitality).

According to the Lubavitcher Rebbe, the Divine Revelation to Abraham was of the very fullest. Abraham was reaching a state of intimate closeness with the Divine he had never attained before. And still he understood that the mitzvah of *hakhnasat orchim* was beckoning him. So he asked the Divine to remain with him *in* this same elevated state while he took care of what appeared to be human beings with physical needs. In this way God remained present with Abraham while revealing the Divine self to the strangers as well, and *this* became part of Abraham's own encounter with the Divine. God didn't depart because Abraham was sensing the Divine Presence *in* the strangers.[6]

The Ba'al Shem Tov (Israel ben Eliezer, eighteenth century, Ukraine) also teaches us that the first three letters of the word *oreyach* (guest) spell the word *ohr* (light), and the final letter, *chet*, has a numeric value of eight, which traditionally represents the infinite (eight on its side is the sign for infinity). And so, when we welcome guests into our homes, offering them food, drink, and comfort, they can provide us with much more: *ohr chet*, infinite light.[7] When we open ourselves to this understanding, the manifestation of the Divine Presence enters our homes.

The Practice

1. Begin with breath awareness.
2. Then, reflect on the text.
3. Move to quieting down your mind.

These three steps are explained in detail in the introduction.

4. Visualize an event in the future. Invite a select group of people over for a meal, perhaps a Shabbat dinner, an afternoon barbeque, or any other occasion that would be ideal to welcome them into your home. Now, issue an invitation to a monarch or a favorite celebrity as well. Everyone will say yes to the gathering!

Once there is agreement on the date and time, begin preparing for the meal. Settle into your inner breathing rhythm — being breathed into with each inhalation, holding and gazing for a moment at the wonder of the gift of life, and then returning this gift with gratitude with each exhalation.

How exciting and what an honor it is to host royalty! What types of food and drinks will you prepare and serve? Where do you shop? How do you cook? How do your table settings befit the extraordinary occasion?

This is how many Jews go about preparing for the traditional Shabbat dinner. In a magnificent and sacred tradition handed down through the generations, the most important guest each week is the Shabbat bride and queen herself, enclothed in the Divine Presence. The invited guests become the bride's and queen's entourage.

At last, after all the intentional and careful preparations, there is a knock on your door. All of your guests — including someone very important and influential — are waiting to be let into your home. Opening the door, you greet each guest individually with a joyful welcome. Do you sense the Ba'al Shem Tov's illumination that each guest brings infinite light into your home? If not, what might you try to do to realize this?

You spend this sacred time with your guests as Abraham and Sarah have taught us — by attending to all of their needs and treating them as the spark of the infinite Divine they are. As your time together draws to an end, do you sense an interconnectedness with your guests? Are they expressing their authentic selves? Are they manifesting gratitude, joy, love?

Soon after everyone has gone, reflect on the evening. What are you feeling? What do you sense?

Perhaps, as I do at times, even after my guests have physically left my home, you sense a piece of their souls, their infinite light, has not. It's the dearest hostess gift I could ever imagine.

Ḥayyei Sarah

Spiritual Protest

> Sarah's lifetime came to be one hundred years and twenty years and seven
> years, these were the years of Sarah's life. Sarah died in Kiriath-arba — now
> Hebron — in the land of Cannan.
>
> Gen. 23:1–2[1]

Where We Are

Sodom is destroyed and Lot, Abraham's nephew, is saved. Isaac is born
and circumcised at eight days old. God assures Abraham that his lineage will descend through Isaac. Hagar and Ishmael are expelled, but
God saves them from dying in the desert and promises Abraham that
Ishmael will also become a great nation. In a famous episode known as
the *Akedah* (the Binding [of Isaac]), God commands Abraham to offer his
son Isaac on the sacrificial altar. Abraham binds him to an altar, and just
as he raises the knife, God commands him not to slaughter Isaac. God
tells Abraham that because he did not withhold his son, his offspring
will be greatly increased.

Following the Binding of Isaac, this Torah portion begins with the
death of Sarah.

At First Glance

Is there some connection between these two events? Rashi (Shlomo
Yitzhaki, eleventh c., France) argues that not only is there a connection —
there is causation! He explains that when the news reached Sarah about
her son's near-death experience at her husband's hands, her "soul flew
from her" and she died.[2]

Rashi also finds meaning in the Torah's depiction of Sarah's lifespan.
Instead of saying 127 years, the Torah says "one hundred years and twenty

years and seven years." Each unit of time was listed alone so that it was understood as a "complete number" in and of itself. "When she was one hundred years old, she was like a twenty-year-old regarding sin. Just as a twenty-year-old she had not sinned, so too when she was one hundred years old, she was without sin. And when she was twenty, she was like a seven-year-old in regards to beauty."[3] Rashi concludes: "The verse then ends with the words 'These were the years of Sarah's life' because her entire life was equally virtuous at every age."

A similar phrasing is later used to describe Abraham's lifespan upon his death—"He lived a total of one hundred years and seventy years and five years" (Gen. 25:7)—but the text does *not* go on to say, "These were the years of his life." The fact that this life summation only appears in reference to Sarah suggests that there is something unique about Sarah's life that does not apply to Abraham's.

A Deeper Dive

We begin our deeper dive from a different vantage point. The Rimanover Rebbe (Tzvi Hersh HaKohen, eighteenth–nineteenth c., Poland) teaches that there's a connection between the salt used during the ritual animal sacrifices in the Temple service and human suffering.[4] He explains: "Concerning salt; too much will ruin the meat and you will be unable to enjoy it. Only when the meat is salted properly can one enjoy it. Likewise with suffering, the amount must be moderated, so the person will be able to receive them, in order so a person will not be damaged by unbearable suffering. For a person to be properly purified by suffering, the suffering must be administered with compassion, in its proper measure."[5]

Connecting this teaching to the Binding of Isaac preceding Sarah's death, the Piaseczner Rebbe (Kalonymus Kalmish Shapira, twentieth c., Poland) pronounces, "If she, Sarah [traditionally considered the greatest of righteous women in the Bible, meaning her faith and trust are the strongest] was unable to bear such pain, how much less so can we."[6] Yet the Piaseczner Rebbe goes on to offer a seemingly contrary understanding. It isn't quite right that Sarah couldn't bear it—she *chose* not to!

The Piaseczner explains how Sarah used her agency to critique what she deemed her unjust allotment of suffering: "It is possible to explain that our mother Sarah herself, who took the Binding of Isaac so much to heart, to the point that her soul flew out of her, acted for the benefit of Israel, in order to demonstrate to God that the Jewish nation is not capable of tolerating such excessive suffering."[7] In other words, she did not die because she was in shock. To the Piaseczner, she died as a protest to God, in effect telling God, *I choose not to live in your world anymore if I have to suffer the way I am suffering. Whatever years are in front of me, I am giving them up.*

What is more, the Piaseczner holds, Sarah's protest from her place of absolute faith in the loving Creator is at its essence a gift to us. As our matriarch, Sarah chose the path of spiritual protest not solely for herself, but on behalf of her whole community, present and future—including all her children alive today. She has thereby given each of us the gift of protest to wield when we are suffering. We too are allowed to implore the Divine, "Help me go on, but not this way." The Piaseczner offers a prayer for the end of suffering: "Therefore, let God quickly send us spiritual and physical salvation, with revealed kindness."[8]

With this understood, the Piaseczner explains the reason why the Torah only refers to Sarah, and not Abraham, with "these were the years of the life of." In the case of Sarah, he says, Rashi's statement that "all the years were equally virtuous" also encompasses the additional years Sarah sacrificed in protest to God by not continuing to live.

The contemporary writer Dr. Henry Abrahamson (twenty-first c., United States) points out that "the Rebbe pushed the theologically challenging material even further, arguing that Moses was not the only biblical figure to protest excessive suffering—Sarah, by allowing herself to die with the shock of the news of Isaac's experience, was also issuing the ultimate statement of dissent, and that 'she did this for the benefit of the Jewish people.'"[9] Scholar Daniel Reiser argues further that the Piaseczner understands Sarah to not only be a righteous woman, but a *melitz yosher*—an advocate and defender—of the people. Notably, he is the first rabbinic figure to ascribe this honor to a woman.[10]

Perhaps each of us might take from the Piaseczner's teaching an encouragement to cultivate the *middah* of spiritual protest wisely. We might choose to use spiritual protest only when we feel we have no other option. And as a sacred *middah*, it may end up bringing us closer to God.

For example, there was a point in my life when I met the limits of my tolerance for suffering. I felt pangs of severe loneliness due to my extreme disconnection from my own inner being. When I could endure it no longer, I called out to God, saying, "I cannot do this anymore. I am protesting my reality." It was as if our matriarch Sarah was gently giving me her gift of permission for me to challenge my Creator with my pure truth.

To my amazement, this spiritual protest opened doors of opportunity for me to flourish in ways I never could have imagined.

The Practice

1. Begin with breath awareness.
2. Then, reflect on the text.
3. Move to quieting down your mind.

These three steps are explained in detail in the introduction.

4. Meditate on the idea that living a Jewish life compels a person to recognize and honor all of one's feelings and emotions — both those that bring joy and gratitude and those that involve suffering and doubt. When experiencing Judaism as a spiritual practice one soon begins to realize that the Torah way of life is not a pretentious, "feel good" way, but rather a "real" and a "connecting" way of living. Namely, the Piaseczner Rebbe teaches, our Creator is asking us to encounter all feelings with a similar question: How can I utilize this feeling in my practice as a tool to cultivate a sense of closeness and nearness to the Divine?

As you settle into your inner self, begin to reclaim — or be aware in the present — of a moment along your life journey that evokes searing pain, loneliness, alienation, insecurity, anger, or any other extreme feeling. This is a very important step along your spiritual journey. This moment is private, intimate, and customized by our Creator especially and uniquely for you. How do you face this moment? How do you transform this into a sacred moment? What do you allow yourself to do with this?

Our matriarch Sarah has bequeathed to us an inheritance. As our mother, with the force and focus of a mother's unconditional love for her child, she gives us the opportunity to transform what could be considered a self-centered and heretical act into a sacred practice. Protest! Push back, argue, yell, cry, demand. Pour out your heart that you cannot bear more pain and suffering. Scream at the Creator that you cannot live like this anymore!

Embrace Sarah's gift. Choose to cultivate closeness to your Creator in what might seem like the most counterintuitive way imaginable. You may yet reap radically amazing results.

Toledot

Spiritual Conflict Resolution

> And God said to her: "Two peoples are in your womb; two nations from within your bowels shall be separated; one nation will gain strength and prevail over the other, and the elder shall serve the younger."
>
> Gen. 25:23

Where We Are

Abraham purchases a burial site for Sarah in Hebron, in Kiryat Arba. Isaac marries Rebekah. Abraham passes away and his two sons Isaac and Ishmael bury him at the family burial site in Hebron, near Sarah.

Isaac and Rebekah hope to have children. In light of Rebekah's prolonged childlessness, Isaac calls out to God to help her conceive a child. His prayer is heard and Rebekah conceives, but the pregnancy is difficult. She is carrying twins and the Torah conveys that "the children struggled with each other within her" (Gen. 25:22).

By exploring this further, we will hopefully come to understand how this births the *middah* of spiritual conflict resolution.

At First Glance

Experiencing great physical pain during her pregnancy, Rebekah goes "to inquire of the Lord" (Gen. 25:21–22). This is the first time in the Torah when someone facing personal difficulty seeks an answer from the Divine. Hers is not an arrogant inquiry, but a humble gesture of seeking meaning for her suffering. God responds with our verse under discussion. Shortly afterwards, Rebekah gives birth to the warring twins, first Esau, then Jacob.

The in utero conflict between the two brothers foreshadows an ongoing sibling rivalry after their birth. They have very different personalities. Esau is driven to fulfill his physical needs in the external world: he is the one who goes out to the fields, hunts, and brings home food for the family. His modus operandi is representative of the first divine step to create the human being: giving this being its physical form. "The ETERNAL God formed the earthling from the soil of the ground" (Gen. 2:7). Jacob focuses on the internal world: he remains inside his tent and devotes himself to being in communion with God, meditating and praying. This is also a way of providing for the family—but spiritually. His modus operandi is said to embody the second divine step after the formation of the physical earthling: infusing it with a soul. "And the One blew into its nostrils breath that gives life, and the human became a living soul" (Gen. 2:7).

Esau and Jacob clash over receiving their father Isaac's love and attention. Favoring Esau's manliness and valuing the sustenance he provides, Isaac rewards him with his attention. Meanwhile, Jacob's basic—and unfulfilled—human need to be loved by his father blinds him into deceiving Isaac—pretending to be Esau in order to receive a special blessing his father wants to give his brother. Metaphorically, then, the brothers' conflict can be understood to spotlight the complex tensions between physical and spiritual needs, between body and soul.

This struggle is basic to the human condition. For example: Which weighs more heavily on my mind, ensuring that I have food, shelter, and clothing or ensuring that I sense purpose, meaning, and human connection in life? My intuitive idealism directs me to answer, "Both!"— and I seek a peaceful resolution between these two. Perhaps it is not necessary to choose.

The conflict between Esau and Jacob is said to extend far beyond the two of them. Our verse says, "Two peoples are in your womb; two nations from within your bowels shall be separated." Jacob becomes the progenitor of the Israelites and Esau the progenitor of the Edomites, who settle to the south and east of Israel. Today the Edomite nation no longer exists, but its predominate traits of conquest and might characterize the many empires that rose and fell in the Middle East and Europe over the past three millennia. The feud between Esau and Jacob can be said to represent the many such nations that have risen up against the Jewish nation.

A Deeper Dive

Shneur Zalman of Liadi (eighteenth c., Belarus) teaches otherwise: that the rivalry between Jacob and Esau represents an inner conflict inherent to the human condition. It is a metaphor for the struggle between two strong primary energies within each of us: the divine soul and the animal soul.[1]

Jewish mysticism understands the animal soul as absolutely essential for our own physical vitality. This soul is enclothed in our blood—"The soul of the flesh is in the blood" (Lev. 17:11)—and our physical blood is the essential life-giving force sustaining our physical bodies and all of its functions. It understands the divine soul as also absolutely essential for our own spiritual vitality. The life-giving breath of the Creator, originally blown into Adam and Eve, continues into the present: we receive this divine gift of life through our inhalation, and then return the gift through our exhalation.

As breath flows through us, animating our soul, blood circulates through us, keeping our bodies alive. What the breath means to our divine soul, the blood means to our bodies—together they can sustain both a healthy body and spiritual vitality. However, when the human condition pulls a person to one of the extremes, we feel an inner tension, even imbalance.

The Piaseczner Rebbe (Kalonymus Kalmish Shapira, twentieth c., Poland) provides an alternative, "two mindsets" framework for thinking about this innate tension. Within the "lower consciousness" of Esau, one yields primarily to the world's physical demands, seeking food, clothing, and shelter as well as physical security, control, and power.

This lower consciousness is absolutely necessary for human survival. Yet it can be perilous if left unchecked. Overprioritizing the physical components of living can lead to hedonism, unhealthy materialism, heartless behavior, and a significantly impaired ability to sense the Divine Presence.

Alternatively, when experiencing the "higher consciousness" of Jacob, one's mindset and heart may gracefully open up to the world. The inclination is toward selflessness, experiencing life beyond surviving. And rather than being limited by natural forces in the physical world, one may actually sense the infinite Divine Presence in them, and thereby fulfill the divine soul's innate need to thrive and connect. This, in turn, creates space for an awareness that connects us to the Creator's world beyond our limited being—one that connects the Creator's life-giving energies within each of us to the same life-giving energies of the creations around us.[2]

Here, too, however, if left unchecked this so-called higher consciousness can lead to a different extreme: asceticism. This also diminishes our human capacity to sense the Divine Presence, because it rejects part of the Creator's world. A truly higher consciousness must include both centers of living.

With these two frameworks in mind, we might ask: How can I cultivate a practice of "spiritual conflict resolution" and reach internal harmony between my inner Jacob and my inner Esau? Is this really possible? I suggest that we can—through love, compassion, mindful practice, and internalization of yet another important teaching in our verse: "the elder shall serve the younger."

The Esau in us, the physical side of our lives, needs to serve the Jacob in us, the spiritual side of our lives. From the inner calling to reach from merely surviving to thriving, we can pursue the quest for meaning. We can act on our drive to pursue a life punctuated by devotion to an idea or a belief greater than our limited selves.

In this way, the ever-present conflict between these two internal powers continues, but the means to resolve it abides as well. We can acknowledge the physical side of ourselves and work to quiet down its urges. From there, we can employ it to help manifest our spiritual side. Giving meaning and providing structure to how we engage with the physical world can actually enhance our devotion to our spiritual center. By gently honoring and harnessing one part of ourselves—rather than trying to viciously destroy it—we may be able to bring harmony and integration not only to our inner lives, but even to the world at large.

By doing so, with love, compassion, and awareness, we cultivate the *middah* of spiritual conflict resolution—a *middah* where our spirit is enriched rather than threatened by the physical, employing the physical to advance and sustain its integrity.

The Practice

1. Begin with breath awareness.
2. Then, reflect on the text.
3. Move to quieting down your mind.

These three steps are explained in detail in the introduction.

4. Visualize a moment when you were in nature. Perhaps spending time at the beach, walking through a forest, picnicking with family and friends at a community park, hiking up a mountain trail, or even gazing into a piece of art in a museum or a book that expresses the artist's rendition of a slice of the natural environment. The goal of this visualization at this point is to sense the plurality and diversity in the Creator's natural world—and the harmony.

What thoughts and feelings arise for you once you are able recognize harmony inherent in the natural world? Serenity? Wonder? Perhaps wanting to also live in harmony when you may feel you do not? Ask yourself then, why don't I?

Consider this as an answer: because the human being may be the only creature that does not participate in this naturally balanced eco-system effortlessly. We humans have been blessed—or to some it seems cursed—with free will. The Creator does not bring the human being into existence with a preprogrammed sense of inner tranquility. We humans must choose to make the effort to cultivate the experience of inner harmony. Why? Because our Creator formed us with two opposing urges: the internal voices of the twins Esau and Jacob.

How do you experience your inner Esau—the parts of you that focus on surviving, on limitations and restrictions, on scarcity, and manifest an overconcern with fulfilling your physical needs? In fact, how do you experience the physical aspects of your life? Do you feel physically healthy, alert, and rested when you wake up? Or not?

Then, begin to explore your inner Jacob. What feelings come up for you now? Do you also experience a sense of thriving, of abundance; does part of you welcome possibilities rather than only probabilities? Do you feel an inner tug to be in service to an idea, value system, or theology that requires reaching beyond your limited daily routine? How do you experience the spiritual aspects of your life? Do you feel self-worth, a sense of purpose in your life, connection to other people and creations—even a sense of closeness to the divine energies within you and around you? Or not?

Our calling as human beings is to recognize that what seems to be an irreconcilable situation is natural to the human condition. Be aware of the feelings this process evokes. Do you feel overwhelmed, cynical, stressed, unbalanced, angry, disappointed, torn apart, and confused? or, perhaps, are you curious and determined to rise to the challenge of what seems to be an impossible calling—inner conflict resolution?

How would you cultivate a life that equally honors your inner Esau and your inner Jacob—honoring your physical and spiritual needs in unison?

The Jewish tradition suggests that with love, compassion, and mindfulness, we can achieve this by prioritizing our inner Jacob as paramount while yet recognizing the need to honor the Esau within us as well. How does this approach feel? Does it resonate for you?

Our physical being plays a crucial role in achieving holistic health, but can you sense how important it is to value your soul, your spiritual being, as most important? Does inner conflict resolution redefined as spiritual conflict resolution bring a sense of hope and optimism to your struggle? Do you see the value of the Eternal's teaching in our verse that this conflict resolves when "the elder will serve the younger?"

Conclude your practice by exploring how you might honor and express your "elder Esau" being in service to your "younger Jacob." How might you meet your physical needs without injuring your spiritual ones? How might you enrich your spiritual sensitivities by intentionally engaging with the physical world?

Va-yetse'

Yearning for a Personal Encounter with God

> Jacob then made a vow, saying, "If God remains with me, protecting me on
> this journey that I am making, and giving
> me bread to eat and clothing to wear, and I return safe to
> my father's house—the ETERNAL shall be my God. And this stone, which I
> have set up as a pillar, shall be God's abode."
>
> Gen. 28:20–22

Where We Are

Esau marries a Canaanite woman, to his mother's chagrin. Isaac decides to bless Esau, his first born (even if by only a few moments). Rebekah schemes a plot whereby her favorite son, Jacob, impersonating Esau, receives the blessing his blind father intends for Esau. Returning home from hunting with a special meal for his father, Esau discovers Jacob has stolen his blessing and swears that after their father passes away, he will kill his brother. Overhearing this, Rebekah tells Jacob he must flee to her brother Laban in Haran and remain there until Esau's anger subsides. To facilitate this, she asks Isaac to send Jacob to Laban on the pretense that Laban will help find Jacob a wife within their family—a more welcome outcome than Esau's choice to marry a Canaanite woman. Isaac agrees.

On his way to Haran, Jacob camps for the night on Mount Moriah. There, he dreams of angels ascending and descending a ladder reaching from earth to heaven. Upon waking, "Jacob took the stone [on which he slept] and raised it as a monument" (Gen. 28:18). He then utters the aforementioned vows.

At First Glance

The syntactical construction of Jacob's oath raises an important question in Jacob's—and, ultimately, our own—relationship with the Divine.

On the surface, the oath consists of two parts: 1) the conditions for its fulfillment and 2) Jacob's promised fulfillment of the oath once the conditions are met.

What is not clear, though, is where the former ends and the latter begins. Verse 20, "If God remains with me, protecting me on this journey that I am making, and giving me bread to eat and clothing to wear," and the first part of verse 21, "and I return safe to my father's house," clearly establish Jacob's conditions that God will need to fulfill in order for Jacob to be bound by his vow. Verse 22 then speaks of what Jacob will do for God: the fulfillment of his oath, "And this stone, which I have set up as a pillar, shall be God's abode."

But what about the second part of verse 21, "the ETERNAL shall be my God"? Is this part of the conditions for the vow's fulfillment, essentially as if the text had read "*and* the ETERNAL shall be my God," or part of Jacob's own vow, in effect "*then* the ETERNAL shall be my God"? To begin to resolve this ambiguity, let's consider this perplexing phrase employing two different names for the Creator: ETERNAL and God.

Based in the Kabbalistic tradition, the name "ETERNAL" refers to the manifestation of the Creator as the Infinite One—beyond this world and transcending everything in it. In fact, the Zohar states that "there is no thought that can grasp or understand this aspect [of the Creator at all]."[1] From this theological standpoint, we are meant to believe in the existence of the Infinite Creator who continuously ensures the sustainability of the physical world, while simultaneously acknowledging that as finite human beings with limited intelligence, we do not possess the capacity to understand—and hence to relate to—this Infinite Creator, the ETERNAL. And yet many of us may find it quite challenging to be in an actual relationship with a theology or an idea, so this identity seems to rule out a deep relationship of mind, heart, and soul with the Divine.

However, the same Kabbalistic tradition has it that the name "God" refers to the manifestation of the same Infinite Creator, but within, rather than beyond, this world. This affords each of us an immanent and visceral experience, intellectually and emotionally and spiritually, of our Creator, and enables an actual relationship with the Creator. God is enclothed in and revealed through nature—within each of us and in the environment surrounding us. From an ultimate point of view, only one reality exists. From the human point of view, we can experience the same Creator in these two different ways.

Through this lens, Jacob's use of "my God" can be understood as his experiencing the transcendent nature of the Divine in an immanent and visceral way. Jacob clearly hopes for this and believes in its possibility. However, returning to the question above, does he view this felt experience as *a condition* for the vow's fulfillment or *as part* of the vow itself?

Rashi (Shlomo Yitzhaki, eleventh c., France) and Nachmanides (Moses ben Nachman, thirteenth c., Spain and Acre, the Holy Land) debate this point. Rashi believes in the "*and* the Eternal shall be my God" interpretation. As one of the conditions for Jacob to make the stone a "house of God," he first needs to experience God as "his God."[2] Solely believing in the existence of the Infinite Creator does not suffice for him to fulfill his oath.

Nachmanides, however, reads "*then* the Lord will be my God"—not as a condition, but as part of the promise itself.[3] Hence, if God provides Jacob with protection, food, clothes, and a peaceful return home, then he will be able to make the ETERNAL his God and the stone will be the symbolic abode for the Divine Presence. In other words, by following God's will, Jacob will naturally be enabled to do the work necessary to sense "his God"—in a unique, personal, and visceral way.

What is the deeper significance of these two interpretations? And why might the Torah recount Jacob's oath in a way that allows for variant readings?

A Deeper Dive

To help us answer these questions, the contemporary Hasidic scholar and rabbi Yanki Tauber (twenty-first c., United States) teaches in the name of the Lubavitcher Rebbe (Menachem Mendel Schneerson, twentieth c., United States) that the key to understanding this ambiguity lies in Jacob's oath, "and this stone . . . shall be God's abode."

Rabbi Tauber explains: "Jacob is promising to make 'the stone'—the brute substantiality of the physical world—into a divine abode. Each one of us therefore possesses the capacity as well to be transformed within our own selves into a 'house of God.'"[4] Jacob is dedicating his intention to fulfill this sacred mission. Employing the physical as a means to reveal the Creator's presence transforms its very existence—and ours.

This is Jacob's response to humankind's inner calling to fulfill the needs of the soul as well as the needs of the body. Jacob, devoted (in one form or another) to experiencing the One as a personal and intimate presence in his life, desires to make a home for God in the lower corporal realms.

And now we can understand the significance of the variant readings of "and" or "then" the ETERNAL will be my God. The ETERNAL becoming "my God"—a direct encounter with the Divine—can really be both: one of the conditions in order to transform "the stone" and the end result of the prior conditions being met that allows us to then do this transformative work. In the spirit of our sages, "These and those are the words of the living God," the Jewish tradition allows for contrasting opinions— and, moreover, we need both Rashi's and Nachmanides' points of views, as these represent two different, authentic ways of experiencing our relationship with the Divine.[5]

Taking this further, the human-Divine relationship may never really be the same from moment to moment. The fluidity in the connection gives it life and a sense of it being true, rather than forced or dogmatic.

I suspect that at times, in the spirit of Rashi's understanding, we may need to first encounter the Divine in a personal way before we can begin engaging in making a home for God in the earthly realm. Perhaps without this, some of us may sense distance from God and even be lonely. At these moments, experiencing God in our lives may become essential. Sensing God's presence internally becomes a way to feel connection and closeness with God, and this then inspires us to embrace and engage in the mission of transforming a stone into a house of God.

And yet at other times, in the spirit of Nachmanides, we may already sense closeness. Therefore, we can dive right into the spiritual work of making a home for God in the lowly realm, of ensuring that "this stone shall be God's abode," by transforming our physical environment into a spiritual reality.

The deeper significance of these two interpretations illustrates how there really is no one way to cultivate this spiritual practice. Hence, the variant readings of either "and" or "then" invite us to consider the many possibilities that await us at any moment.

The Practice

1. Begin with breath awareness.
2. Then, reflect on the text.
3. Move to quieting down your mind.

These three steps are explained in detail in the introduction.

4. Visualize a moment in your life when you sensed the urge to explore a deeper and perhaps less known part of yourself—your spiritual side. Or, if you've never felt the urge to do this, imagine yourself as a curious explorer about to begin a new adventure—spiritual exploration. The objective of spiritual exploration is to encounter the invisible component of what keeps you alive and breathing. Think of this as searching for a nonphysical dimension of living your life that affords you a sense of inner serenity and equanimity. We cannot see this but we may be able to sense this. We may intuitively become aware of its existence—and its importance in living a healthy life.

As a curious explorer, what provisions do you need prior to setting out? What conditions need to be met before you can gain access to your inner world? Are there physical needs to be fulfilled before you can immerse yourself in this encounter? What may these be? What is your emotional landscape? What do you need to do to be ready?

Continue visualizing this journey as you move deeper and deeper. Imagine sensing your own unique encounter with the one Source of your life, your Creator. What would that be like? What would you want this to be like? What *is* it like, right now?

If you sense yourself experiencing your internal being, consider the possibility that in your spiritual exploration you are encountering the Divine Presence. For some of us, this discovery comes to fulfill an innate yearning to encounter the Divine Presence within us that we have searched for along our life journeys.

Imagine infusing your everyday actions with this newly discovered awareness.

During the course of the day, accept the invitation to become aware if you sense the Divine Presence. Do you sense that expressing your spirituality brings feelings of closeness with the Divine? What are you experiencing and realizing?

Do you experience that you are transforming your awareness of the ETERNAL into your own personal God with whom you have a visceral relationship?

In this vein, we all possess the potential to transform "this stone" into a "house of God"—in one way or another.

Va-yishlaḥ

Transforming Heel Consciousness to Face Consciousness

Jacob was left alone. And a figure wrestled with him until the break of dawn. When he saw that he had not prevailed against him, he wrenched Jacob's hip at its socket, so that the socket of his hip was strained as he wrestled with him. Then he said, "Let me go, for dawn is breaking." But he answered, "I will not let you go, unless you bless me." Said the other, "What is your name?" He replied, "Jacob." Said he, "Your name shall no longer be Jacob, but Israel, for you have striven with beings divine and human, and have prevailed."

Gen. 32:25–29

Where We Are

Jacob arrives at Haran. He marries Leah and then Rachel. Each bring their maidservants, who become Jacob's concubines. The four women give birth to eleven sons. After two decades of working for Laban, Jacob wishes to leave his father-in-law and return home with his new family.

Jacob sends messengers to Esau to let him know he is returning home. Esau replies he is coming to meet him. The two brothers haven't seen each other since Esau vowed to kill Jacob twenty years ago.

On his way to meet Esau, Jacob separates from the rest of his entourage for the evening. While his whole family crosses a river, he remains on the far bank for the night, alone. And then, out of nowhere, a mysterious figure appears and begins to wrestle him.

At First Glance

Who is this figure? Rashi (Shlomo Yitzhaki, eleventh c., France) believes this was not a mere mortal man, but Esau's guardian angel, intent on hurting Jacob, whereas the prophet Hosea proclaims that Jacob "strove with an angel and prevailed" (Hos. 12:5), with the traditional Jewish understanding that angels are messengers from God, sent to relay to a human a special divine communication.[1]

Rashi also points out that the Hebrew word *avak*, translated as "wrestle" in the verse, connotes an additional meaning of "dust," that is, the wrestling results in raising a lot of dust.[2] Menachem ben Sorek (tenth c., Spain) suggests that *avak* derives from the Aramaic *aveiku*, meaning to intertwine or join together. Hence, Jacob's efforts to defeat his opponent result in his becoming entangled with his opponent as well.[3] In these ways we may understand the wrestling match as serving to introduce the delivery of a divine message.

After wrestling all night and sustaining a leg injury that leaves him limping, Jacob seems to prevail over this force. At first, while wrestling through the night, he may have thought, as Rashi suggests, that this was Esau's "guardian angel" coming to hurt him, but it would seem that, as Hosea suggests, this is really an angel sent by God to convey a message bearing extreme importance for Jacob's life.

The angel begs Jacob to let him go at daybreak (the tradition teaches that at sunrise there is a sort of changing of the guard that requires this angel to depart), but Jacob sets a condition for the angel's release: "I will not let you go unless you bless me." In response, the angel gives him a spiritual and identity-affirming name-change. His birth name was Ya'akov—Jacob, which derives from "heel," because he was grasping onto his brother Esau's heel, wanting to hold him back so he could be born first. He now receives the name Yisra'el—Israel, which conveys, "You have striven with beings divine and human and have prevailed."

Ultimately *this* was the purpose of the wrestling match—forcing Jacob to struggle with his own identity. As we will see, he wrestles with who he is or isn't, and for the first time in his life achieves victory— being faithful to his true self. Hence the angel blesses him with a name change befitting the success of this existential encounter and marking a paradigm shift in Jacob's consciousness. The wrestling episode springs Jacob from "heel consciousness" to "face consciousness."

A Deeper Dive

Rabbi Jonathon Sacks (twentieth–twenty-first c., England) teaches about this paradigm shift: "One thing . . . stands out about the first phase in Jacob's life: he longs to be Esau. More specifically, he desires to occupy Esau's place" because "Esau is everything Jacob is not."[4] As the firstborn, Esau holds special status in the family. As a "man of the field" (Gen. 25:27), he exemplifies the persona of a "man's man" who possesses the strength and skill to fight and win. More to the heart of the matter, Jacob likely longs to be Esau to possess what his father has bestowed solely on his brother: love and affection.

This fateful night can thus be understood as Jacob's inner battle with his own existential truth. Who *is* he now? Is he only a man who longs to be Esau? Can he only imagine his life in terms of another? Or is he his own man, called to a different destiny?

This brings us to Jacob's demand, "I will not let you go until you bless me" and the unnamed stranger's gift of a name change as an unexpected return. The American thinker Rabbi Yael Levy (twenty-first c., United States) understands Jacob's demand for the blessing as an inner plea to the Divine to "find the blessing in all this conflict and pain."[5] Notably, both of his names, Jacob and Israel, signify "struggle," but Jacob's struggle and Israel's struggle are not the same. Rabbi Sacks explains:

> The terms of the conflict have been reversed. It is as if this adversarial force said to him, "In the past, you struggled to be Esau. In the future, you will struggle not to be Esau, but to be yourself. In the past you held on to Esau's heel. But in the future, you will hold on to the Divine face to face. You will not let go. And the Divine will not let go of you. Now let go of Esau, so that you can be free to hold on to God!" Before Jacob could be at peace with Esau, he had to learn that he was not Esau, but Israel—he who wrestles with God and never lets go.[6]

Jacob's newfound willingness to be himself precedes—and enables—this revelatory encounter. Twenty years earlier, when his father Isaac had asked his name, he had lied and answered, "I am Esau." This time, when the angel asks him, "What is your name?" he replies truthfully, "Jacob," and from this truth his blessing—his name change—flows: "Said he, 'Your name shall no longer be Jacob, but Israel'" (Gen. 32:29).

Jacob does seem to "find the blessing" he seeks "in all this conflict and pain." Before this encounter he was denying his own true self and trying to grab onto Esau's identity—heel consciousness. Now he is embracing his own self-identity—face consciousness. His blessing is no longer suffering from self-estrangement.

All the more, Jacob no longer suffers from divine estrangement. He connects to the Divine as he connects to his true self. Immediately after the angel departs Jacob calls the place of the struggle Peniel, "face of God," and this paradigm shift of identity accompanies him to his encounter with Esau. Instead of maintaining his modus operandi, running away from Esau, Jacob "went on ahead and bowed low to the ground seven times until he was near his brother" (Gen. 33:3–4). The *Aderet Eliyahu* (of Rabbi Yosef Hayyim, nineteenth c., Baghdad) teaches that "Jacob was prostrating himself to the Divine Presence that he beheld, and not Esau [as many assume]."[7] When the brothers finally reunite, Jacob (now as Israel) proclaims to Esau: "To see your face is like seeing the face of God" (Gen. 33:10).

Enhancing this understanding, the Hebrew word for "face" is *panim*, which derives from the same word as *penimiyut*—inner or internal. When Jacob sees himself "face to face," we can understand this as his beholding the Divine Presence in his internal self. And when he sees Esau face to face, he can behold the Divine Presence within Esau as well.

From this eventful night, the Torah invites each of us to wrestle, as Jacob did—maybe not alone, maybe not at night, but most likely in the depths of our soul. Through this we can discover the face, the name, and the blessing that is ours alone. Once we reach this place, we are no longer trying to catch up to or flee in heel consciousness. Rather, we are encountering ourselves and each other face to face, in face consciousness.

The blessing is not that we will not struggle, but that we *will* struggle— and when we do, we will prevail and be the better for it. The struggle itself may reveal the higher self. And prevailing does not mean that we will be perfect; it means we will be honest. We are not perfectly righteous. We are not always Israel. The struggle does not annihilate the Jacob within. Sometimes we slip into Jacob consciousness and begin to mimic Esau again just to survive.

Yet *this* is what is meant by the higher self. When we honor the place where we struggle because we see the face of God in it, we cultivate the *middah* of transforming heel consciousness into face consciousness. And then we honor the person with whom we struggle—another person or ourselves—because we can now see the face of God in this human being too.

The Practice

1. Begin with breath awareness.
2. Then, reflect on the text.
3. Move to quieting down your mind.

These three steps are explained in detail in the introduction.

4. Visualize a time you struggled with your self-identity. What is the content? What is your emotional landscape? When you look into the mirror from this place, who do you see? Are you running away from yourself, desperate to be someone you're not—a heel grasper? Or are you running toward yourself and others?

If you sense that at times you are living with heel consciousness, what does this feel like? Painful emotions (such as guilt, shame, self-loathing, jealousy) may arise when we are not living our true selves. This practice invites us to be open to those feelings, recognize them, and perhaps see them as angels, divine messengers, with whom we wrestle. We are invited to wrestle with them—whether we prevail this time or not.

If you also sense that at times you are living with face consciousness, what does *this* feel like? Both positive emotions (such as self-confidence, self-assurance, trust that you are experiencing a glimpse of who you are truly meant to be) and more difficult emotions (such as fear, anxiety, hesitancy) might accompany a square confrontation with yourself. Pause, and experience the capacity, potential, and strength enclothed in all of this.

Now, as you receive life through the breath, imagine you are receiving face consciousness. Pause and reflect on this experience of receiving this blessing. As you return the breath, gently let go of heel consciousness. Pause and reflect on the experience of bidding farewell to the angels with whom you struggled.

Do you allow yourself to honor your inner Jacob and to celebrate your inner Israel?

This is the practice. This is the struggle. This is the sacred moment: "To see your face is like seeing the face of God" (Gen. 33:10). This is the higher you, when you honor the place where you struggle because you see the face of God within it.

Va-yeshev

Navigating Our Inner Opposing Personalities

Israel said to Joseph . . . , "Your brothers are pasturing at Shechem. Come, I will send you to them." He answered, "I am ready." And he said to him, "Go and see how your brothers are and how the flocks are faring, and bring me back word." . . . When Joseph came up to his brothers, they stripped Joseph of his tunic, the ornamented tunic that he was wearing, and took him and cast him into the pit. . . . Then Judah said to his brothers, "What do we gain by killing our brother and covering up his blood? Come, let us sell him to the Ishmaelites, but let us not do away with him ourselves. After all, he is our brother, our own flesh." His brothers agreed.

Gen. 37:13–27

Where We Are

Jacob (now also known as Israel) and Esau reconcile and part from each other in peace. Jacob's wife Rachel dies while giving birth to Benjamin, the twelfth son. Jacob and his father Isaac are reunited in Hebron. Isaac passes away.

Jacob settles down in Hebron. Joseph, the first of the two sons of Jacob and Rachel, recounts to the family dreams of ascending to such power and fame that his own father and brothers will bow down to him. His brothers are enraged. Our verses continue this narrative.

At First Glance

Rashi (Shlomo Yitzhaki, eleventh c., France) draws our attention to Joseph's response to his father's request that he catch up with his brothers. He answers, "*He'nei'nee*—I am ready." Whenever this phrase is used in the Bible, "it is an expression of humility and readiness," Rashi explains.

"Here he is enthusiastic to fulfill his father's request, even though he knew his brothers hated him."[1]

As Joseph wanders in the fields of Shechem in pursuit of his brothers, the text tells us that "a man came upon him" who, upon Joseph's inquiry, tells him his brothers decided to go to Dothan. Who is this stranger, and how could he know who Joseph and his brothers are? Rashi comes to explain that this mystery man is in fact the angel Gabriel.[2]

As it so happens, Joseph's encounter with the "man" becomes a pivotal moment that determines the rest of Jewish history.

However, right now Joseph does not know that. And ostensibly he has already fulfilled his father's wishes at this point—Jacob had requested he go to Shechem, and he has. Not having found his brothers here, he could simply return home.

But Joseph continues to search for his brothers, despite his awareness that their future encounter is liable to be discordant and tense. Rashi interprets the stranger's guidance to Joseph, typically translated as "they have gone from here," as "they have departed from all feelings of brotherhood."[3] Perhaps, then, the angel Gabriel is warning Joseph: proceed with caution or go home.

Why doesn't Joseph return home? His decision to pursue the search for his brothers seems to exemplify two opposite character traits. On the one hand, he models prioritizing others: he fulfills the mitzvah of respecting one's parents by exerting the extra effort to do so. Yet Joseph also prioritizes self-perfection, seen both in his dreams of ascending to power and fame, and here by what might be his inner drive to succeed at even an unpleasant task.

In this light, Joseph's act of persistence has utmost significance for what happens next. Joseph's encounter with his brothers in Dothan sets the next major chapter in the evolution of the nation of Israel in motion, as it eventually leads to Jacob moving his family to Egypt, to the Israelites becoming enslaved by the Egyptians, to the Exodus from Egypt, and to the covenant at Sinai. At this moment, though, those realities are far in the future. Joseph's brothers have flung him into a pit. His brother Judah now takes the lead in preparing to sell him into slavery.

In this episode Judah confidently assumes a position of leadership—itself a form of self-actualization—while his brothers acquiesce to his suggestion and follow his lead (Gen. 37:27). Yet, later, he comes across as a humble person dedicated to being in the service of others. When, for example, he publicly proclaims that he wronged Tamar, "She is more in the right than I, inasmuch as I did not give her to my son Shelah [when I should have]" (Gen. 38:26), he opts to confess his own wrongdoing in order to spare his daughter-in-law's reputation. Again, we see two ostensibly contradictory inclinations existing simultaneously within both Joseph and Judah.

A Deeper Dive

The Lubavitcher Rebbe (Menachem Mendel Schneerson, twentieth c., United States) develops this idea in a different light when he asserts that Judah and Joseph possess irreconcilably opposite impulses, as manifested in each of their views of their purpose in life.[4] Joseph—whose name means "to add"—desires ongoing growth, self-fulfillment, and achievement, whereas Judah—whose name means "to acknowledge or admit"—seeks to be in service to that which is greater than self. The Rebbe teaches that these two seemingly antithetical forces—personal achievement and giving over of self—are contained within each of us as well:

> The Joseph/Judah conflict is a dichotomy that extends to every area of life: the conflict between growth and self-fulfillment on the one hand, and dedication and commitment on the other. There are many identifiable motives to human actions, many formulas for the articulation of a purpose to human life. All, however, fall under one of two general categories: 1) For ourselves (to enjoy life, realize our potential, achieve transcendence, etc.) 2) In service of something greater than ourselves (society, history, G-d).

Indeed, we sense both to be ever-present forces in our lives. On the one hand, we are strongly driven to better ourselves, to "get the most" out of every experience and opportunity. We also sense that this is not a shallow selfishness, but something very deep and true in our souls — something implanted in us by our Creator as intrinsic to our identity and purpose.

On the other hand, we are equally aware that we are part of something greater than ourselves — that if our existence has meaning, it is only because it serves a reality beyond its own finite and subjective self.[5]

Might we view these two forces as not condemned to remain in opposition? The Rebbe concludes: "There is a point at which the two converge and unite. This is the moment when we recognize that the refinement of self can itself be an act of service — when it is undertaken because we sense, *This is what the Creator desires of me*."[6] In effect, the reconciliation happens when the Judah persona absorbs and employs the Joseph persona for higher purpose.

This absorption seems to manifest in Joseph when he promises to honor his father's request to bury him in the family burial site in Caanan. Joseph utters confidently, "I will do as you have spoken" (Gen. 47:30), because, as second-in-command over the Egyptian empire, he has the authority to facilitate his father's request — and so he does.

Similarly, this absorption seems to manifest in Judah when he asks the Egyptian vizier to enslave him instead of his younger brother Benjamin: "Therefore, please let your servant remain as a slave to my lord instead of the boy, and let the boy go back with his brothers. For how can I go back to my father unless the boy is with me? Let me not be witness to the woe that would overtake my father!" (Gen. 44:33–34). Judah's commitment to his father to ensure Benjamin's safe return home emboldens him to voice an objection and substitute plan that might well have led to his being sentenced to death — had Joseph not been the (disguised) authority evaluating the proposition.

These insights on harmonizing the "Joseph" and "Judah" aspects of us have been transformative in my own life. Several decades ago, I was deeply immersed in the ultra-Orthodox world. My Jewishness exemplified the "Judah" life of being in service — to such a painful extreme that living the "Joseph" life of self-fulfillment seemed unimaginable. Intuitively I sensed that I did possess the ability to fulfill the deep but faint call to leadership and live a life actualizing more of my own inner potentials. However, the demands and expectations of me emphasized external performance and observance of the mitzvot. Some of my teachers attempted to convince me that my own sense of purpose in realizing personal potentials paled in importance with dedicating my life to being in service to God. In a sense, I was expected to negate my own individual self.

Somehow, I deeply intuited that I could honor both approaches. I had to cease ignoring the Joseph in me by only living my inner Judah. A better self, I realized, is a self who is better resourced to fulfill its purpose in creation. Indeed, the making of this better self may actually represent the ultimate service of God.

I felt hopeful that I could honor both of my Joseph and Judah dispositions. And over time, I came to glean wisdom, including the teachings here, that helped me to better harmonize the two.

I believe that if we can attain this textured service for the Divine, then the Judah and the Joseph in us can exist in full harmony. Our Judah may reign sovereign—the ultimate criterion is, of course, service to the Divine—but the passions and ambitions of the Joseph in us will receive full expression for that divine service. Navigating our inner opposing personalities may actually reveal their potential to enhance each other by being in harmony with each other. Indeed, the lines between them might even blur and dissolve.

The Practice

1. Begin with breath awareness.
2. Then, reflect on the text.
3. Move to quieting down your mind.

These three steps are explained in detail in the introduction.

4. Direct your awareness to embodying the Joseph force. Visualize yourself manifesting your Joseph force in the world. Lean gently into this driving force that develops your potential, manifests innate talents and skills, and cultivates a sense of self-worth. What is your

Joseph energy like? What are your thoughts? What feelings does this awaken, intellectually, emotionally, bodily, spiritually?

Then, while you're still in the Joseph energy, try to lean softly into the Judah energy, the space of being in service to something greater than your finite self. Can you be present with both energies simultaneously? Or, if you're having trouble experiencing this, can you imagine a scenario where you feel called to yield to something greater than your own inner world while you simultaneously aspire to refine yourself to be a "better you"?

With either scenario, what thoughts and feelings awaken in you? Is there tension between the two leanings, or do you find yourself able to strike a balance, giving both the Joseph and Judah energies a platform for expression? How might you navigate your inner Judah and Joseph from here?

Mikkets

Removing Our Disguises to Show Our True Selves

> Now Joseph was the vizier of the land; it was he who dispensed rations
> to all the people of the land. And Joseph's brothers came and bowed low
> to him, with their faces to the ground. When Joseph saw his brothers,
> he recognized them; but he acted like a stranger toward them and spoke
> harshly to them. He asked them, "Where do you come from?" And they
> said, "From the land of Canaan, to procure food." For though Joseph
> recognized his brothers, they did not recognize him.
>
> Gen. 42:6–8

Where We Are

The Ishmaelites sell Joseph to the Egyptians. Potiphar, a prominent member of Pharaoh's court, purchases Joseph and finds favor with him—until Potiphar's wife, spurned in her attempts to seduce Joseph, slanders him to her husband, and Potiphar has Joseph imprisoned. Pharoah imprisons both his royal cupbearer and baker as well, and Joseph accurately interprets their dreams.

Pharoah wants to understand his own dreams. His royal cupbearer (his sentence now commuted) tells Pharoah about Joseph's prescient interpretation of his dream. Summoned, Joseph interprets Pharaoh's dreams, forecasting seven years of plenty followed by famine. Pharoah promotes Joseph to viceroy, second in command only to himself, and when the famine happens as projected, entrusts him with distributing Egypt's stockpiled food to the needy world.

After twenty-two years, Joseph and his siblings meet again—but the situation could not be more different. When last they saw each other, his brothers, enraged at this favored son who shared his dreams of ruling over all the family, sold him into slavery. Now, through an inconceivable course of events, his brothers arrive in Egypt to beg him for food. The prophetic nature of his original dream begins to manifest as his brothers "bowed to him, faces to the ground" (Gen. 42:6)

At First Glance

How can we understand the verse telling us that Joseph recognized his brothers, but they did not recognize him? Rashi (Shlomo Yitzhaki, eleventh c., France) explains that when they last saw each other, the brothers were all already bearded, while young Joseph had had no beard and now was bearded and unrecognizable.

Ibn Ezra (Abraham ibn Ezra, eleventh–twelfth c., Spain) suggests that Joseph first recognized the group as his brothers and then recognized each brother individually.[1] So while the brothers saw a high-ranking Egyptian in front of them, Joseph saw his family.

Yet he decides to keep this knowledge and his identity a secret. Rashi explains Joseph's acting "like a stranger toward them" to refer to his "speaking harshly."[2] Expanding on this, Sforno (Obadiah ben Jacob Sforno, fifteenth–sixteenth c., Italy) says Joseph masked his voice and mannerisms and "spoke to them in Egyptian [while] having everything he said translated into Hebrew by an interpreter."[3]

Why didn't Joseph reveal himself to his brothers straightaway? Is anything gained by this ruse? The text does not answer these questions. The answers may be revealed in deeper spiritual commentaries.

A Deeper Dive

The scene of Joseph recognizing his brothers all the while they mistake him is one of four "type-scenes" in Genesis in which one character dons a disguise to deceive another. First, Jacob misleads Isaac by pretending to be his brother Esau (Gen. 27:1–27). Next, Leah misleads Jacob into thinking he has wed her sister Rachel, who Jacob loves, rather than her (Gen. 29:25). Then, Tamar misleads Judah into thinking he is lying with a prostitute, rather than his own daughter-in-law, in hopes of (eventually) convincing him to let her marry his last son Shelah (Gen. 38:11–16). Finally, Joseph misleads his brothers about who the viceroy of Egypt truly is.

Rabbi Jonathan Sacks (twentieth–twenty-first c., England) suggests that all four characters choosing disguises share the need to be loved by the people they deceive. However, their deceptions do not lead to this, but to something more important:

Jacob, Leah, Tamar and Joseph discover that, though they may never win the affection of those from whom they seek it, God is with them; and that, ultimately, is enough. A disguise is an act of hiding—from others, and perhaps from oneself. From God, however, we cannot, nor do we need to, hide. He hears our cry. He answers our unspoken prayer. He heeds the unheeded and brings them comfort. In the aftermath of the four episodes, there is no healing of relationship but there is a mending of identity. That is what makes them not secular narratives but deeply religious chronicles of psychological growth and maturation. What they tell us is simple and profound: those who stand before God need no disguises to achieve self-worth when standing before humankind.[4]

Rabbi Sacks suggests that if we lack the awareness of the Divine in our lives, we may wind up relying on other people to define our sense of self-worth. This can lead us to project a disguise to others, with the hopes of fulfilling our human need to be loved. The Hasidic masters—knowing the importance of cultivating the inner life as the key to self-worth—emphasize the need to encounter the Divine within. Then a disguise is never necessary.

Rabbi Sacks's teaching may hint at why Joseph didn't reveal himself to his brothers straightway. Many of us experience inner emptiness when our need to be needed by others is unmet; conversely, the fulfillment of this need contributes to our well-being. Earlier, Joseph's brothers had clearly demonstrated they did not need him. Now, while disguised, the brothers clearly express they do.

Nonetheless, given the brothers' desperation, even if Joseph had revealed himself to them, they still would have needed him! This leads to the question of whether anything is gained by this ruse. Rabbi Sacks answers with an emphatic yes. While the text does not explicitly state this, Sacks seems to be teaching that by the very act of not revealing himself to his brothers, Joseph senses the Divine Presence in his interaction with them. Why? Perhaps because Joseph now realizes that his true self can never hide in a disguise before his Creator. His true unmasked self remains the only image he can show to the Divine.

As the story unfolds, Joseph does allude to having a connection with the Divine at an earlier (unspecified) point, perhaps during the type-scene of disguise. Revealing his true self to his brothers at last, he proclaims, "God has sent me ahead of you to ensure your survival on earth, and to save your lives in an extraordinary deliverance" (Gen. 45:7). And this divine connection is what allows him to forgive his brothers: "Now, do not be distressed or reproach yourselves because you sold me hither; it was to save life that God sent me ahead of you" (Gen.45:5).

Delving deeper, Joseph himself may have yearned to sense the Divine Presence in his life without success until he saw his brothers once again. Without conscious awareness, he may have been inclined to remain incognito so as to experience God's presence in this potent moment. Perhaps, in a circuitous way, Joseph was so desperate to be reunited with his brothers in a loving and compassionate way, he subconsciously realized that only when he sensed the Divine Presence, would he then be able to truthfully connect with his brothers.

And yet, the Piaseczner Rebbe (Kalonymus Kalmish Shapira, twentieth c., Poland) warns in general (not specific to this Torah portion) about "living out of alignment with our inner truth."[5] The nature of the Divine is Truth, he says, and so lying about our identity is a force that undermines one's authentic living. Ultimately, donning disguises not only raises a veil between us and another person, but also between ourselves and the Divine. To counter the impulse to bend the truth about who we are, he prescribes "wholeheartedness and simplicity":

Plant life sprouts with wholeheartedness and simplicity, with no external intent and motive. Rather, its soul compels it to sprout and grow. Just in this way, a small child behaves in all of his affairs with simplicity and wholeheartedness, in accordance with the existence of his soul, as it spreads forth. Were an adult also to behave in all of his affairs and engage in all of his thoughts, guided by the light of his soul, he also would be wholehearted and truthful.[6]

In our Torah portion, the implication seems to be that Joseph's immediately revealing his true identity to his brothers would have exemplified his acting "guided by the light of his soul" with "wholeheartedness and simplicity." The irony is not lost here: Joseph's wearing a disguise leads him to the same place that living truthfully likely would have led him: to an awareness of the Divine. The former eventually led the masked Joseph to need an awareness of the Divine before proceeding further with his brothers. The latter would have led the unmasked Joseph to manifest his awareness of the Divine when proceeding further with his brothers. Two different paths to the same end destination.

All the while, removing our disguises to show our true selves can lead to our feeling loved for who we truly are.

The Practice

1. Begin with breath awareness.
2. Then, reflect on the text.
3. Move to quieting down your mind.

These three steps are explained in detail in the introduction.

4. Visualize a moment that brings you into direct contact with a part of yourself that you associate with wearing a disguise. Allow your heart to open up to whatever feelings this engenders. Has wearing masks led to fearfulness (of being rejected, unloved, or exposed), shame (in not believing in your own self-worth), confusion? Does mask wearing play a powerful role in your day-to-day living?

We all share basic human needs: for connection, respect, attention, inclusion, and love. Just as much, we all need to feel needed and experience a sense of self-worth. Ponder two questions: Does hiding my true self serve me well? Does showing myself to the world in disguise fulfill these needs?

Anything within us that can influence our lives strongly is worthy of attention and awareness. In our practice, we need to recognize and even honor the mask-wearing part of ourselves. So as you begin to excavate perhaps a darker side of yourself, pause! I invite you not to run away. Remain where you are and soften your awareness of what you are thinking and feeling. With the curiosity of an explorer, review what caused you to don the disguise. What needs were not being met that led to this deception of self?

Imagine accepting wholeheartedly that Rabbi Sacks's insight, "Those who stand before God need no disguises to achieve self-worth when standing before humankind," includes you! How might it look and feel to take up the Piaseczner Rebbe's guidance to cultivate "simplicity and wholeheartedness" as the way you show up in the world?

Doing this work as a spiritual practice can open us up to both loss and liberation.

Va-yiggash

Seeking and Granting Forgiveness

> Then Judah went up to him and said, "Please, my lord, let your servant
> appeal to my lord, and do not be impatient with your servant, you who
> are the equal to Pharoah."
>
> Gen. 44:18

Where We Are

Having recognized his brothers who sold him into slavery, Joseph—
now the vizier of Egypt, in charge of distributing food to the famine-
stricken world—remains incognito. Joseph incarcerates Simeon and
conditionalizes his release on the brothers' returning with their youngest
brother, Benjamin. When they bring him, Joseph frames Benjamin for
theft and arrests him.

Judah, who had originally suggested selling Joseph to the Ishmaelites (Gen. 37:26–27), now intervenes on his younger brother's behalf. A
little later, he offers himself as a slave in Benjamin's stead (Gen. 44:33).

At First Glance

From Judah's plea that Joseph "not be impatient" with him, Rashi (Shlomo
Yitzhaki, eleventh c., France) says that "you can learn that Joseph spoke
to him harshly."[1]

In this framing, with trepidation, Judah approaches an ill-tempered
magistrate from whom he requests mercy. Alternatively, Sforno (Obadiah
ben Jacob Sforno, fifteenth–sixteenth c., Italy) paints a much more asser-
tive Judah, teaching that this line should be read, "And do not become
impatient when I tell you that you have caused this injustice against our
will."[2] By this understanding (with support from the previous verse, in
which Joseph refuses to arrest all the brothers along with Benjamin

because it would be "degrading" for him to "pervert justice"), Judah is "sweet talking" the magistrate by appealing to his bend toward justice.[3]

In either reading, Judah is standing up for his youngest brother. Here again Judah is in the position to give up one of his brothers, but this time he offers up himself (not Benjamin) as a slave to the Egyptian vizier. Shedding light on *why* Judah protects Benjamin — because of his own guilty conscience (having betrayed Joseph many years ago) or as a result of a true change of heart, Rambam (Moses ben Nachman, twelfth–thirteenth c., Egypt) teaches that when we are put in the same situation in which we once misstepped and make a different choice, it is considered a full return to God (in Hebrew, *teshuvah*).[4]

Perhaps Joseph even contrived these circumstances to allow Judah to complete his personal *teshuvah*. We might therefore equate Joseph's behavior toward Judah as his yet-to-be-revealed desire to forgive Judah.

A Deeper Dive

The Maggid of Mezritch (Dov Ber Friedman, eighteenth c., Ukraine) sees this request not only as an interpersonal one but also as a testament to Judah speaking with the inner Divine Presence. Creatively rendering *bee* — which normally translates as "please" — as "in me," another of its other meanings, he proposes an alternative reading of the above verse, "Please, my lord, let your servant appeal to my lord, and do not be impatient with your servant":

> Then Judah approaches [the Divine] in prayer and speaks to the Eternal *in me*, "Please, my GOD, let Your servant appeal to my GOD, for Your sake, for behold I am a portion of the Supernal God, and do not be impatient with Your servant. Do not let the accusers persecute me, for all I intend is to bring blessing to the portion of the Creator that resides within me. *For in me is my* GOD and through me the Divine speaks."[5]

In this case, by reading "my lord" as "my GOD," we may understand the Maggid to mean that Judah's plea to become the Egyptian viceroy's slave in place of Benjamin extends beyond Judah speaking to Joseph and also God. I would suggest we can view this as the indwelling Divine speaking *through* Judah to Joseph—as if simultaneously Judah speaks to the Divine within him, and *this* plea is what Joseph hears.

In essence, prayer can now act as the bridge between the micro and the macro, with the individual becoming the mouthpiece for the Divine. Our particular needs mirror a bigger heavenly need. Here, Judah seems to be bringing to Joseph more than his own personal need to be heard and heeded. Rather, it appears that the indwelling Divine is revealing to Joseph a lack in the Higher Realm that sorely needs to be filled, and Joseph can be the instrument through which this manifests: the *middah* of forgiveness, which hitherto the Creator had yet to introduce into the world—and does for the first time now.

Indeed, through this influx of spiritual awareness, Joseph does hear the indwelling Divine speaking through Judah. Hence, in a dramatic turn of events, his response to Judah's plea to be enslaved instead of Benjamin goes far beyond what even he originally may have intended to do until he heard Judah speak. At this point, "Joseph could no longer control himself before all his attendants, and he cried out . . . to his brothers, I am Joseph. Is my father still well? But his brothers could not answer him, so dumbfounded were they on account of him" (Gen. 45:1–3).

And now we bear witness to the first time in the Torah one human being forgives another. Joseph asserts: "Now do not be distressed or reproach yourselves because you sold me hither; it was to save life that God sent me ahead of you. . . . It was not you who sent me here, but God" (Gen. 45:5,8).

Rabbi Jonathan Sacks (twentieth–twenty-first c., England) teaches that Joseph's response was one of those "moments that change the world," because it was "the first recorded moment in history in which one human being forgives another" following the latter's repentance.

However, the actual word "forgive" is not used; rather, Joseph says his brothers should not be "distressed." Rabbi Sacks suggests, "That is why the Torah recounts a second event, [seventeen] years later, after [their father] Jacob had died. In the next Torah portion, *Va-yeḥi*, the brothers sought a meeting with Joseph fearing that he would now take revenge." They concoct a story of their father having reminded them to ask Joseph for forgiveness after his passing (Gen. 50:16–18), likely because they had not yet felt forgiven. Rabbi Sacks adds: "Joseph weeps that his brothers did not originally understand that forgiveness is precisely what he meant."[6]

We might return to the Maggid's teaching that what enabled Joseph to forgive his brothers was actually hearing God's voice speaking to him through Judah to consider how it might apply to our own seeking and granting of forgiveness. When we can sense the Divine Presence within a person who has hurt us and seeks forgiveness—or even before that forgiveness is sought—it can become easier for us to forgive. It may seem as if the Divine Voice is gently whispering to us to be forgiving.

In this sense we can view the next Torah portion, *Va-yeḥi*, as a continuum of this portion. In fact, the Torah scroll itself suggests this idea. *Va-yeḥi* is the only Torah portion Rashi identifies as "closed," meaning the only one in which no extra space appears between it and the prior Torah portion (our current parashah, *Va-yiggash*) in the text of a Torah scroll.[7] This oddity connotes an unusually strong connection between these two portions, and forgiveness bookends both: *Va-yiggash* begins with Joseph forgiving his brothers and *Va-yeḥi* ends with his brothers not feeling forgiven, so forgiveness needs to be extended again.

But why didn't the brothers feel that Joseph truly forgave them? Might it be in part because they did not forgive themselves? Just as one needs to forgive other human beings, those people need to forgive themselves. For many of us this can be terribly difficult.

Seeing one's life through a spiritual—rather than ego-oriented—lens can help. Joseph endeavors to help his brothers let go of the past with spiritual guidance: "Besides, although you intended me harm, God intended it for good, so as to bring about the present result—the survival of many people" (Gen. 50:20) This does not disregard our mandate to assume responsibility for making amends and seeking forgiveness when we engender harm. Yet at some point after we do that, we might just come to realize that the offense was part of the divine plan.

Can we forgive ourselves? Yes! Why? Because the part of our inner being that will always forgive us is the Divine Presence dwelling within each of us. When we believe that God resides within us (see *Va-yishlah*), we may come to rely on this Divine Presence to forgive us. And when our Inner Being forgives the actions of our external being, this also becomes a means of encountering the Divine within.

Hence, the practice of forgiveness actually includes three, rather than two, components: 1) the seeking of forgiveness from another, 2) the granting of forgiveness to another, and 3) the forgiving of oneself. All the more, cultivating the *middah* of forgiveness can help each of us reveal our godly selves.

The Practice

1. Begin with breath awareness.
2. Then, reflect on the text.
3. Move to quieting down your mind.

These three steps are explained in detail in the introduction.

4. Going into the visualization feeling relaxed, focused, and open-hearted, invoke a time when someone hurt you, intentionally or not. If you can, gently lean into your feelings of betrayal, pain, and being taken advantage of. Are you still hurting?

If you can give yourself permission to do this, despite the discomfort, it may become your first step toward forgiving the person who caused you to suffer. If, however, you are not ready for this—because the practice might bring up painful residual trauma—visualize what a kinder and more compassionate world would look and feel like. Could forgiveness play a role in advancing the world to this redeemed and healed place?

Even if you feel able to continue the practice, you might question why you would forgive this person. As Joseph's descendants, we have inherited his capacity to forgive. Imagine encountering your inner Joseph—opening up to the possibility that what has happened is part of a divine plan, for reasons that may be clear or may not.

Is it possible for you to sense a Divine Presence in the perpetrator of your hurt? Is it possible for you to reach into your spiritual toolbox and take out compassion, a tool that can allow us to see reality in a deeper way?

Now, invite the divine energy within you to manifest. This is the piece of you that is pure.

Gently pause.

Redirect your awareness to your breathing cycle.

Imagine a time in your life when you were the one who hurt another and now seek forgiveness. Imagine the pain of the person you hurt. Do you sense hurt within you as well?

If you have been able to forgive another person during this practice, does that act of forgiveness support you in seeking forgiveness from the person you have harmed? And from yourself as well if need be?

Are you moved to cultivate the practice of *teshuvah*—returning to your higher and more pure self, the source of forgiveness?

Va-yeḥi

Finding Favor in Others

> And when the time approached for Israel to die, he summoned his son
> Joseph and said to him, "Please, if I have found favor in your eyes, please
> put your hand under my thigh and deal kindly and truthfully with me,
> please do not bury me in Egypt. For I will lie down with my fathers and
> you shall bring me out of Egypt and bury me in their tomb."
>
> Gen. 47:29–30[1]

Where We Are

Joseph forgives his brothers for having sold him into slavery. They return
to Canaan to share the good news with their father Jacob, who has long
believed that Joseph was killed. God tells Jacob: "Fear not to go down
to Egypt, for I will make you there into a great nation" (Gen. 46:3). The
family of seventy settles in Egypt and Pharaoh grants them some of his
best land. Seventeen years after settling in Egypt, Jacob, on his death-
bed, asks Joseph to swear that he will bring his body back to Canaan to
be buried with Leah, his parents, and his grandparents.

At First Glance

Rashi (Shlomo Yitzhaki, eleventh c., France) explains that Jacob directs
his wish to Joseph and not any of his other eleven sons because Joseph,
second-in-command in Egypt, was the only one "who had the power in
his hands to do what he was about to ask."[2] Ultimately, Pharoah would
have to approve the burial of one of his subjects outside of Egypt—which
Pharoah was liable to perceive as a disrespectful affront to his monarchy.
No one but Joseph could even have hoped for Pharoah's permission.
Pharoah does grant Joseph's request, and Joseph follows through with
the burial (Gen. 50:4–13).

Still, it is not clear from our verse why Jacob had conditioned his request to be buried in Canaan on whether he found *hein* (favor) in Joseph's eyes ("Please, if I have found favor in your eyes . . . I will lie down with my fathers and you shall bring me out of Egypt and bury me in their tomb"). Given the cultural value of honoring one's parents, why didn't Jacob simply expect Joseph's loyalty to suffice?

To answer this puzzling question, we need to better understand what *hein* means. Traditionally the word invokes sentiments of favor or acceptance, though Onkelos (first c., Jerusalem) translates *hein* as "compassion" and its precise definition remains unclear.[3]

The first mention of "finding *hein*" occurs in the Torah portion of Noah—"But Noah found *hein* with GOD" (Gen. 6:8)—and then recurs six more times in the Hebrew Bible (Gen. 18:3, Gen. 30:27, Gen. 33:10, Gen. 47:29—our passage—Judg. 6:17, and Esther 5:8). In all, then, "finding *hein*" only appears seven times—a rare biblical usage that compounds the challenge of comprehending its meaning here. Further challenging our quest, the commentaries do not explain "finding *hein*" either.

A Deeper Dive

Returning to the original question, "Why did Jacob insist that Joseph find this quality (*hein*) in him?," we might view the lack of traditional guidance on how to interpret "finding *hein*" as its own clue to its definition. We might presume that *hein* is particular and specific to each person, so much so that this uniqueness contributes to it lacking an absolute and objective definition. In fact, we may understand that *hein* assumes a relative meaning—the quality trait within each of us that defines and distinguishes us as being our unique selves. Finding *hein* in oneself and in another now becomes the subjective experience of that person's unique character.

Through this lens, perhaps Jacob was hoping Joseph would see in him his own importance, specialness, and individuality—that he, as his particular self, mattered, beyond his being Joseph's father. With Jacob's full knowledge of the outlandish, possibly dangerous nature of his ask, it may have been even more important to him that Joseph thought him worthy of being buried in the family plot in Canaan. *Hein* must perhaps be understood as a relational awareness—not only of how we subjectively experience ourselves and our fellow human beings but also of how we experience our awareness of the same.

Supporting this idea of self-discovery of inner *ḥein*, Rebbe Nachman of Breslov (eighteen–nineteenth c., Ukraine) teaches, "For in every Jew there is something precious, an aspect of a [point], which their friend does not have."[4] I would suggest by extension that this refers to all human beings. And this unique preciousness in each of us enhances the uniqueness of *ḥein* within each person. *Ḥein* may in fact be the unique gift that our Creator has bestowed upon each of us.

Rabbi Shmuel Weiss (twenty-first c., Israel) posits a unique understanding of *ḥein* while addressing the spiritual malady known as *sinat ḥinam*, "baseless hatred." Usually, the word *ḥinam* means for free, or baseless—having no reason. If so, he notes, a person might surmise that its remedy would be *ahavat ḥinam*, "baseless love," but: "'The phrase '*sinat chinam* [*ḥinam*]' literally means 'hatred of others' *chein* [*ḥein*].' *Sinat chinam* is the denial of another's right to exist, the belief that they contribute nothing valuable to this earth. That attitude is an affront not only to the other person, but also to God Who made that individual. The antidote to *sinat chinam*, then, is not really 'free love,' but rather the respect of every other person's unique place in God's universe."[5]

If this is the case, Jacob may have sought from Joseph the love of his own unique place—his *ḥein*—in the Creator's universe. We might then ask, "What was so particularly special about Jacob that for that reason alone, Joseph swore to fulfill his father's request?" The text never conveys what Jacob had hoped his son would see in him, or what Joseph did in fact find uniquely special in his father. Instead, we might take to heart the teaching in the condition Jacob imposed on Joseph: to discover this precious aspect of his father.

I would suggest an additional interpretation of the word *ḥein*. In Hebrew, *ḥein* is spelled *ḥet-nun*, which can also be read as an acronym for *ḥein nistar*, "hidden wisdom." (Perhaps this is why *ḥein* may be difficult to translate into one or two words; it may very well be hidden even from ourselves!) Each of us possesses the precious jewel of hidden wisdom. However, many people lack the awareness of their own inner hidden wisdom, and, like me, may live for years without knowing they even possess it. Maybe we are being asked to uncover and reveal this treasure of awareness that lays deep within us. Just as for Jacob finding this precious jewel of *ḥein* took on great significance, he may be inspiring us, his descendants, to do the same.

An understanding in this vein may very well raise the question: If finding our own *ḥein* may be a daunting challenge, is it any wonder that someone else would not see our *ḥein* when they look at us? Perhaps we have to first become aware of our own *ḥein* to then see *ḥein* in others—and for others to find *ḥein* in us.

Might this be why Jacob asked for it from Joseph? Perhaps he wanted to give his son the gift of being able to find his own *ḥein* first, which would then enable him to see his father's.

Today, it becomes a special moment and source of gratitude when any of us experiences what makes us individually and uniquely who we are. And from this awareness and appreciation of our inner *ḥein*, we may be opened to seek out, experience, and value the inner *ḥein* of others.

So it is that manifesting our individual *ḥein* into the world may become a powerful, compassionate, and effective way to cultivate connection with others. This then becomes a transformative process: from *sinat ḥinam*, "hating another's uniqueness," to *ahavat ḥinam*, "loving another's uniqueness."

There is a beautiful Hasidic teaching that the day each of us was born is the day the Creator decided the world can no longer exist without you in it.[6] Our individual uniqueness is the Creator's gift to each of us—and our own gift to each other, to encourage each other to discover this gift within every one of us.

The Practice

1. Begin with breath awareness.
2. Then, reflect on the text.
3. Move to quieting down your mind.

These three steps are explained in detail in the introduction.

4. Visualize yourself gently dropping into your internal self with the curiosity of an explorer. As you gaze into the mirror of your own identity, what do you believe makes you uniquely "you"? Imagine that *ḥein* is the Creator's middle name for you (David Ḥein, Debra Ḥein, Dana Ḥein, etc.). What best describes your unique *ḥein*? How does your existence—your very life—matter, so much so that the Creator decided the world can no longer be sustained without you in it?

Do you sense *this* is your authentic true self? What feelings come up for you?

Might *this* be what you are meant to share with the world?

Would you wish other people to find your *ḥein* in you? Would you wish to find the *ḥein* in others?

Now, as you immerse yourself in these purifying waters of *ḥein* energy, direct your awareness to an individual you connect with. Do you experience their finding favor—*ḥein*—in your eyes? Do you find favor—*ḥein*—in this person's eyes?

2

Exodus (Shemot)

Shemot

Overcoming Habitual Behaviors

> When GOD saw that he had turned aside to look, God called to him out
> of the bush: "Moses! Moses!" He answered, "Here I am." And [God] said,
> "Do not come closer! Remove your sandals from your feet, for the place
> on which you stand is holy ground!"
>
> Exod. 3:4–5

Where We Are

Shortly before Joseph passes away, he adjures his family to ensure that
when the Hebrews are redeemed from what will soon be their harsh
enslavement, they will bring his bones up to Israel for interment in
the holy land.

A new king arises over Egypt who enslaves the Hebrews. Yocheved
lays her newborn son Moses in a handmade basket among the reeds
in the Nile in hopes of saving him from the mandatory drowning of all
newborn Israelite boys. Pharaoh's daughter finds and adopts Moses, and
for forty years he grows up in the King's palace. He smites an Egyptian
for striking a Hebrew slave and then flees to Midian, where he marries
Zipporah, daughter of Yitro, the Priest of Midian. He lives with his new
family for the next forty years.

The Eternal decides that the time of salvation for the Hebrews
has arrived, and Moses will be the redeemer. As Moses goes about
his daily shepherding of the flock, God appears to him in a blaze of
fire from within a bush—and yet, extraordinarily, the bush is not
consumed. Moses approaches the bush, seeking to understand why
it is not burning.

Moses' revelation of God is replete with wonder: "a blazing fire out of a bush" (Exod. 3:2).

Rashi (Shlomo Yitzhaki, eleventh c., France) points out that the root of the word *labat*—"blazing"—is *lamed-bet*, which means "heart." Thus, he teaches, the messenger of God appeared to Moses in the "heart of the fire."[1]

This is Moses' first encounter with the Divine, and while Rashi does not comment on how the "heart of the fire" may relate to Moses himself, I would suggest an important connection. Perhaps Moses' witnessing of this extraordinary external phenomenon affected him very deeply, as if—as is the case with many transformative experiences—he experienced the "heart of his own fire."

Nachmanides (Moses ben Nachman, thirteenth c., Spain and Acre, the Holy Land) compares the divine requirement that Moses remove his sandals ("'Remove your sandals from your feet, for the place on which you stand is holy ground!'") to other such mandates in the Bible, among them Joshua 5:15: "The captain of GOD's host answered Joshua, 'Remove your sandals from your feet, for the place where you stand is holy.' And Joshua did so." Nachmanides concludes that Moses (and the others) must remain barefoot because of the holiness permeating the site.[2]

Yet, what defines this ground as holy, and why would that necessitate the removal of footwear?

A Deeper Dive

According to the Zohar, the primary source of Jewish mysticism, the first word in the Torah—*bere'shit*, meaning "in the beginning"—is alluded to in every weekly Torah portion.[3] Just as the brain (in the head) of a person gives life to every cell in the body via neurotransmitters, the head of the Torah—its "in the beginning"—does the same for the entire body of the Torah.

In our current Torah portion *bere'shit* is inferred from *shal nalecha m'al raglecha*, "remove your sandals from your feet." How? The gematria, or numerical value of the letters,—of both *bere'shit* and *shal nalecha m'al raglecha* equals 913.[4] And this numerical equivalence suggests an important teaching: Moses' removal of his shoes, seemingly a minor action, actually starts the gears turning for beginning his new role as redeemer of the Hebrew slaves. Moreover, this "in the beginning" is not only a life-changing moment for Moses, but a holy moment beginning the next major chapter in the history of the Jewish people. In Jewish tradition the word *kadosh* ("holy") refers to any object, moment, or event uniquely set apart from the everyday. What is unprecedented here is not Divine Revelation, which occurs sporadically throughout Genesis (from the creation of Adam and Eve through the death of Joseph), but the first breaking of the laws of nature. A burning *and* unconsumed bush is radically special—*kadosh*.

And why was Moses commanded to remove his shoes?

The answer appears to lie in the many double entendres in the original Hebrew, "remove your sandals from your feet." First, the root of the word "remove" (*nun-shin-lamed*) is the same as the word "to cast out." Next, the root of the word "sandals or footwear" (*nun-ayin-lamed*) also denotes "locks." Lastly, the root of the word "feet" (*reish-gimmel-lamed*) can also mean "habitual behavior." Thus, the verse can be understood spiritually to read, "God said to Moses, 'Do not come closer until you cast out from yourself the consciousness of the locking in of your accustomed habitual behavior, for you are standing on holy ground.'"[5]

This alternative reading suggests that God is asking Moses to be ready to accept a new mission in his life—one so radically unfamiliar it equates to a new beginning along his life journey. He will need to transition out of living a quiet and predictable life as a family man shepherding his father-in-law Jethro's flock of sheep to redeeming the Hebrew slaves, starting by confronting Pharoah in the name of God, "Let My people go" (Exod. 5:1). His hitherto "locked in" behavior—working devotedly in the family business—will impede him from stepping up into this life-changing role. A mindset that used to be an asset, serving him well, has now become a deficit. He must "cast [it] out."

This reading also helps us understand why "the place on which you stand is holy ground." Yes, a burning, unconsumed bush is *kadosh* ("holy"), a word that can refer to any radically special moment or event. Yet something beyond physicality can also define this place as *kadosh*. A direct divine encounter charging Moses with a new life mission that will require a paradigm shift of consciousness—the nature of this new spectacular calling itself makes the place where it happens *kadosh. The encounter itself* transforms an ordinary place into a sacred one—wherein even a mundane bush manifests the holiness in the moment. Perhaps by the Eternal manifesting a phenomenon that moves beyond God's own habitual behavior, breaking the customary laws of nature, Moses will likewise be inspired to move beyond his own "locked in" behavior.

This alternate understanding may also explain Moses' response in the subsequent verse, "And Moses hid his face, for he was afraid to look at God" (Gen. 3:6). Rabbi Jonathan Sacks (twentieth–twenty-first c., England) understands Moses to fear a "profound and radical" shift in which he is "most likely be[ing] forced to understand the world in a totally new way."[6] After forty years of shepherding, suddenly God says to him, "Come, therefore, I will send you to Pharaoh, and you shall free My people, the Israelites, from Egypt" (Exod. 3:10).

Possibly what is being asked of Moses is to surmount the inherent human resistance to change in order to embrace his new mission as sacred work. The Piaseczner Rebbe (Kalonymus Kalmish Shapira, twentieth c., Poland) writes that "human beings are so deeply enmeshed in the force of our habits of perception that it is nearly impossible to overcome them."[7] Logically, we can assume that Moses wants the Hebrews to be free; forty years earlier, he killed an abusive Egyptian taskmaster (Exod. 2:12). But emotionally, he strongly resists the radical consciousness shift that will require *him* to be the catalyst for this momentous mission.

Similar to Moses, when first given the opportunity to be redeemed, a great many of us resist. Our challenge may very well be to approach our own inner liberation, being mindful that for us, too, some type of consciousness shift may be required. As with Moses, this shift might also include a personal encounter with a divine call to release ourselves from habitual behavior that may no longer serve us well.

Just as Moses' encounter at the burning bush represents the beginning of his eventual embrace of the divine plan for him, the episode may also model a redemptive paradigm shift in each of us. For some of us, this may mean shifting toward a Judaism that prioritizes practices that manifest and enhance awareness of the Divine. Like Moses, we might begin to sense the nonphysical inherent in the physical—to sense God in an unconsumed burning bush.

Our *bere'shit*, our own new beginning, may then involve overcoming "our locks"—our daily habits that lock us into feeling physically, psychologically, or spiritually far from the Divine. Undertaking such a new beginning would necessitate that we release ourselves from whatever holds us back. Should we embark on this journey, we can take heart: the nature of this new beginning marks the ground we stand on as holy as well.

And so if at times we hide our faces from fear, as with Moses, let us recognize and honor that moment. As long as we know we are not condemned to remain in that place of constriction forever, we can then hear the call as our own, to "remove your sandals from your feet, for the place on which you stand is holy ground!"

The Practice

1. Begin with breath awareness.
2. Then, reflect on the text.
3. Move to quieting down your mind.

These three steps are explained in detail in the introduction.

4. Visualize yourself at the burning bush. It is *you* that God is talking to. It is *you*—you with the spark of Moses within you—that God is calling to become a redeemer. Now, though, the Divine is calling you to redeem yourself. The time has now arrived for you to unlock your own habitual behaviors that keep you enslaved.

What are these habitual behaviors? What keeps you enslaved to them?
How might you begin to overcome them?
What would it take for you to no longer be enslaved?
What might your self-liberation be like?

Va-'era'

Awareness of the Divine in Our Midst

> Say, therefore, to the Israelite people: I am God; and I will free you from
> under the labors of the Egyptians and deliver you from their bondage.
> I will redeem you with an outstretched arm and through extraordinary
> chastisements. And I will take you to be My people and I will be your God.
> And you shall know that I, the ETERNAL, am your God, Who freed you
> from the labors of the Egyptians. I will bring you into the land I swore to
> give to Abraham, Isaac, and Jacob, and I will give it to you for a possession,
> I GOD.
>
> Exod. 6:6–8

Where We Are

Eighty-year-old Moses accepts the calling to become the redeemer of
the Hebrew slaves. He returns to Egypt. With his brother Aaron as his
spokesperson (since he has a speech impediment) Moses approaches
Pharaoh, invokes God's name, and demands that Pharoah let the Hebrews
go free. Pharaoh responds by increasing the burdens on the enslaved
Hebrews. God reassures Moses that they will be redeemed.

At First Glance

The midrash explains that the Israelites needed all four divine actions
in our passage—"I will free you," "and deliver you," "I will redeem you,"
and "I will take you to be My people"—to become fully liberated from
enslavement. Each action denotes a new step. First was liberation from
harsh labor, which began as soon as the plagues were introduced. Next
was deliverance from servitude, on the day the Israelites left Egypt.
Third was the splitting of the sea that foiled the Egyptian pursuers,
after which the Israelites felt completely redeemed. Fourth was God's

taking the nation as a holy people at Sinai with the giving of the Torah.[1] Today, Jews commemorate all four actions by drinking four cups of wine during the Passover seder.

Yet five cups of wine appear on the seder table. The fifth cup parallels a fifth biblical act of redemption, "And I will bring you into the land." In a simple understanding of the verse, this act of redemption took place thousands of years ago. Forty years after the Eternal promised "and I will bring you into the land," Joshua crossed the Jordan River and entered the Land of Israel. And for the last some thirty-four hundred years, the Jewish people have maintained a presence in the land.

But we can understand the fifth cup and its associated charge, "and I will bring you into the land" in terms of another biblical theme—not of a past event, but of a deeply hoped-for realization in the future. This fifth cup hints at the ultimate redemption for all humanity.

The biblical prophets foretell that the Messiah will bring this final redemption to the world. A redeemed era will usher in universal awareness of the Creator, global peace, and an ideal, utopian world. As the prophet Isaiah proclaims, "And they shall beat their swords into plowshares" (Isa. 2:4)—representing a yearned-for era when swords of war will be transformed into life-bringing plows, a time of peace. Soldiers who previously killed each other will now become civilians who provide food for one another.

The prophet Malachi understands Elijah the prophet to return to earth as the forerunner of the Messiah, acting as the messenger announcing the prophesied arrival: "Lo, I will send the prophet Elijah to you before the coming of the awesome, fearful day of GOD [the Messiah]" (Mal. 3:23). From here the tradition refers to this fifth cup as the "cup of Elijah." By placing the fifth cup on the table, but not drinking it, we are reminded we have yet to realize this ultimate step in experiencing world peace, unity, and prosperity.

A Deeper Dive

In the introduction to his Passover Haggadah, Rav Kook (Avraham Yitzchak HaKohen Kook, nineteenth–twentieth c., Jerusalem) asks, "What is the difference between a slave and a free person?" Answering his own question, he asserts that this difference refers not only to "social standing" but also to a person's spiritual disposition: "It is possible to find an educated slave whose spirit is full of freedom, and conversely, a free person whose spirit is servile. What is characteristic of freedom is the exalted spirit whereby a person or a people is able to be faithful to its inner essence, to the image of God in its midst. . . . The spirit of servility is quite the opposite."[2]

Rav Kook teaches that the consciousness of freedom means awareness and mindfulness of our inner being—our soul, as this represents the image of God "in our midst." Human beings can maintain fidelity to this awareness even if they are physically enslaved. Conversely, people who live in physical freedom may still live a life enslaved by societal and cultural expectations rather than faithful to their inner core being.

Among many factors contributing to this "psychological enslavement," the absence of sensing the Divine Presence may play a significant role. The Me'or Eynayim (Menachem Nachum Twersky, eighteenth c., Ukraine) teaches: "The secret meaning of the Egyptian exile is that true awareness was in exile; people were unable to attain the awareness required to be in service to our blessed Creator."[3]

The Me'or Eynayim identifies lack of awareness of God as the key element of the Egyptian exile, an exile both physical and spiritual. He views the Hebrews' physical enslavement as the main obstacle to their being in a visceral relationship with the Divine. The harsh conditions the Egyptians laid upon the Hebrews likely precluded them from entertaining the existence of their Creator. And spiritually, in alignment with Rav Kook, the Egyptian taskmasters became those psychological forces that people then and now empower over themselves.

So grounded, we can contemplate the teaching of Rabbi Arthur Green (twenty-first c., United States): "To be free, to be liberated from Egyptian enslavement, is to be aware of God as fully as you are able."[4]

A mystical insight on the divine role in inner liberation may also resonate here. It lies in the tiniest of spelling differences between *goleh* ("exile") and *geulah* ("redemption"). *Goleh*, spelled *gimel-vav-lamed-heh*, represents exile, disconnection, and fragmentation—spiritually reframed as the absence of knowledge of God. *Geulah*, spelled *gimel-aleph-vav-*

lamed-heh, represents redemption, unity, and harmony — spiritually understood as the restoring of the knowledge of God. What is the difference? Orthographically, *geulah* is the same as *goleh*, except it also includes an *aleph*, the first letter of the Hebrew alphabet, which itself signifies "one."[5]

When a person's consciousness does not include a godly consciousness, the mystics define that mindset as being in spiritual exile, and one may easily sense fragmentation and division both within and without in the world. When we add the *aleph* — i.e., consciousness of the One — to our awareness, we now experience a kind of spiritual redemption from enslavement to others' definitions of us and expectations for how we are to live our lives. And, as discussed in the previous commentary, we may find ourselves in need to redeem ourselves from yet another form of spiritual enslavement — our own habitual behavior — or to other ideas and feelings that we discover within ourselves, i.e. our fears, holding a grudge, low self-esteem. The key factor that these various spiritual redemptions share, both external and internal, is probably they all include the awareness of the Divine Presence within us.

Returning to the four aforementioned divine actions on behalf of the people, we might notice that with each one, the Hebrews were passive beneficiaries. At Sinai — after the Giver of the Torah "takes" the Israelites to be a new and unique nation — they enter into an active relationship with their Creator, epitomized by the instruction: "And you shall know that I, the ETERNAL, am your God, Who freed you from the labors of the Egyptians." Only then do the Hebrews arrive at the fifth and final action expressing God's ultimate act of liberation: "and I will bring you" to the land. In other words, while originally no conditions were laid upon the Hebrews for the first four steps moving them from exile to redemption, in order to proceed to the fifth and ultimate stage, they are required to be actively involved by cultivating awareness of God in their midst ("And you shall know that I, the ETERNAL, am your God").

We can understand "you shall know" as the collective achievement of the new nation and also as individual knowledge uniquely experienced by each person present at Sinai. Regardless, by either understanding, the previous enslavement of every Israelite to Pharaoh is undone by entering a willing partnership with the Divine. And so it is that cultivating awareness of the Inner Dwelling of the Divine becomes a key to each Israelite's own redemption. Conceivably, then, as mentioned earlier, awareness of God might be a precondition for our own personal redemption as well.

Returning to the significance of the fifth cup of wine as a symbol of the final redemptive stage for all of humanity, we've seen that the Passover seder is not only a celebration of our national and historical liberation from Egyptian enslavement; it can also celebrate our own inner liberation. And the fifth cup of wine—the cup of Eliyahu, the cup of redemption—can serve as a reminder that both personally and collectively, we have not yet reached the ultimate state of freedom: the era when not only all of humanity will live in peace, but each of us as individuals will experience inner tranquility and holistic peace of mind, body, heart, and soul.

With this recognition, when we place the fifth cup on our seder table, we can imbue it with a testamentary meaning: our personal commitment to develop and deepen our own growing consciousness of the Divine. The more conscious we are of being in the Creator's presence, connecting with our Source of Life, and sensing closeness with the Creator, the less we are likely to be enslaved to those inner "Pharaohs" often chained to societal expectations.

Then we just might fully celebrate the traditional reference of Passover as the "season of our freedom." And if that fifth cup reminds each one of us to do our part in cultivating the consciousness of personal redemption within, it may well draw us all closer to global redemption.

The Practice

1. Begin with breath awareness.
2. Then, reflect on the text.
3. Move to quieting down your mind.

These three steps are explained in detail in the introduction.

4. Revisit your life journey as if you are writing your memoir. Can you recall a time when you became aware of the Divine Presence in your

life? If so, begin to gently visualize this moment. Allow it to become more and more in focus. Was this a time that you identified as being sacred and spiritual? What does that feel like? If not, what would you imagine a moment like this to be like?

Are you feeling any sense of liberation, of freedom to be more of your true self?

Now, gently focus on allowing yourself to be your genuine self.

Do you sense the Divine Presence dwelling with you in this moment?

Bo'

Inner Self-Renewal

> God said to Moses and Aaron in the land of Egypt: "This month shall mark for you the beginning of the months; it shall be the first of the months of the year for you."
>
> Exod. 12:1–2

Where We Are

The Hebrews' redemption from Egyptian enslavement begins with nine plagues that God brings upon the Egyptians: blood, frogs, lice, wild beasts, pestilence, boils, hail, locusts, and darkness.

God delivers the first commandment in the Torah addressed to the entire Israelite people: designating a first month, to be determined by witnessing the new moon. While the commandment is given directly to Moses and Aaron, God tells Moses to relay it to all of Israel.

At First Glance

The sages assign the name "Nissan" to this "first month," which then becomes the beginning of the "Torah New Year" (not to be confused with the "New Year" of Rosh Hashanah) upon which all Jewish holidays are based. For example, we learn the date for Yom Kippur in the verse, "Mark, the tenth day of this seventh month is the Day of Atonement" (Lev. 23:27)—which means the "seventh month" relative to the "first month" of Nissan. Note that Rosh Hashanah, the New Year commemorating the Creation of the world, also occurs in the Torah's "seventh month."

We learn that a new month begins when witnesses bear testimony to the appearance of a new moon—the origin of the tradition's adoption of a lunar calendar. The Hebrew wording itself associates a "month" (*chodesh*) with something "new" (*chadash*).

Rashi (Shlomo Yitzhaki, eleventh c., France) offers perspective on the connection between the new month and the new moon. After God informs Moses and Aaron, "This month shall mark for you the beginning of the months," he says: "Moses was in perplexity regarding ... how much of [the moon] must be visible before it is proper to consecrate it as new moon: [God] therefore pointed it out to him in the sky with the finger and said to him, 'Behold it like this, and consecrate it.'"[1]

We come to see that differentiating time into monthly units was a novel idea for the Israelites. The fact that God had to instruct Moses in what constituted a new moon indicates that this was the Hebrew slaves' first experience of a month in time.

Sforno (Obadiah ben Jacob Sforno, fifteenth–sixteenth c., Italy) suggests why that was. Prior to their liberation, the Hebrews had no need to construct a time measurement system. As slaves, they had been deprived of another essential freedom: the freedom to manage their own time. Sforno imagines God now speaking plainly to the newly freed Hebrews: "From now on these months will be yours, to do with as you like ... [unlike when] you were enslaved [and] your days, hours, minutes even, were always at the beck and call of your taskmasters."[2]

These interpretations share the ushering in of a new reality. By sanctifying a moment in time, the appearance of the new moon, the Hebrews are beginning to experience the early stages of redemption from their enslavement. We might ask, what is the relevance of these ancient teachings for us today? After all, we moderns are well used to marking time, and science replaces the ritual need for the human eye to witness a new moon.

A Deeper Dive

The Netivot Shalom (Sholom Noach Berezovsky, twentieth c., Israel) teaches that the moon represents a reality both constant and ever-changing in its cycles.[3] The traditional liturgy encourages this awareness through the ritual of reciting *Kiddush Levana*, the "Sanctification of the Moon" prayer, during which a community of worshipers acknowledges the presence of a newly waxing moon. The Talmud additionally teaches: "One who blesses at the proper time the new month by reciting the 'Sanctification of the Moon' prayer is considered as if that person is actually encountering the face of Divine Presence."[4]

This raises the question: What is the connection between this ritual recitation and experiencing a revelation of the Divine Presence? Understanding the unique nature of the lunar calendar upon which this monthly ritual is based may point us to the answer.

The lunar cycle begins from a place of darkness. To the naked eye, the new moon may appear invisible! However, the very next day we see its first sliver, and *that* is what begins the new Hebrew month. Its light grows increasingly visible as it emerges to its fullest illumination in the sky—and then it begins to wane and once again become invisible.

Spiritually, this resembles times when, sensing our own inner darkness, we may become despondent and despairing. When we lack "illuminating clarity" and feel confused, ambivalent, or even lethargic, we may lose hope that our circumstances can change. Thus the continuous cycle of the moon symbolizes that our individual capacity to spiritually renew is likewise possible, sustainable, and ongoing. In our darkest moments, we can draw hope from the lunar cycle.

This well describes the life of the People of Israel. It can be said that the lunar calendar itself reflects the history and life of the Jewish people. Our history has been a recurring theme of darkness, suffering, despondency— and resilience, followed by surviving and even thriving against all odds. With faith, trust, and experience we Jews can remain hopeful and move through the trying cycle of darkness toward a renewal of light and illumination. Part of the monthly ritual sanctifying the new moon proclaims, "And God directed the moon to renew itself as a crown of glory to those He carried from the womb, whose destiny is likewise to be renewed."[5]

Building on this foundation, we might take in another connection between God, the moon, and ourselves. Just as the Creator formed the moon to renew itself, God created human beings for each of us to renew ourselves, too.

Opening ourselves up to this teaching may help us cultivate faith and trust in the Creator. Just as the moon waxes and wanes yet is always present, so too one can maintain fidelity to one's relationship with the Divine during times of both darkness and light.

It is thus fitting that God's first commandment to the budding Israelite people was to recognize the new moon—the mirror image reflecting and defining their spiritual path. The Netivot Shalom explains that this mitzvah was given to the nation specifically in Egypt, because there the enslaved Hebrews lived in perpetual spiritual darkness. Their own despair preceded the mitzvah. It was precisely from this depraved, dark place that the Hebrews needed to be liberated.

At first, he says, the Hebrews experienced sanctifying the new moon as imbuing them with hope for redemption. Their capacity for spiritual renewal was itself a divine gift leading them toward redemption. From this point, when Moses conveys to the Israelites the mitzvah to sanctify the new moon, the lunar cycle becomes the basis of the Torah calendar.

We might then say that this marking of lunar time relies on human beings becoming a copartner with the Creator. Consider that a twenty-four-hour day is a solar unit, with Shabbat, on the seventh day, demarcated through such a solar reckoning. In a sense, this is fully the Creator's domain. We humans do nothing to confirm that a day is in fact a day. In contrast, as we've seen, the Jewish holidays have been set in time by their relationship to the "Torah New Year" ("Mark, the tenth day of this seventh month is the Day of Atonement"—Lev. 23:27)—which, being lunar based, depends on human beings sanctifying the new moon, which then translates into a new month. We may be able to imagine this as the Creator inviting the Jewish people to be in partnership in the acknowledgment of time—as if God were saying, "I am in charge of Shabbat, being a solar unit of time, and you direct the festivals, determined by the lunar calendar." Now, imagine what it would have been like for people enslaved for over two centuries to have been given this invitation to acknowledge time as a sacred encounter with the Divine!

This teaching has profound ramifications for how we, too, live our lives. Jewish thinking asserts that a person's life journey is not destined to be set in stone. We human beings have been created with freedom of choice, and with this freedom to choose we can mobilize our inner resources to experience self-renewal. The capacity to always be moving along the trajectory of renewing—even, and specifically, during those moments of emotional darkness and suffering—transforms from a divine gift to a basic spiritual resource we can have at our disposal. As we wane, we can wax. As we wax, we realize that even this is temporary. Once again, as the cycle of life unfolds, we shall wane. And then wax again.

Returning to the earlier question, we may now understand the connection between the monthly ritual of sanctifying the new moon and recognizing the Divine Presence. As "moon people," the Jewish culture can be said to mirror the waxing and waning lunar cycles through each of our individual experiences of sensing the Divine Presence in our lives. The experience itself waxes and wanes. At times the Divine Presence is evident and at other times remains concealed.

The Jewish people's belief, faith, and capacity for self-renewal have sustained us through the cycles of loss and life, despair and hope for thousands of years. And the ritual of sanctifying the new, waxing moon sensitizes us to this stunning reality.

The Practice

1. Begin with breath awareness.
2. Then, reflect on the text.
3. Move to quieting down your mind.

These three steps are explained in detail in the introduction.

4. Re-create in your mind a few times that you have gazed up at the evening sky, taking in the light of the moon. How do you experience these varied experiences of viewing different degrees of moonlight, from night to night, as it waxes and wanes?

As you are being breathed into by the Creator, through your inhalation, visualize you are receiving the potential to behold the moon's ever changing and self-renewing property. Then hold your breath for a moment, and simply gaze at the moon (in your mind). As you return your breath to the Creator, through the exhalation, visualize yourself actualizing an expression of your own self-renewal. Again pause, and gaze at your own inner lunar cycle. Imagine that the moon's ongoing capacity to renew itself can inspire you to do the same.

What would inner self-renewal be like for you?

What might you do differently today, tomorrow, the day after tomorrow...?

This practice invites you to ask yourself: What do I need to know in order to do something new today, at this very moment?

Contemplating even the smallest of changes can feel overwhelming when we experience ourselves as immersed in a very dark space. The practice invites you to ask yourself: What do I need right now for me to believe I *can* move into the light in my life?

What are the signs that you may be experiencing self-renewal?

Be-shallaḥ

Jumping into Our Own Sea of Mystery

> Then Moses held out his arm over the sea and GOD drove back the sea
> with a strong east wind all that night, and turned the sea into dry ground.
> The waters were split, and the Israelites went into the sea on dry ground,
> the waters forming a wall for them on their right and on their left. . . .
> Then GOD delivered Israel that day from the Egyptians. Israel saw the
> Egyptians dead on the shore of the sea.
>
> Exod. 14:21–22,30

Where We Are

After Moses and Aaron receive the mitzvah to sanctify the new month,
the Eternal brings the tenth and final plague: the smiting of all firstborns
in Egypt at midnight. Meanwhile, the Hebrews partake in the festive
meal of the Paschal lamb, matzah, and bitter herbs, followed by their
Exodus from Egypt.

By the seventh day, the newly freed Hebrew slaves—now chased
by the Egyptians, who regret Pharaoh's decision to let their slaves go
free—arrive at the Sea of Reeds. God then commands them to journey
forward into the waters.

After hesitating, the Hebrews go forward and experience the miraculous splitting of the sea. Once they reach the other side, the waters
return to their normal state, drowning all the pursuing Egyptians and
thus finally rendering the Hebrews a liberated people.

At First Glance

After the Israelites crossed the sea, they "saw the Egyptians dead on the
shore of the sea" (Exod. 14:30) and began to sing and celebrate: "Then

Moses and the Israelites sang this song to GOD. They said: I will sing to GOD, who has triumphed gloriously" (Exod.15:1). Following Moses' song of praise to God, "Miriam the prophet, Aaron's sister, picked up a hand-drum, and all the women went out after her in dance with hand-drums. And Miriam chanted for them: 'Sing to GOD, who has triumphed gloriously'" (Exod. 15:20–21).

Is the text suggesting that the Hebrews were celebrating the Egyptians' deaths?

A biblical verse clarifies for us that the Jewish tradition frowns on celebrating the deaths of our enemies: "If your enemies fall, do not exult" (Prov. 24:17). The Hebrews were celebrating that they were now free—not only from enslavement, but also from pursuit. Sforno (Obadiah ben Jacob Sforno, fifteenth–sixteenth c., Italy) explains: "Until the Egyptians died, [the Hebrews] had been compared to slaves running away from their masters."[1]

The Rabbis incorporated this life-affirming value. They insisted that death was not a cause for joy by instituting the practice of reciting only an abbreviated version of the week-long celebratory holiday liturgy after the first day of Passover.[2] We temper our joy out of respect for the Egyptians' deaths while celebrating our own people's liberation from slavery.

When considering this focused value on life, the Hebrew slaves' jumping into the sea that soon splits before them can be seen as even more momentous than their original Exodus from Egypt seven days prior. This action led them to finally experience living as free people.

A Deeper Dive

The midrash teaches that when the verse says "the waters were split," this refers not only to the water in the Sea of Reeds, but actually to all the waters in the world, which were split as well.[3] Rabbi Yanki Tauber (twenty-first c., United States) writes in the name of the Lubavitcher Rebbe (Manachem Mendel Schneerson, twentieth c., United States) that this expansive understanding of the water splitting wasn't only limited to physical water, but encompassed "the individual sea of every soul, to the cosmic sea that suffuses the deepest secrets of creation."[4] He continues:

After "the Israelites had marched through the sea on dry ground" (Exod. 14:29), the waters [resumed] their natural course. Again, the sea world was obscured, again the subconscious became a mystical and secret place. But a precedent had been established, a potential implanted in our souls. Never again was the sea to be impregnable, never again were the revealed and hidden in man to constitute two hermetic worlds. With the splitting of the seas, God empowered us to penetrate our individual seas, to blaze pathways of dry land on the ocean floors of our souls.[5]

From this teaching, we may come to understand that ever since this miraculous event, the Divine has given each of us an opportunity to become aware of a dimension of living usually concealed under our own "sea." Similar to the scuba diver who realizes there is a new reality lying beneath the sea waiting to be discovered, we are also given the opportunity to discover what is occurring underneath our apparent and external reality. And discovering what dwells under our individual waters, what is latent and heretofore unrealized, may in fact be our own path to personal freedom: to encountering our authentic and true selves.

To do this we may very well face a similar situation as the Hebrews: jumping into the sea—of our concealed self—without any knowledge of what will happen. When the Hebrews approached the sea with the Egyptians poised to attack, they panicked. We too may be filled with trepidation about drowning in what might lie beneath.

But when Moses beseeched God on the Hebrews' behalf, "God said to Moses, 'Why do you cry out to Me? Tell the Israelites to go forward'" (Exod. 14:15). And once they moved forward, "God drove back the sea with a strong east wind all that night and turned the sea into dry ground. The waters were split, and the Israelites went into the sea on dry ground. . . . Then God delivered Israel that day from the Egyptians. Israel saw the Egyptians dead on the shore of the sea."

We too may come to realize that the journey of self-discovery leads us to this point where we must simply dive in. And the act of jumping into our own sea may likewise bring redemptive consciousness: for us, a newfound recognition of who we truly are. In this light, we may recast the drowning of the Egyptians metaphorically for our own spiritual journey as the submerging of all the forces that hold us back from living a life free to be our authentic selves.

Those of us who already dedicate time to cultivating mindfulness may find ourselves continuously arriving at our sea. Immersion is always a different experience—since we, along with all of creation, continuously evolve. In the traditional morning liturgy, we proclaim, "In goodness, [the Creator] continuously renews each day the act of Creation." Each time we jump into our internal selves, each time the waters that conceal cognizance split, we may emerge with a new jewel of inner awareness lying at the bottom of our sea.

And as we gain clearer insight—not always crystal clear—of what lies beneath our own surface awareness, we just may discover and then encounter the Divine within us, hidden under a misty sea of limited consciousness.

The Practice

1. Begin with breath awareness.
2. Then, reflect on the text.
3. Move to quieting down your mind.

These three steps are explained in detail in the introduction.

4. Visualize a time when you felt as if you were living someone else's life—enslaved by external or internal forces that held you back from living your own life of inner truth and integrity. Do you feel cornered? Do you feel as if you are breathing in someone else's breath?

From this painful place, do you feel the urge to pray or cry out as the Hebrews did on the shores of Egypt?

Gently inhale your painful feelings, honoring them as you would this very breath of life, and then as you exhale, gently cry out (or in) and give expression to your feelings. Then imagine, as if your prayers are answered, a shift inside of you. Unable to fully understand how or why, you somehow no longer feel held down by these "Egyptian" forces preventing you from manifesting your true self.

Now, as you receive your next breath, breathe in the energy of curiosity to dig deeper within yourself. As you return your breath, imagine yourself asking about what you discover. Have these demons convinced me that it is acceptable to live like a slave? And where do they come from? Are they residing within me, masquerading as other people's voices?

When you are ready, on your next inhalation, as you receive breath, imagine you are receiving the life force of increased awareness. As you exhale this energy of awareness, what is manifesting for you? Imagine your sense of self now beginning to shift as you realize the voices actually belong to you. What feelings surface at this crucial moment? Hope? Worthiness of breaking free? Jubilation? Fright? Wariness of what liberation might really mean?

Now gently breathe in the energy of possibility. As you release this breath back into the universe, imagine your situation changing. Begin to visualize yourself as one of the Hebrews during the Exodus from Egypt. You will no longer be shackled and restrained to live a life that is not yours. You begin to shed the fetters of bondage, asking yourself with wonderment, Who am I? How do I cultivate a life of fidelity to my inner pure truth? What do I need to know?

And then, you reach your sea—that body of water that covers and conceals all the wisdom that you need to know to continue further. You even sense the demonic voices beginning to reappear as they pursue you, attempting to manipulate you and annihilate your newfound freedom. What do you do now?

Again, you cry out in prayer and desperation! And you hear the deep calling within as your Source proclaims, "Jump in!" And you do!

And then those poisonous voices pursuing you drown and die out!

Begin to now receive the breath of closure. You are preparing to softly move out of the practice to begin leaning into what you intend to do next. As you return the breath of potential closure, visualize yourself leaning into that next step.

What are you feeling now? How would you describe the experience of leaping into your unknown self?

If new awareness has not yet been revealed to you, it may simply not be the right time. Spiritual work cannot be forced, but with dedication to your own practice, the process is likely to manifest what you seek. Sometimes this happens when we least expect it. What is most important, and in this we each have control, is to engage in the practice. That in itself begins to fertilize your inner garden of awareness to sprout.

As you conclude your practice, inhale the energy of realizing your hopes, and as you exhale, drop in to that place of actualization. Imagine the possibility of awareness. Somehow, in some way you do not understand, you are able to discern a small part of you that has long evaded your self-awareness.

What does it feel like to glimpse more of who you truly are?

Yitro

Spiritual Intimacy

> God spoke all these words, saying: "I, the ETERNAL, am your God who brought you out of the land of Egypt, the house of bondage: You shall have no other gods besides Me." . . . All the people saw the thunder and the lightning, the blare of the horn and the mountain smoking; and when the people saw, they fell back and stood at a distance.
>
> Exod. 20:1,1[1]

Where We Are

Having heard about the miracles of the Exodus, Moses' father-in-law Jethro joins the Israelite caravan traveling in the wilderness and shares his leadership wisdom with Moses.

After forty-nine days, the Israelites arrive at Mount Sinai.

The Israelites hear the "Ten Utterances" (also known as the Ten Commandments).

At First Glance

What in fact *did* the Eternal say and the Israelites hear? The midrash comments: "The Holy Blessed One said all ten utterances in one word."[2]

While such a phenomenon stretches human comprehension, the tradition does not lack other interpretations. As one example, the Torah recounts that after the first two utterances, the Israelites protest to Moses that this intense direct communication by God is too much for them to bear. "You speak to us," they said to Moses, "and we will obey; but let not God speak to us, lest we die" (Exod. 20:16). From this, the Talmud reasons that since the gematria or numeric equivalent of the four Hebrew letters composing the word "Torah" (*tav-vav-reish-heh*) equals 611 and there are 613 total mitzvot, the Israelites heard two of the utterances directly (those cited above), and Moses taught the remaining 611.[3]

Then there are multiple understandings of how the Israelites reacted after "the people saw [the thunder, the lightening, the blare of the horn, and the mountain smoking]." According to THE JPS TANAKH: Gender-Sensitive Edition (RJPS), "They fell back and stood at a distance" (Exod. 20:15). However, a midrash holds that rather than "fell back," the people trembled: "The [Hebrew] root nun-vav-ayin of the word va-yanu'u in the text actually denotes trembling."[4] In essence, after leaving Egypt as a complete nation only seven weeks earlier, watching the Sea of Reeds first split open and then recede to liberate them, seeing what is usually heard and now witnessing the smoking mountain, the Israelites were at once highly excited, vulnerable, and unsettled.

Yet Ibn Ezra (Abraham ibn Ezra, eleventh–twelfth c., Spain) comments, "It is impossible to maintain that va yanu'u means: and they trembled. For if they did not move from their place, how did they stand far off?"[5] The Israelites could not have "stood at a distance" if they remained in their places trembling. Therefore, he says, yanu'u must mean, "they fell back."

But Sforno (Obadiah ben Jacob Sforno, fifteenth–sixteenth c., Italy), connecting "seeing the thunder" and "falling back," states: "The word 'saw' in our verse is to be understood in the same way as in Ecclesiastes 1:16, 'and my mind [literally "heart" — lev] has zealously absorbed wisdom and learning.' Just as the heart cannot see, so people cannot 'see' sounds. The meaning is that they understood the meaning of these sounds."[6] How the Israelites cognitively internalized the moment frightened them, he says, and fear impelled them to back away.

The common thread tying these diverse commentaries together is the understanding that the Giving of the Torah was like no other moment in the Israelite nation's experience, arousing awe in everyone who beheld it. Taking this further, a stunning midrash proclaims that all Israelites — past, present, and future — were present at Sinai. Commenting essentially on "I make this covenant, with its sanctions, not with you alone" (Deut. 29:13), the midrash says: "But rather the generations that have yet to come were also there at that time."[7] Then, responding to the next verse, "But both with those who are standing here with us this day before the ETERNAL our God and with those who are not with us here this day" (Deut. 29:14), the midrash states: "R. Abahu said in the name of R. Samuel bar Nahmani, 'Why does it say, "those who are standing here . . . and with those who are not here" [without using the word, standing]? Because all the souls were there, [even] when [their] bodies had still not been created.'"[8]

If, spiritually, we all participated in this momentous event of some thirty-four hundred years ago, might we be able to reenact it in our own spiritual practice today? The mystics would reply encouragingly, "By all means."

A Deeper Dive

Historically, the Giving of the Torah at Sinai represents the establishment of the biblical version of a constitution. However, this involved much more than the revelation of laws and commandments. Hasidism posits that the Giving of the Torah ruptured what had hitherto been the status quo of God's interaction with human beings. Before this remarkable event, mere earthlings (except for rare individuals) were unable to experience personal closeness with God. For the first time, the Creator united the spiritual realm from above with the physical realm from below. Giving the mitzvot to the Israelites now allowed them a means to infuse physical behavior and objects with spiritual meaning—for example, the mitzvah of lighting candles and uttering a blessing to acknowledge the sacred act of welcoming Shabbat. These acts could connect each of them—and, hence, each of us—deeply with our Creator.

Symbolically, then, we can understand the verse (in Exod. 19:20), "GOD came down upon Mount Sinai, on the top of the mountain, and GOD called Moses to the top of the mountain and Moses went up," as the moment that introduces this new paradigm. Perhaps we might imagine the scenario as two lovers uniting on their wedding day. Indeed, the sages compare the Giving of the Torah to the celestial wedding between God and the Israelites (represented by Moses) meeting at their *chuppah* (marital canopy).[9]

The Piaseczner Rebbe (Kalonymus Kalmish Shapira, twentieth c., Poland) teaches that, like the intimacy between two marriage partners, the revelation at Sinai introduces spiritual intimacy between humanity and the Eternal—an otherworldly attachment experience of being one with the One:

> There is a teaching from the Baal Shem Tov... on the verse "my soul went out when he spoke" (Songs 5:6), that part of the soul of the speaker leaves at the time of speaking.... And herein is the greatness of the connection between God and the Jewish people at the time of the receiving of the Torah. Because God spoke to them, and connected Himself to them, it was the essence of the Speaker connecting with them. It was the very essence of "I" in the phrase "I the ETERNAL am your God." (Exod. 20:2). The Hebrew word for "I" in the first of the Ten Utterances is *Anochi* rather than the more common *Ani*. *Anochi* is an acronym, an Aramaic acrostic, reading *Ani Nafshai Katavit Yahavit*—"I My Soul have Written and Given."[10] God has, so to speak, written and given My soul which becomes revealed to the Jewish people through the Torah that God teaches us. Therefore, whenever we learn Torah, this becomes a time when the Blessed Holy One is speaking with us, and the very essence of *Anochi*— "I"—is being revealed.[11]

At heart, the gift of Torah that the One gave at Sinai—and continues to give to the Jewish people as we learn and live the Torah in all diverse ways—is the very essence of Oneness.

This teaching reimagines an important spiritual practice. While the tradition refers to this event as *Matan Torah*, "the Giving of the Torah"—which clearly limits it as a holiday that we revisit annually—the Piaseczner refers to this holiday as *Kabbalat Torah*, "the Receiving of the Torah," which transforms a moment into an ongoing event. By learning and living the Torah, we can embrace an ongoing practice of receiving the "same Torah," with each "receiving" resembling the first time. Yet if we infuse our physical behaviors with the newness inherent in a learning experience, our "receiving" of the "same Torah" can be different each time, too.

All the more, the Piaseczner says, shifting the language from "giving" to "receiving" Torah invites us into experiencing intimate encounter with the Divine — Soul to soul — as determined by how each of us individually receives the Torah. The act of "receiving" is active, engaging, ever present. The one God gave the one Torah at one place at one time; each individual since then can cultivate the practice of ongoingly receiving the Torah in a uniquely personal way.

The Piaseczner encourages each of us to give all of ourselves to this process. "It should not be that we stand outside of it and look upon Torah, but rather that we give our entire selves to Torah and enter our entire soul into Torah."[12]

However devoted we may be, we will never fully understand God. The mystery may very well be what keeps us engaged. The Piaseczner couples the "mysteries of Torah" with "'the hidden God' (Isa. 45:15) . . . concealed in the Torah."[13] Hence, the mystery of Torah is contained both in the revelation of God and in each of our souls, hidden there until we unlock that piece of ourselves through the body of wisdom we singularly come to learn.

The "Giving of the Torah," now also the "Receiving of the Torah," becomes much more than a constitutional framework within which to govern the new nation. It becomes a prime pathway for cultivating spiritual intimacy with our Creator.

The Practice

1. Begin with breath awareness.
2. Then, reflect on the text.
3. Move to quieting down your mind.

These three steps are explained in detail in the introduction.

4. Visualize your closest intimate relationship with another person, or what you would want that relationship to be like. Picture this loved one's face. Hear their voice. Hold their hand. Inhale their scent. What are you feeling?

Now conjure up different moments shared with this person. What was it like to feel closeness, connection, vulnerability, respect, love? What about separation, hurt, upset, disconnection? And, hopefully, a sense of openness and healing? Try to notice your embodied experience.

Remaining still within your breathing rhythm, explore how these varied feelings and sensations enhance your connection—or do not. Imagine reaching out with your arms and hugging and holding whatever sensations your body communicates and whatever emotions your heart expresses. Each becomes an important building block that nurtures the rawness and wondrousness of this intimate relationship.

Still holding onto these sensations and feelings, gently invite the image of the person to fade away.

Then begin to imagine the energy of the Divine Presence.

You can now hear the Divine Voice guiding you to discover secret parts of your internal self. Imagine yourself feeling held, hugged, and even loved by the Divine's Torah. The Divine is teaching you about your hidden spirit.

Now imagine the Divine has given you an invaluably precious gift: a jewel of your own hidden wisdom.

Would you give anything in return? If so, what? If not, why?

Do you sense that this too is an intimate relationship—one of spiritual intimacy, soul with Soul?

Mishpatim

Doing before Understanding

> Then he took the record of the covenant and read it aloud to the people.
> And they said, "All that GOD has spoken we will do and understand!"
> Exod. 24:7[1]

Where We Are

After the Israelites receive the "Ten Utterances" (also known as the Ten Commandments) at Mount Sinai, the Eternal gives Moses several laws related to civil and criminal damages and, subsequently, on the establishment of three festivals: Passover, Shavuot, and Sukkot. Once Moses writes down and conveys all these mitzvot to the Israelites, they reply with our verse, "All that GOD has spoken we will do and understand."

At First Glance

What does it mean to do the mitzvot ("All that GOD has spoken") before understanding them?

The Rashbam (Samuel ben Meir, twelfth c., France) explains the phrase as referring to two different time periods. "We will do" concerns everything God has commanded *so far*, and "[we will] understand" means that *from now on* the Israelites will first understand the commandment in order to fulfill it.[2]

Alternatively, the midrash teaches that this refers to the Israelites proclaiming their allegiance to fulfill the Eternal's commandments, regardless of whether they understood them or not. By this interpretation, the Hebrew word *nishma'*, thought to signify "understand" (or "hear"), should instead be understood as "heed": "All that GOD has spoken we will do and heed."[3]

Over the course of Jewish history, countless Jews have proclaimed this phrase as an expression of their ultimate dedication to fulfilling the mitzvot—among them those who, influenced by the midrashic approach, do not seek to cultivate understanding in tandem with their action. And yet, even if this paradigm works for some people some of the time, in my view blind faith is liable to lead to robotic behavior and the inability to sustain an enlivening relationship with the Divine. It undoubtedly lacks the messiness, contradictions, and uncertainty inherent in cultivating God relationally. With human relationships, too, the integrity of our relationship is tested when we may not hear, understand, or comply with another's bidding. In fact, though, our struggle to understand or to reach a place of acceptance despite gaps in our connection may even strengthen the fabric of both our Divine and human relationships, as these weather profound tests over time.

Perhaps, then, a core message in our verse is that God does not expect us to mindlessly fulfill the mitzvot. To be in an active relationship with the Divine, we are invited "to do and understand"—to continuously "hear the mitzvot" by thinking, questioning, and understanding them.

If so, then what significance might "doing preceding understanding" have on our spiritual practice of cultivating God consciousness?

A Deeper Dive

The Piaseczner Rebbe (Kalonymus Kalmish Shapira, twentieth c., Poland) opens the window to a more comprehensive and all-encompassing view when he retranslates the Hebrew word *na'a'seh* from the traditional "we will do," to its other Hebrew meaning, "we will make." He then asks, "What will we make?" and follows by suggesting "ourselves." He continues: "In the making of our inner selves after the Giving of the Torah, the Torah will give birth to the hidden essence of the person and with this deeper awareness we will understand."[4]

Hasidism equates this hidden self-essence with our soul, which derives from the infinite divine life force, continuously keeping us alive. When we become aware of our souls, through learning the Torah, we become aware of the Divine Presence dwelling within us. Because God's infinite existence defies limitations of time and space, our God consciousness of our souls encounters not only our hidden self-essence, but its infinite nature.

Are you perplexed? Rabbi Shneur Zalman of Liadi (eighteenth c., Ukraine) teaches that a human being can never totally grasp this infinite nature of God consciousness.[5] He quotes Maimonides (Moses ben Maimon, twelfth c., Spain and Egypt), "This is not within the power of any human being to fully comprehend."[6] The Zohar also proclaims, "There is no thought that can fully grasp [the Infinite One's] greatness."[7]

Returning now to the Piaseczner's guidance that "we make . . . ourselves . . . [to] give birth to [our] hidden essence," the making of a self as a container, to hold an evolved awareness, illustrates how a reconceived directive can become a spiritual practice. While our hidden essence, being infinite in nature, can never be entirely revealed, our search for our hidden self-essence possesses a dynamic vibrancy and fluidity. The new self we make today by heeding and understanding our godly self as best we can then becomes tomorrow's history. Each new day we are invited yet again to experience a higher God consciousness. And, because of God's infinite nature, a God consciousness opens up endless possibilities of "making ourselves." This spiritual work recognizes moments of spontaneity, ups and downs, rising and falling, stepping forward and retreating backward—all the messiness, uncertainty, and contradictions we encounter in real living.

The Me'or Eynayim (Menachem Nachum Twersky, eighteenth c., Ukraine) enhances this idea with his novel and complementary insight. Life is not linear nor smooth, and both the low places and the high places are equally necessary entry points when cultivating the spiritual practice of "doing before understanding":

Why does a person have to fall? . . . One reason is the possibility of attaining a yet greater perception than the one previously experienced. When you want to proceed to a higher consciousness, you need to lack something first. . . . When you are in such a fallen state, you need to exert much effort to sense the Divine within your current fallen existence. How? You need to have faith that "the whole earth is filled with God's glory" (Isa. 6:3), and "there is no place devoid of

God."[8] God is there in your present state of being, though in a more subtle and perhaps less apparent way. This is the doing that precedes the understanding.[9]

The Me'or Eynayim is suggesting that we may cultivate divine awareness even during the lowest times in our lives. From a place perhaps of pain, loneliness, and disconnection, we may be able to reflect on the lack of awareness of the Divine, which then may mysteriously lead *to* the recognition of the Divine's presence. Similar to jumping on a springboard, we may go down in order to then rise up to a higher rung of consciousness. In this light, the deeper meaning of "we will do" equates with committing ourselves to do the necessary work regardless of where we may spiritually be. When we are in a low place, we can remind ourselves that we are not condemned to remain there. We may be able to sense the Divine Presence in that low place. And, from this place of cultivated awareness, we may then understand and heed the Divine Will.

Yet how is it possible for us to sense the Divine Presence when we feel so painfully distant in this low place? The Me'or Eynayim encourages us to start by reflecting on the fact that "God is the 'Life of life.'" He teaches: "God is the life-force within all that lives. When you are in that fallen state, think of this: 'Am I not alive? Who is this life-force within me? Is it not the blessed Creator? God is indeed present right here.'"[10]

When we ask and then contemplate, "What is the life force within me?," the very question may reveal to us the secret of how "to do" before "understanding." Here, the "doing" is opening ourselves in all our vulnerability to seek an answer to this basic existential question. Once we immerse ourselves in the quest, we may well discover that God is the Source of our life force. Then, we may sense the connection between ourselves and this Source.

This approach permeates "doing and understanding" with the aliveness of life as it truly is. Assured faith, which many of us do not possess all the time, is not a bedrock of this ultimate proclamation. Rather, as contemporary rabbi Arthur Green comments, "We only need to pay attention to life itself."[11]

Both the Piasezcner Rebbe's and the Me'or Eynayim's teachings encourage us to see ourselves where we truly are and not where external forces dictate we should be. While the two teachings suggest different ways of "we will do," they equally share the belief that awareness of the Divine plays an essential role in "we will do and understand."

Cultivating this *middah* of "We will do and understand" through this lens can blossom into endless and varied pleasures of simply being alive with our Creator.

The Practice

1. Begin with breath awareness.
2. Then, reflect on the text.
3. Move to quieting down your mind.

These three steps are explained in detail in the introduction.

4. Visualize and imagine a few scenarios in your life in which you felt obligated to act because someone else asked you to, despite your not fully understanding the rationale for the other person's request. Perhaps your parents expected certain behaviors of you as a child. Perhaps a work supervisor or director asked you to take on a new task. Perhaps a close friend or intimate partner made a special ask.

What feelings begin to arise? Resentment, annoyance, being taken advantage of, disrespected? Or, perhaps, enthusiasm, happiness (to be able to help this person), a sense of purpose on behalf of the relationship? If you feel differently depending on the ask, the circumstances, or the person, why is there a difference? With curiosity, ask yourself: If I do not understand the reason, what would have to happen for me to respond heartily?

Now, focus your thoughts on one of these people. Can you take in this human being's meaning in your life?

Returning to your awareness of your breathing cycle, sense the breath entering your body as giving you the potential to go deeper into the practice. As you return your breath through your exhalation, actualize this by imagining you are now being asked to discover within yourself a more trusting and loving person. Might this be the Divine Presence residing within you?

Practice this breath imagery a few times, receiving potential through your inhaled breath and actualizing this potential through your exhaled breath. What would this authentic, intrinsic you feel like?

Pause for a few cycles and simply enjoy receiving life.

Then, once again direct your awareness through your inhalation to receiving the potential to move even deeper. As you exhale and return your breath, sense how this might affect your response to the last request made of you. How might this also affect your response to the others?

Do you experience, "I will do—and then maybe understand"?

Terumah

Creating the Inner Home for the Divine

And let them make Me a sanctuary that I may dwell among them.

Exod. 25:8

Where We Are

The Eternal asks Moses to instruct the Israelites on how to make a *terumah* (offering) to the nation's treasury. Worthy gifts include precious metals, fabrics, animal skins, acacia wood, olive oil, spices for incense, and gemstones, all to be used to build or adorn the portable sanctuary accompanying the Israelites along their journey to the Promised Land.

At First Glance

Addressing why Exodus 25:8 (our verse) refers to this structure as a *mikdash* (holy sanctuary), but in the next verse God asks Moses to construct a *mishkan* (Tabernacle or dwelling place), Ibn Ezra (Abraham ibn Ezra, eleventh–twelfth c., Spain) teaches us that "this building is holy because it is a dwelling place specifically for the Divine."[1] In fact, the word *mishkan* derives from *shohhen*, to dwell.

The Or HaHayim (Hayim ibn Attar, eighteenth c., Morocco and Jerusalem), comments on what appears to be a grammatical error in the verse — the use of the plural "dwell among them" rather than "within it" — to explain that, spiritually, this means the "place that God will sanctify to dwell is within the children of Israel."[2] In effect, the *mishkan* establishes a physical home for the Divine to dwell while simultaneously conferring a spiritual dwelling within each person journeying to the Promised Land.

Perhaps we can now appreciate that the commandment to build a dwelling place for the Divine includes both physical and spiritual components. Yet, even so, the subsequent verses are solely devoted to explaining in exacting detail how to build the physical external structure. There are no explicit instructions regarding how to create a spiritual inner home for the Divine, or why doing so would bear significance.

We will need to delve deeper for guidance.

A Deeper Dive

Even earlier in the Israelites' history, a verse in the song they sing after the splitting of the sea illuminates the idea that a person may desire to become a dwelling place for the Divine. This verse (from Exodus 15:2) usually translates as, "This is my God whom I will enshrine." However, Rashi (Shlomo Yitzhaki, eleventh c., France), relying on the Aramaic translation ("This is my God and I will build a sanctuary for Him") of Onkeles (first c., Jerusalem), explains that *v'an'vei'hu* (whom I will enshrine) also means *naveh* (home). As such, Rashi reads the sung verse as "This is my God for whom I will make a home."[3] Consistent with this interpretation, the wish to build an inner home for the Divine would have surfaced in the Israelites' consciousness considerably before the divine commandment to build a *mishkan*. Likewise, both the Kotzker Rebbe (Menachem Mendel Morgensztern, eighteenth–nineteenth c., Poland) and Samson Raphael Hirsch (nineteenth c., Germany) understand this segment of the song at the sea to mean, "I will make *myself* a sanctuary for Him, for the greatest of all sanctuaries is a human being who makes themselves holy."[4]

Expanding on this desire to make oneself a fitting sanctuary for the Eternal, Rav Adin Steinsaltz (twentieth–twenty-first c., Israel), comments on a verse from Psalms (27:4), "One thing I ask of GOD, only that do I seek: to live in GOD's house all the days of my life, to gaze upon GOD's beauty and to frequent the temple: 'To live in GOD's house' points not towards something physical, but rather expresses the sense of attachment a person experiences when feeling that they are spiritually dwelling in God's home. The experience translates to the sheer pleasure one experiences when encountering the Divine in one's life.'"[5]

Rav Steinsaltz is teaching the connection between living in the house of God and closeness to the Divine, what he calls "the sense of attachment." It may be that the place where we feel most at home and closest with ourselves is also the inner space where we feel closest with the Divine. Conversely, if we feel estranged from our inner self, we may feel spiritually blocked or distant from the Divine, and vice versa. If this seems true for us, we might consider that the existential quest to feel comfortable with ourselves may intertwine with an equally deep internal need to sense the Creator's presence in our lives.

In my own experience of having felt distant from myself, I also felt the same regarding the Divine. When I first entered the ultra-Orthodox world many decades ago, I felt excited at the prospect of feeling closer to God, without knowing what that would entail. The more immersed I became in keeping the mitzvot, the more that observance seemed to resemble that of a trained circus animal, distancing me from my own true sense of how God wanted me to practice my Judaism. I began to feel estranged from myself, not even recognizing myself in the mirror—and estranged from God, too. I was not at home with me, so how could I have sensed being at home with the Divine?

After fifteen years of living a Jewish life that did not express my soul, I left the ultra-Orthodox way of living a Torah life—and the Torah way of life in general. I had no energy left within me to continue a charade, especially since all I really wanted to do was to feel close to God and that had totally evaded me.

In time I realized I could not stay away from Jewish life. I painfully missed the Torah way of living. After a period of deep meditations and contemplative practices, I began to return to my Jewish tradition. This time, though, I deeply prayed to the Eternal to guide me along a path of truth in my relationship with my soul and with the Divine. Finally, I began to feel at home with my Jewish self—and my human self as well. And, finally, I felt the Divine Presence dwelling with me as I began to live in God's house. Being at home with my deeper self thus equated to my being at home with the Divine.

I view the mitzvah to "make for me a sanctuary" as an invitation to dedicate our whole selves to this sacred "building project," and hope that you can as well. The Netivot Shalom (Sholom Noach Berezovsky, twentieth c., Israel) stresses involving both mind and heart in this endeavor:

Each person contains within them two aspects of a spiritual Sanctuary. One is in the brain—the powers of the intellect—and the other is in the heart—the seat of the emotions. This is alluded to when the Torah reviews all the materials that were used to build the Tabernacle: 'These are the records of the Tabernacle, the Tabernacle of the Pact...' (Exod. 38:21). The word Tabernacle appears twice, alluding to the two aspects of the spiritual Sanctuary within the individual.[6]

By integrating both our intellectual and emotional selves, we can draw on our full authentic selves when establishing our inner home for the Divine. We can then build within our whole self a complete sanctuary for God. In this way, kedushah (holiness) dwells and manifests within all of us.

An earlier verse in our Torah portion then guides us on the way to build a holy sanctuary within our whole selves: by identifying and bringing to this sanctuary what each of us is most passionate about. In Exodus 25:2, God tasks Moses to "accept gifts for Me from every person whose heart is so moved." We are to give a terumah (offering) from our hearts, and each of our hearts uniquely inclines us to certain aspects of living more than others. How each of us reveals the image of the Creator within us depends on our unique bouquet of resources. Building our inner mishkan can be understood as a heart-led practice of calling upon these distinctive assets with the spirit of a generous heart.

For the Maggid of Kozhnitz (Yisroel Hopstein, eighteenth–nineteenth c., Poland), "this means that you are now sanctified and invited to be with the blessed Creator; and when you do this [build your inner mishkan] then I will dwell among you, literally within you—in the chambers of your heart... then My place will be within you."[7] Contemporary American rabbi Josh Feigelson then suggests: "For the Maggid, the Tabernacle exists... to open up space in our hearts. It is a calling to a life of capacious awareness of the Divine working through us."[8]

From these varied teachings we may consider that the central point of our authentic selves—our godly selves—lies within our hearts. Mirroring the blood that flows from our heart, through our veins, and back to our heart, the divine life force moves through us and reaches every crevice of life in our being—beginning and ending in the heart. When we cultivate this heart-led *middah* of creating a home for the Divine, when each of us in all of our uniqueness becomes more of our godly selves, then our home is a real sanctuary.

The Practice

1. Begin with breath awareness.
2. Then, reflect on the text.
3. Move to quieting down your mind.

These three steps are explained in detail in the introduction.

4. Visualize building your dream home, without any budgetary restraints. What will it look like? What is the architecture (e.g., cape, ranch, castle)? What is the style (historic, classic, contemporary)? What are the building materials (stone, brick, wood)? Where is your dream home (the city, the country, by the beach, high up in a mountain village)?

What is your favorite room in this home, the place that feels most like your personal sanctuary? What does this physical sanctuary look like with all of its dream furnishings just as you would wish them to be?

Pause now for a few breathing cycles, allowing you to relax into the next step. When you are ready, direct your breath awareness to inhale the actualization of your dream home. As you exhale, imagine yourself walking slowly up to your dream home, and then into your sanctuary room, for the very first time. Open your heart to the experience of what you are feeling. What makes it *your* home? What parts of the physical space express a strong, heartfelt feeling that you are at home in your home?

Pause again for a few breathing cycles that will now move you gently into the next and concluding step. When you feel ready to begin, imagine you are inhaling the potential to transition into entering your spiritual home—the home you are building to be the sanctuary for the Divine Presence within you—your soul.

Now organically visualize moving inwardly from your physical home to enter your spiritual home. Open your heart to the experience. Can you sense you are building a home for the Divine in this magical physical dwelling? Does it feel like *your* spiritual home?

What is revealed in the intersection of your two homes?

Tetsavveh

Being in Service

> You shall further instruct the Israelites to bring you clear oil of beaten
> olives for lighting, for kindling lamps regularly.... You shall bring forward
> your brother Aaron, with his sons, from among the Israelites.... Make
> sacral vestments for your brother Aaron.... Next you shall instruct all
> who are skillful.
>
> Exod. 27:20, 28:1–3

Where We Are

After the Eternal gives Moses the blueprint for building the *mishkan*
(Tabernacle), the Torah describes the importance of constructing a con-
tinually burning lamp.

The next chapter enumerates various priestly garments and acces-
sories the *Kohanim* (Priests) need to wear when performing *mishkan*-
related rituals.

At First Glance

While the content appears clear and direct, these verses depart from
the typical structure of how God usually speaks to Moses. The familiar
phrase, "And GOD spoke to Moses, saying: 'Speak to the Children of
Israel, saying...'" does not appear. Moreover, Moses' name is omitted—
which is especially strange, since the opening verse in this Torah portion begins with an ambiguous "you." The commentators assume the
"you" refers to Moses; the Ba'al HaTurim (Jacob ben Asher, thirteenth-
fourteenth c., Germany), for one, states, "This is the only portion in the
Torah since Moses first appears in which he is not mentioned."[1] Still,
textually, whom God is addressing remains unclear. What might we
learn from this textual oddity?

While the divine directives that follow comport with Moses' obligations as the leader in service to the Israelite nation, the general use of the word "you" may denote a deeper message: that the fundamental calling to be in service to that which is greater than our limited selves applies to all humanity.

We see an indication of this when the Israelites gather at Mount Sinai to witness God giving the Torah to Moses and the Eternal tells the budding nation: "You shall be to Me a kingdom of Priests" (Exod. 19:6). How are we to understand what the role of a Priest implies here? Nachmanides (Moses ben Nachman, thirteenth c., Spain and Acre, the Holy Land) teaches, "This means you shall be a kingdom for Me of people in service."[2] In fact, *Kohen*, the Hebrew word for Priest, derives from the root *kaf-heh-nun*, meaning "to be in service."

To God, it seems, the role of the Jewish people in the world parallels the role of the Priests in the Israelite nation. We can understand the Israelite Priests' role of being in service to the rest of the Israelite nation through performing the Temple rituals, but at first it is not clear to whom the Jewish people are to be *kohanim*, to be in service. The YaShaR (Isaac Samuel Reggio, nineteenth c., Italy) clarifies: "All the nations in the world are like one nation, and you [the Israelites] are the Priests to this one nation."[3] It seems the divine mandate for the Jewish people is to be in service to all humanity.

Inquiring further, we may ask, how is the Jew expected to be in service to humanity? What does this entail? Sforno (Obadiah ben Jacob Sforno, fifteenth–sixteenth c., Italy) teaches, "By teaching and instructing all of humankind to call out in the name of God and for all humankind to be in service to God together."[4] By extension, this may be the mandate for all human beings: to be in service together. As one global nation, we are to be aware of the Creator and better the world.

What, then, might we learn from Moses as an exemplar of the sacred role of being in service?

A Deeper Dive

The kabbalisitc tradition describes how each soul continuously returns to the world to complete its unique mission of service, in a process called *gilgul* (reincarnation.) The soul is the Divine's life force enlivening the human body. We experience this life force through our breathing cycles—entering us, circulating throughout our body, and then exiting as it returns to its Source. The mystics also say this life force transcends limited time and space. A soul may inhabit different bodies throughout generations in order to fulfill its mission in its entirety.

The idea of *gilgul* offers one explanation for the ambiguity of our verse. Addressing Moses as "you" rather than by name may reflect the spiritual connection between Moses and the earlier biblical figure of Noah. Rabbi Adam Jacobs (twenty-first c., United States), extrapolating from the teachings of the renowned kabbalist Isaac Luria (sixteenth c., Jerusalem), explains: "Though Noah was considered a righteous man, he is faulted for failing to take responsibility for his generation and allowing them to be destroyed by the flood. The Hebrew word for the boat he built [and that saved humanity] is '*teyva*.' This word is only used one more time in the Torah [to refer] to the little raft that Moses' mother made to hide him from the Egyptians."[5]

The limited use of the word *teyva* provides the textual context for connecting Moses with Noah, and the two leaders' contrasting responses to God's avowed plan to annihilate either all or some of humanity becomes the focal point of their connection. When God tells Noah about the impending flood that will destroy humanity, Noah neither protests to God nor prays on humanity's behalf. However, when the Eternal tells Moses of the divine plan to annihilate the Israelites for worshiping the golden calf, Moses audaciously protests: "Now, if You will forgive their sin [well and good]; but if not, erase me from the record that You have written!" (Exod. 32:32). Rabbi Jacobs thus surmises that Noah's soul was reincarnated into Moses' body. When Moses is given the same opportunity the Eternal gave to Noah, he corrects Noah's response (or lack thereof). Moses' upright stance demonstrates what God may have sought from Noah: to live in the spiritual state of both being strongly connected to the Eternal and, simultaneously, strongly connected to the Eternal's Creation, humankind.

The Noah and Moses scenario may suggest that being in service to a mission that exceeds our own limited self is the common denominator that connects everyone. This may be humanity's universal purpose. Yet how we each fulfill this collective mission is particular to our unique selves.

Returning to "now, if You will forgive their sin [well and good]; but if not, erase me from the record that You have written!," the Eternal responds to Moses' ultimatum by accepting his plea and forgiving the people. It would appear that the status quo is now peacefully restored—but our tradition leaves us in a quandary.

The Talmud astonishingly teaches, "The curse of a sage comes true in some way, even if it was conditional and the condition was not fulfilled."[6] In other words, we might logically assume that since God acquiesces to Moses' plea by saving the Israelites from annihilation, God would not need to proceed with Moses' original demand to be erased from the Torah otherwise. And yet, through the lens of the talmudic sages, Moses' wish for his name to be erased if God does not grant forgiveness becomes his curse—on himself—that then *has* to come true.

But wouldn't that mean that Moses' name would have to be completely erased from the Torah? Literally, yes! Thus we are faced with two opposing truths. Of course Moses' name is *not* erased from the Torah—and, equally so, the Talmud in essence would "force" God to do exactly that!

Rabbi Bahya (Bahya ben Asher ibn Halawa, thirteenth–fourteenth c., Spain) suggests: "Even though [Moses'] prayer, namely forgiveness of the sin of the Jewish people, was accepted by God, Moses' name does not appear in the entire portion of *Tetsavveh* as a direct consequence of his uttering the words 'erase me from the record that You have written.' Whereas God forgave the grievous sin of the golden calf, He did in fact execute Moses' curse and honor the talmudic adage by 'erasing' Moses' name from this portion."[7]

Expanding on this idea of "you" replacing Moses' name, and taking this in another direction, we might consider that if *we* immerse ourselves in our mission by being in service to better God's world, perhaps our individual names may not matter as much as *what we do* with our particular names.

We may not know the details of the Divine's intention for each of our souls—our specific part in *tikkun*, healing or fixing. Still, the universal element seems to emphasize being in service, even if it means we may feel "erased"—unacknowledged or unrecognized—while carrying out our mission. Moses exemplifies the determination to be unconditionally committed to serving his fellow Israelites—so much so, the sages say, he doesn't need name recognition. In fulfilling his mission to be in service to improving the world, his actions, not his name, are significantly more important.

His example can encourage us to strive for the same, to be so invested in service that we do not even need recognition.

The Practice

1. Begin with breath awareness.
2. Then, reflect on the text.
3. Move to quieting down your mind.

These three steps are explained in detail in the introduction.

4. Visualize your breath as it moves throughout you as your soul, energy within your body that keeps you alive and well.

Ask yourself: What does being in service conjure up for me?

Then: What is my unique *tikkun*? What kind of fixing, healing, bringing of unrealized potential to fulfillment ought I, might I, do I engage in?

And then: Does my sense of purpose somehow relate to being in service to the Creator's world?

When we cultivate mindfulness, as here, a particular result is less important than the actual practice. By picturing in your mind what being in service conjures up for you, *this* is already cultivating a spiritual consciousness, a consciousness in service.

Ki Tissa'

The Inherent Value of Every Person

GOD spoke to Moses, saying: When you take a census of the Israelites according to their army enrollment, each shall pay GOD a ransom for himself on being enrolled, that no plague may come upon them through their being enrolled. This is what everyone who is entered in the records shall pay: a half-shekel by the sanctuary weight—twenty *gerahs* to the shekel—a half-shekel as an offering to GOD.

Exod. 30:11–13

Where We Are

The Torah describes the ritual to officially induct the *Kohanim* into priestly service.

God tells Moses to take a census of the Israelite men of army age. However, it is to be facilitated in an unorthodox way. Instead of counting people, each person is to contribute a half-shekel coin. The sum total of the coins will be counted, and the collected funds will facilitate building the foundational sockets for the *mishkan* (Tabernacle), upon which the walls rest.

At First Glance

Why does the Eternal command Moses to take a census?

Rashi (Shlomo Yitzhaki, eleventh c., France) asserts that counting the Children of Israel is an expression of how dear the people are to God.[1] But if this is the case, why does Moses proceed to count the half-shekel coins and not the people themselves? Rashi explains: "When we wish to know the sum total of the population, we do not count them by the head, but by their half-shekel contribution. When counting people, a plague may come upon them as we see during the time of King David."[2]

When King David commanded his army commander Joab to execute a census, Joab respectfully attempted to dissuade his king from carrying it out, to no avail. The people were counted, and a deadly plague ensued. King David admitted he sinned and sought God's forgiveness for having counted the people (2 Sam. 24).

While averting a plague would appear to be a strong argument for not counting people in a census, I believe we can go deeper. The preferred way to facilitate a census may teach us about recognizing the inherent value of every human being.

A Deeper Dive

Returning to our verse, the Netivot Shalom (Sholom Noach Berezovsky, twentieth c., Israel) addresses what appears to be its awkward phrasing. Why does it say that the value of a half-shekel is half of "twenty *gerahs*"? Why doesn't the verse simply refer to a half-shekel as ten *gerahs*? Even more so, why doesn't the verse simply state, "a half-shekel or ten *gerahs*"? He teaches:

> While the obligatory contribution equaled ten *gerahs*, the commandment employs the term "half shekel" instead of ten *gerahs* to accentuate the fact that everyone had to have a part in the *mishkan*—yet everyone had to realize that they were only a "half." In the building of the *mishkan*, the Torah requires a collaborative effort. Each individual is never more [or less] than a half, until that person unites with another. In fact, each person contributes their half-shekel to the greater "other half"—the Israelite nation.
>
> In this way each person contributes equally towards the nation becoming united as one whole. This unity, as the fundamental and essential building block of both the macro *mishkan* and the micro inner *mishkan*, allows the *Shekhinah* to dwell and manifest its Presence.[3]

In other words, the commandment text prioritizes communal efforts that intentionally lead toward interconnectedness. God's mandate to the people manifests the dual recognition that everyone possesses something of value to contribute and that the whole is in fact each person's "other half."

Emphasizing this radical equality, the Torah states just a couple of verses later: "The rich shall not pay more and the poor shall not pay less than half a shekel" (Exod. 30:15).

Maimonides (Moses ben Maimon, twelfth c., Spain and Egypt) clarifies: "Even a poor man who derives his livelihood from charity is obligated [to make this donation]. He should borrow from others or sell the clothes he is wearing so that he can give a half-shekel."[4]

From here we might understand one reason why the Torah appears to be quite rigid in this mitzvah: to emphasize the core Jewish tenet of the inherent value of each individual. Each person must be counted by contributing the same amount, regardless of the donor's financial status, because each person's contribution equally matters. The *mishkan* would be incomplete without every person's equal contribution. It would seem that the *Shekhinah* (Divine Presence) dwells only in a complete sanctuary—one equally represented by all.

That half-shekel coins were used specifically to build the foundational sockets of the *mishkan* emphasizes this point. While all other parts of the *mishkan* derived from the people's freewill contributions, the foundation to which everyone contributed equally was built upon the single attribute that everyone equally possessed: the inherent value of having been created equally in the image of God.

This inherent value, the idea that the very imprint of the Divine is embedded in the spiritual DNA of each of us, is meant to give rise to a person's sense of self-worth. The term "*ki tissa*" itself conveys the idea of self-worth. While it is often translated as "when you count [the heads of the people]," it literally means, "when you elevate and raise [the heads of the people]." If "when you count" was in fact the intended meaning, "*ki tifkod*," which clearly conveys taking a census, would have been the more precise rendering. But *ki tissa'* appears instead.

From its usage, we may learn that this census avoided counting people in a way that would reduce them to mere numbers. In an extreme case of such dehumanization, the Nazis branded each of their Jewish victims with a number to render them owned and nameless, like cattle. Henceforth, Jews have become all the more sensitive to the dehumanizing effect of reducing a person to a number. The Torah census appears cognizant of just that.

The Ishbitzer Rebbe (Mordechai Yosef Leiner, nineteenth c., Poland) probes this idea further:

> Each person's head was "elevated" at the moment they passed before Moses to contribute their half-shekel. At that moment a person's consciousness [their head] was raised to now realizing their unique purpose in the world. God revealed to each person at that moment that the *mishkan*—and the world itself—would be incomplete without their contribution. Also, at that moment each person realized that the same was true for everyone else. No matter how many highly evolved and spiritually sensitive people contributed their half-shekel, the *Shekhinah* would not dwell in the *mishkan* until each and every individual made their contribution as well—regardless of perceived status in the community.[5]

The Ishbitzer Rebbe's insights help us understand how two elements may lead us to recognize our inherent value. First, he points out, the "raising of the head" equates with raising our consciousness to become aware that we each have a unique purpose in our lives. This knowledge alone may inspire us to believe that our lives matter and are of high value. Second, our own sense of self-worth may lead us to realize that without everyone's contributions, including our own, the world would be incomplete. We equally really do need each other.

In this respect, Rabbi Jonathan Sacks (twentieth–twenty-first c., England) points to the danger inherent in counting Jews, promoting as it might a gross misunderstanding that the value of a people lies in their numbers:

> The danger in counting Jews is that if they believed . . . that there is strength in numbers, the Jewish people would long ago have given way to despair. How then do you estimate the strength of the Jewish

people? You do not need numbers. You need dedication, commitment, study, prayer, vision, courage, ideals and hope. You need a people who are instinctively inclined to give and to contribute. Give, then count the contributions: the finest way ever devised to measure the strength of a people.[6]

I suggest that Rabbi Sacks's sentiments may be extended beyond the Jewish world to include all of humanity. Strength lies not in numbers of bodies, but rather in what each individual person contributes to our world.

Might the Divine be asking each of us to become aware of our inner half-shekel—our inherent self-worth? Rabbi Dr. Avraham J. Twerski (twentieth–twenty-first c., United States and Israel) observes that the "substantial majority of emotional or behavioral problems [in the world today] are due to one common underlying factor: an unjustified and unwarranted feeling of low self-esteem."[7]

We each possess something of substantial worth to contribute to the world—no more and no less than anyone else's—and simultaneously, we each need everyone else's "half" to become whole and complete. Cultivating the *middah* of recognizing our inherent value allows us to participate fully in making this world a dignified, compassionate, and sacred home for the Divine—a true *mishkan*, within us and beyond.

The Practice

1. Begin with breath awareness.
2. Then, reflect on the text.
3. Move to quieting down your mind.

These three steps are explained in detail in the introduction.

4. Visualize a half-shekel coin. For this practice, any round, gold coin with a "half" or "½" inscription will work.

Allow yourself to move into your heart, the receptacle for your half-shekel coin.

Gazing at the half-shekel there, imagine that this golden coin represents your potential contribution to your relationships, to your community, and to the world.

What do you possess of worth to contribute to the world? Can you sense your inherent value?

Can you believe your life really does matter? Can you sense how the world needs the contribution of your half-shekel? Can you sense that you need everyone else's?

Do you sense that your own life calls upon you to contribute this half-shekel to the larger half-shekel of society?

Might this ennoble you to show up in the world as your best self?

Va-yak'hel / Pekudei

Transforming the Ordinary into Wonder

> Moses then convoked the whole Israelite community and said to them:
> These are the things that GOD has commanded you to do: On six days
> work may be done, but on the seventh day you shall have a sabbath of
> complete rest, holy to GOD.
>
> Exod. 35:1–2

Where We Are

Moses conducts the census. God appoints Betzalel as chief architect of the *mishkan*. There is another reminder of the importance of abstaining from work on Shabbat.

The Torah then returns to something that historically occurs earlier, after Moses ascends Mount Sinai to receive the Torah. After forty days, Moses descends with the two tablets to witness the Israelites worshiping the Golden Calf. He smashes the tablets and then ascends for a second forty days, during which he successfully pleads with the Eternal not to destroy the Israelite nation. Moses descends to inform the people that they will live. He then ascends for the final forty days, bringing two freshly carved stone tablets, as the Eternal instructs. God renews the covenant with the Children of Israel and again inscribes the Ten Utterances (alternatively, Ten Commandments) onto the second set of stone tablets. Moses descends with these. The Eternal and the Israelites have now been reconciled and their relationship renewed on what becomes the first Yom Kippur, the Day of Atonement.

The two verses under discussion occur the day after Yom Kippur.

Rashi (Shlomo Yitzhaki, eleventh c., France) observes that the directive to build the *mishkan* is given right after an exhortation to observe the Sabbath. The proximity of these verses teaches that even building the holy *mishkan* does not supersede the observance of Shabbat.[1]

While the directive of "a sabbath of complete rest, holy to GOD" is clear, the text does not explain with what attitude the Israelites are to approach their work of building the *mishkan* during the remaining six days of the week—and, by extension, how we might best approach creating and working six days a week in our own time.

What messages might lie underneath the surface of our text?

A Deeper Dive

For decades I pondered what it means to be truly religious. My inner idealist always imagined that if I encountered a person who really did "walk with God" (Deut. 30:16), I would sense an aura of wonder enveloping this person. I entered the ultra-Orthodox world in hopes of finding many who exuded this sense of wonder.

When my hopes were not realized, I began to explore texts teaching how to bring the sacred nature of Shabbat into the ordinary moments of the week. On Shabbat, I realized, my capacity to experience the Divine Presence was more acute—and this consciousness might continue to flow into my workweek. This, then, just might fuel the religious wonder I was seeking.

Abraham Joshua Heschel (twentieth c., Poland and the United States) eloquently articulated this ideal: "The higher goal of spiritual living is not to amass a wealth of information, but to face sacred moments."[2] Heschel viewed an awareness of the Divine as a key component of the religious experience—both on the sacred Shabbat and during what appears to be the less sacred weekdays. The practice of transforming the ordinary into a sacred moment—through the awareness of the Divine Presence in the mundane—defines the moment as a "wonder."

The Me'or Eynayim (Menachem Nachum Twersky, eighteenth c., Ukraine) depicts such an approach in relation to our passage. Regarding

Moses' instructions to the whole community, "These are the things that GOD has commanded you to do: On six days work may be done, but on the seventh day you shall have a sabbath of complete rest, holy to GOD," he questions why the verse states "work may be done" in the passive form, rather than "you may do work" in the more popular active form. He asks rhetorically if the verse implies that the work is done by itself. Then he segues to explain the meaning of a verse from Proverbs (3:6), "In all your ways, acknowledge [God]": "A person needs to realize that everything they do, or notice is in alignment with the 'Torah energy' that lies within it. And they need to fully believe in this. For the Torah directs all of creation's behavior."[3]

Here, "Torah energy" refers to the broad understanding of Torah being the Creator's will for a creation to continue existing. The Me'or Eynayim elaborates: "This means that the person realizes that it is not the actual human being conducting a business transaction and other earthly endeavors, rather the 'Torah energy' embedded within the action. Therefore, the activity in fact does occur on its own—meaning we do not do it. The 'Torah energy' within it is revealed by being enclothed in the human being's limbs and words."[4]

It turns out that when the Me'or Eynayim asks if the passive phrase "work may be done" hints that the work happens on its own, it may not be as rhetorical as we initially thought. His commentary points to a deep belief that yes, in fact, it does! Due to the abstention from human creative work on Shabbat, the Divine Presence becomes revealed as the "Doer" that orchestrates all that occurs on this special seventh day. Shabbat spotlights the Creator taking center stage.

In actuality, he is teaching, the godly force revealed on Shabbat remains the same during the week, despite this "Torah force" appearing more subtly and possibly even being concealed as human endeavors take center stage. It is all too natural, then, to overlook the presence of the Divine. Those of us who are Shabbat observers may make the mistake of assuming that our workweek activities are less godly than our Shabbat traditions. Yet from the Me'or Eynayim's understanding, when during the workweek our physical hands reach for a credit card, or a keyboard, or a dinner plate, our hands are not actually doing the work. The godly force that continuously breathes life into our bodies also breathes life into our actions.

This spiritual awareness births the consciousness that can allow us to transform the ordinary into wonder. While the external action remains the same, we may come to recognize it as a "sacred moment" by perceiving the Divine Presence within it. Our own awareness of the concealed internal reality can define any moment—this moment—as sacred.

The Me'or Eynayim goes on to contrast the Shabbat-revealed and weekday-concealed energies through comparing the names we apply to each:

> We refer to the six days as *chol*—the mundane, the everyday, the ordinary. This contrasts with Shabbat as *kodesh*—special, unique, wonder.... Please God, with the revelation of the Messiah ... all the concealments of the Divine will no longer exist and only the revealed holiness of the One will remain. However, until then, while we remain in spiritual exile from obvious awareness of the Divine, we must actively draw out the holiness hidden in the *chol*. For now, the forces of concealment prevent *kodesh* from being recognizable. Consequently, we must actively reveal the *kodesh* through fulfilling the verse, "In all your ways, acknowledge [God]"—not allowing the *chol* to remain as a boundary and barrier to awareness of the Divine.[5]

This novel approach encourages us to harness the energetic flow of the Divine that we may experience on Shabbat to strengthen our capacity to "acknowledge God" in "all our ways" during the weekday too.

We can bring a refined *chol* consciousness into our Shabbat *kodesh* consciousness, too. As we move closer to Shabbat during the week, this awareness of *kodesh* within *chol* can sensitize us to the revealed divine aura on Shabbat, heightening our recognition of the revealed Divine Presence. And again, from there we can bring Shabbat *kodesh* consciousness into weekday *chol* consciousness, transforming the ordinary because of our increased awareness of wonder. Shabbat influences the weekday mindset, which influences the Shabbat mindset, and so it continues. What may have seemed like opposed energies existing in discrete segments of time can merge into each other, blurring the line between them and actualizing an enhanced experience of both.

Through this lens, the Piaseczner Rebbe (Kalonymus Kalmish Shapira, twentieth c., Poland) interprets the talmudic teaching that "if only Israel would keep two Sabbaths, they would be redeemed immediately" as an invitation to weave together Shabbat and weekday energies: "While the first Shabbat is the obvious seventh day, the second Shabbat occurs during the six weekdays—by drawing the *kodesh* of the Shabbat consciousness into the weekday *chol* consciousness—to a degree where it actually pervades and transforms the weekday *chol* consciousness into Shabbat *kodesh* consciousness."[6]

By undertaking "in all your ways, acknowledge [God]" as a spiritual practice, we may begin to transform seemingly mundane acts of the workweek into sacred moments. And by cultivating this practice, we may come to experience, in a personal, micro way, the long-awaited messianic redemption our prophets have yearned for. All the more, by transforming the ordinary into wonder, we just might transform, one person at a time, a broken and fragmented world into a healed and redeemed one.

The Practice

1. Begin with breath awareness.
2. Then, reflect on the text.
3. Move to quieting down your mind.

These three steps are explained in detail in the introduction.

4. Visualize a moment when you have experienced wonder and amazement. Relive this special time in your mind. What feelings come up for you? What *is* awesome about this time? Do you sense increased energy within you? If yes, what is this energy like? How does it affect your sense of wonder?

Begin to direct your awareness to your breathing cycles. Sense with each new inhalation the possibility of finding more wonder in your life. Sense with each exhalation what this may be like.

Imagine now transporting this feeling of wonder into an ordinary moment from today. Hold the feeling of wonder and then invest it into this moment. Bring to this moment the belief that the sensation of wonder—your enthusiasm, joy, excitement—is fully transferable. Sense with each inhalation the prospect of finding more wonder in this moment. Sense with each exhalation what this is like.

What is surprising you? What in this very moment might rise up to the level of awe?

3

Leviticus (Va-yikra')

Va-yikra'

Hearing Our Individual Calling

> [GOD] called to Moses and spoke to him from the Tent of Meeting, saying:
> Speak to the Israelite people, and say to them: When any of you presents
> an offering of cattle to GOD: You shall choose your offering from the herd
> or from the flock.
>
> Lev. 1:1–2

Where We Are

Moses reiterates all the directives regarding construction of the *mishkan* and its various ritual objects, and the work begins. Upon completion, Moses approves the work, and the Divine descends to dwell in the Tabernacle. This completes the book of Exodus.

The book of Leviticus begins with Moses receiving the general rules of the sacrificial offerings.

At First Glance

The first Hebrew word in Leviticus is *vayikra*, "[GOD] called," and the Hebrew title of the biblical book, Va-yikra', acquires its name from it, just as the other four books of the Torah are named for one of the words in their first verse. Derived from Greek, the English name, "Leviticus," reflects that much of the book's content is devoted to the Levite Priests' rituals.

Why our verse begins with "[GOD] called to Moses and spoke to him," rather than the more common "And GOD *spoke* to Moses" is unclear. Rashi (Shlomo Yitzhaki, eleventh c., France) suggests that "the word 'called' expresses endearment and that the Voice went out and only reached Moses' ears."[1] For undisclosed reasons the Creator desires this moment of divine calling to Moses to be private and intimate.

A Deeper Dive

The fact that "[GOD] called to Moses and spoke to him," rather than instructed Moses at the outset, may indicate that the deeper message of this passage has to do with the very act of divine calling to Moses, not the content of that calling. We might then understand that "[GOD] called to Moses" to advance a mission unique to Moses, since as the leader of the nation, he is responsible for ensuring that all Temple-related rituals are properly performed.

If God calls to Moses with a task that only he can do, might we too possess an individual divine mission for which each of us was created, even if we cannot yet conceive of it?

I believe that this is so. Unlike all other divine creations, who were originally created in the plural, the Eternal created the first human being in the singular: "And God created humankind in the divine image, creating *it* in the image of God" (Gen. 1:27). The very fact that God created each human being as an individual indicates to me that the Divine intended each of us to possess an individual life mission as well. To this point, when the talmudic sages discuss various reasons why the human being was created in the singular, they proclaim: "Since all humanity descends from one person, each and every person is obligated to say: The world was created for me, as one person can be the source of all humanity, and recognize the significance of their actions."[2] The Talmud recognizes that each of us human beings has been created with a special divine plan solely for us alone.

And yet, we might ask, what if I don't know the divine plan for me? How are each of us to know what our individual missions entail?

One way, as for Moses, may be that the Eternal enlightens us to our unique purpose through a calling. In the summer of 1971, as I was turning twenty years old, I found myself thirty-five thousand feet in the sky enroute to a beach lover's paradise: backpacking from beach to beach in southern Europe. Suddenly, for the first time in my life, I heard "the calling." I heard within me, "Go to Israel." At first, I thought I just imagined this. Being on my first transatlantic flight with all the excitement and insecurity this would naturally cause many of us to feel, I wondered if this directive was real.

But then I heard it again, and again. And I intuitively sensed I needed to heed the voice.

Three simple words, "Go to Israel," radically changed the course of my life. Prior to hearing my calling, I never imagined I would someday live in Israel, raise children to be proud Israelis, adopt traditional Jewish practices, pursue a career in Torah scholarship, teach and lecture on Jewish sacred texts and guide meditation gatherings both in Israel and around the globe. So, too, prior to this crucial moment, the trajectory of my life had not guided me to glean any knowledge of my unique purpose. Those three words led me to incredible clarity about my purpose in having been born.

Even now as I reflect back on that voice, still crystal clear as if it just occurred, I wonder about this "calling." What was more startling—that I heard this uninvited calling or that I actually honored it?

My background lacked any context with which to understand this calling. While I had always believed in the idea of an omnipotent Creator, I had never given much thought to being in an actual relationship with the Divine. Yet the message I was receiving was loud and clear. Deep in my bowels and despite my best logic, I felt pressed to heed this counterintuitive directive. It didn't matter that I hadn't planned for any of this. After landing in Europe, I simply boarded the next flight to Israel, as if that had been my original plan.

I came to learn later that Jewish scholars refer to the voice I heard calling and guiding me to my next step as *nevuah l'hadrakhah*, "prophecy for personal guidance." But prophecy is said to have ended more than two thousand years ago with the biblical prophets. How could this be? And yet, how could this not be? How else am I to understand what happened in that life-changing moment en route to Europe?

The Piaseczner Rebbe (Kalonymus Kalmish Shapira, twentieth c., Poland) teaches that although an external voice from above predicting the future no longer exists, the internal prophetic voice for personal guidance has not ceased.[3] Hearing this internal voice renders the moment sacred.

Elaborating on the Piaseczner's teaching, Dr. Henry Abramson (a contemporary American scholar and historian) explains: "The spiritual enlightenment engendered by Hasidism [i]s intrinsically related to the phenomenon of prophecy. . . . The Rebbe contended that God continued to maintain an open broadcast channel, and that with the appropriate spiritual training, Hasidim could receive Divine inspiration. . . . The development of this spiritual sensitivity was the primary goal."[4]

As this teaching implies, not all of us hear our inner calling—what the first book of Kings calls the "soft murmuring sound" (1 Kings 19:12). To develop spiritual sensitivity, the Piaseczner encourages us to become aware of the Divine Presence in our lives: "In general, become a person who seeks out the Divine Presence everywhere. . . . And when you seek Him out, you will indeed find Him. Where will you find Him? In yourself and in everything around you."[5]

It may be that when we consciously seek the Divine Presence in our lives, we are more likely to hear our calling. I imagine that much of my own existential searching was for an encounter with the Divine, albeit in my case without my ever being cognizant of this. When I heard my own calling, I sensed emptiness in my life and was searching, though for what I did not know. Earlier in my life I had not been on a conscious search either for meaning or for a connection with God. I wonder whether at that moment in the skies I was finally ready for a divine encounter.

The Me'or Eynayim (Menachem Nachum Twersky, eighteenth c., Ukraine) notes that the Hebrew slaves did not hear their calling immediately upon their redemption. In fact, God's call to the people to build their own homes for the Divine to dwell in only occurs after the plagues in Egypt, the splitting of the Sea of Reeds, the people's liberation from slavery, and their arrival at Sinai with all its dramatic and startling sights. Only after all these external wonders does God command, "Make Me a sanctuary that I may dwell among them" (Exod. 25:8). The Me'or Eynayim explains:

This is compared to a person who has always been in a dark place and has never seen light. If someone were to suddenly take this person out of the darkness to the bright sunlight, they would not be able to bear it. Therefore, they need incremental steps to accustom themselves to seeing light—first a small crack through which to peek; then it can be widened into a window, and then the person can be led outside into the full brightness of the day.[6]

Contemporary Rabbi Arthur Green points out that this parallels Plato's famous allegory of the cave.[7] When the people finally leave the dark cave, their eyes hurt and they quickly return.

The Or HaHayim (Hayim ibn Attar, eighteenth c., Morocco and Jerusalem) comments that when the Egyptians enslaved the Israelites, the nation was steeped in spiritual darkness. When God tells Moses that the Hebrew slaves will be liberated, "I have come down to rescue them from the Egyptians and to bring them out of that land to a good and spacious land" (Exod. 3:8), it is because the Hebrews' "souls [had sunk and] had been contaminated with levels of impurity."[8] God has to lower Himself, as it were, and then raise up the Israelites' souls to freedom.

In this vein, had the Eternal at that time revealed the Divine Presence within the people with its accompanying calling, it probably would have overwhelmed them. Instead, a progression of external wonders helped prepare the Israelites for the eventual internal wonder of hearing their calling at Sinai.

If we consider all the varied perspectives here, they seem to share two components. First, an individual calling gives life meaning. Second, while the pathway to recognizing one's calling may not be clear-cut, we seem to need to be ready to hear it, so we can heed it when it does arise. In this light, the Piaseczner's urging that we "seek out the Divine Presence everywhere" may prove a valuable practice.

What might lead you to cultivate readiness to hear your divine calling?

The Practice
1. Begin with breath awareness.
2. Then, reflect on the text.
3. Move to quieting down your mind.

These three steps are explained in detail in the introduction.

4. Visualize opening up to hearing your calling. As you inhale, imagine you are breathing in your calling. As you exhale, imagine accepting being called. Gently lean into this visualization through breath awareness for a few moments. Where is this happening in your external environment? How, internally, have you prepared for this?

Now, pause and be with the rhythm of your breathing cycle. In essence, drop into your own self. As you experience this centering, what do you imagine happening when you hear your calling? Do you hear an actual voice from within? Do you have an intuitive sense of your inner "soft murmuring sound" guiding you? Or?

Might you be ready to accept divine guidance to continue your life with more clarity and purpose?

Tsav

Keeping Our Inner Fire Burning

A perpetual fire shall be kept burning on the altar, not to go out.

Lev. 6:6

Where We Are

The first five chapters in Leviticus give a detailed accounting of the extensive array of ritual offerings the *Kohanim* are to facilitate in the *mishkan*. The Torah then addresses the fire that burns upon the sacrificial altar.

This brings us to our current verse, where the text emphasizes the importance of keeping the fire upon the sacrificial altar burning continuously. In addition, the fire must never be extinguished.

At First Glance

How are we to understand the seeming redundancy in our verse: God's exhortation, "A perpetual fire shall be kept burning on the altar, not to go out"?

Since Jewish tradition holds that every word in the Torah contains specific meaning, and the Torah would be incomplete without every word in it, the tradition itself compels us to refute the ostensible redundancy by somehow deriving two distinct meanings from the two injunctions.

As a result, various commentators have asked, what does the second instruction—that the fire is "not to go out"—intimate that the first, "A perpetual fire shall be kept burning on the altar," does not?

Chizkuni (Hezekiah ben Manoah, thirteenth c., France) says that the two commands contain two different ideas. "The phrase 'a perpetual fire shall be kept burning on the altar' means the fire will be tended to even on the Shabbat [as during the week]."[1] Except for this instance, and in the case of saving a life, Shabbat observance prohibits starting or stoking a fire. Chizkuni interprets the second phrase "[it is] not to go out" to mean "Even while the Israelites were journeying through the wilderness, God's honor required taking precautions to ensure that the fire be kept burning."[2] Otherwise, when the Israelites were busy erecting and disassembling the *mishkan* at each encampment, unintentionally they might have let the fire be extinguished.

A Deeper Dive

Our verse may also be addressing another fire: the spiritual fire of our souls. As we will see, keeping our spiritual inner fire burning and ensuring that we do not extinguish it seems to mirror the directives on how to maintain the physical fire on the sacrificial altar in the *mishkan*.

The Bible explains that "A mortal's life breath [soul] is GOD's lamp" (Prov. 20:27). In Hebrew the word for breath, *neshima*, derives from the same etymological root as soul, *neshama*. We learn this from the Creation story in Genesis, when the Creator brought the first human being into the world: "The ETERNAL God formed a Human from the soil's humus, blowing into his nostrils the breath of life [*nishmat hayyim*]: the Human became a living being [*nefesh haya*]" (Gen. 2:7). The verse itself equates breath with soul, employing another Hebrew word for soul, *nefesh*, as well. The verse in Proverbs seems to expand on this idea of breath/soul giving the first human being life by comparing the soul to GOD's lamp.

Ibn Ezra (Abraham ibn Ezra, eleventh–twelfth c., Spain) teaches: "This alludes to the noble soul given by God that provides illuminating intellectual awareness."[3] His interpretation offers a novel framework from which to understand a common response to those "aha!" moments when we grasp someone else's perspective, "Oh, I *see* what you mean." It is as if, before, we were groping in the dark, but suddenly the intellectual qualities of the soul "shed light" on the matter.

For most of the world's history, external light was provided by fire. (The electric light bulb was invented relatively recently, in the late nineteenth century.) I would suggest that our soul's inner fire continues to fuel both our mind's capacity to think and our heart's capacity to feel.

Rav Kook (Avraham Yitzchak HaCohen Kook, nineteenth–twentieth c., Jerusalem) compares the fire on the ritual altar to the inner fire inherent in each of us:

> It is forbidden to extinguish the thirst for Godliness that burns and rages with a strong flame in the heart. If an individual were to extinguish the spark or ember upon the physical altar, they would transgress the prohibitive commandment "[it is] not to go out." (Lev. 6:6) So much the more so, one who extinguishes the spiritual supernal spark that burns upon the spiritual altar, which permeates a person's sacred life in their heart. As well, one needs to continually add fire from the realm of the human being below: "A perpetual fire shall be kept burning on the altar . . ." (Lev. 6:6)[4]

Rav Kook's teaching reflects the traditional belief that every human being contains a "thirst for Godliness that burns and rages with a strong flame in the heart." Even if only subconsciously, we all yearn for an intimate encounter with our Creator.

He speaks further on the existence of two spiritual fires intertwining on the spiritual altar in our hearts. The smaller one from below, belonging to the realm of the human being, continuously rises toward its Source, the larger fire above.

By way of comparison, we might notice a phenomenon. When a small flame, such as a lit match, is placed in close proximity to a larger flame, say a multiwicked candle, the match flame naturally gravitates toward the candle's flame, as if it is being pulled within a magnetic field.

Rav Kook continues:

> A person needs to continually add fire from "below," from the realm of the human being, [and not to rely solely on the fire that miraculously descended from "above."] This spiritual fire that the human adds to the altar [their heart] from "below" consists of applying one's intelligence, with wisdom and understanding, with the light of learning Torah, and with the light of fulfilling a *mitzvah*. All of this in order for

the lofty flame within to rise and increase in its strength and power, affecting all aspects and levels of one's life.[5]

I would expand on Rav Kook's teaching of what it means for a person to "add fire on their altar" to encompass how each of us *expresses* our soul, thereby keeping the fire of our soul alive. The ways in which we think, speak, and behave as we manifest and shine the light of our soul can infuse the world with goodness, kindness, and compassion.

Rabbi Yaakov HaLevi Filber (twenty-first c., Israel) enhances Rav Kook's interpretation that we must add our own fire from the human realm to the higher fire of our soul from the supernal realm:

> The Torah is not satisfied solely with this fire that descended from the heavens. Rather, the Torah commands us to bring fire as well from the human being. Why is the Torah not satisfied with the fire that descended from the heavens and therefore commands us to bring additional fire from the human being? Because this combination of a Heavenly act with a human-made act contains guidance and direction for the role of the human being in God's world.
>
> The role of the human being is not merely to abstain from spoiling and destroying the Blessed Holy One's world, because the human being was not created to be a passive creation who does not make nor create anything. Rather the fundamental role of the human being is to enhance and complete the world.[6]

We may now realize that "the fire from below" that each of us can add to the already existing "fire from above" gives each of us the capacity to be in a relationship with the Divine as an active partner. We human beings are born into an incomplete world that needs our engagement to realize its potential as a space whereby the Divine Presence becomes revealed and indeed recognized. Hence, this partnership brings these two fires together—the upper fire of the Divine descending into our hearts and the lower fire ascending to the Divine through our spiritually sensitive behavior.

"A mortal's life breath [soul] is GOD's lamp" (Prov. 20:27) is one of many teachings here devoted to encouraging us to keep the divine spark within our hearts alive. All of us receive an opportunity to shine our inner healing light to a broken world. If each of us brings our own fire from below to enhance the fire from above, and if innumerable others do as well, together we just might make the world the ideal we dream for it.

The Practice

1. Begin with breath awareness.
2. Then, reflect on the text.
3. Move to quieting down your mind.

These three steps are explained in detail in the introduction.

4. Visualize a warm, companionable fire. Perhaps you are on a camping trip, and after dinner you're sitting around the campfire, gazing at the jumping flames, feeling warm and comfortable. Or perhaps you are at home, on a winter's night, sitting by your inside fireplace, if you have one or can imagine one, with family and friends, relaxing and taking in the fire's warmth, both physically and emotionally. Or?

How does this feel?

Moments later, feel the fire beginning to dwindle. The sensation of being a bit chilly is replacing the warmth. What can you do to help the fire resume its original state?

Now, visualize a spiritual fire within you. There is radiant energy inside of you keeping you "warm." What does this feel like? How do you experience your inner warmth, your inner fire, your inner illumination?

After some time has passed, as with the external fire, you notice your spiritual fire beginning to diminish in its intensity and brightness. What can you do now? How might you add spiritual fire to your inner flame?

Shemini

A Time to Remain Silent

> Now Aaron's sons Nadab and Abihu . . . offered before GOD alien fire—
> which had not been enjoined upon them. And fire came forth from GOD
> and consumed them; thus they died by God's will. Then Moses said to
> Aaron, "This is what GOD meant by saying: 'Through those near to Me I
> show Myself holy. . . .'" And Aaron was silent.
>
> Lev. 10:1–3

Where We Are

The Torah delves into the laws relating to the Priests' sacrificial service.
The Priests are inducted, their services commence, and the Divine Presence (missing since the Golden Calf catastrophe) returns. The people
rejoice and fall on their faces.

Two of Aaron's sons, Priests like their father, bring an offering clearly
outside the bounds of a Priest's acceptable sacrifice to the altar. They
die. Moses speaks to Aaron about his sons' deaths. Aaron stays silent.

At First Glance

Aaron's silence after witnessing the deaths of two of his sons introduces
us to the *middah* of choosing silence. At certain moments in our lives,
remaining silent may be the best response.

Jewish tradition recognizes silence as a value. Ecclesiastes (3:1,7)
says, "A season is set for everything, a time for every experience under
heaven. . . . A time for silence and a time for speaking."

With regard to our verse, Rashi (Shlomo Yitzhaki, eleventh c., France)
teaches that because Aaron remains silent, refraining from questioning
God in the midst of his trauma, the Eternal rewards his passive restraint

by speaking to him directly (in verses 9–11). Up until now God has always spoken to Aaron through Moses.[1]

Nachmanides (Moses ben Nachman, thirteenth c., Spain and Acre, the Holy Land) suggests, to the contrary, that Aaron did respond, but not through speech. He first wept profusely and only then remained silent.[2] It seems that to Nachmanides, any words Aaron could have spoken thereafter would have only diminished the emotional outpouring of his heart. Aaron's grief found greater expression within this space of silence. His silence did not equate to passivity, but rather to active intentionality.

Sforno (Obadiah ben Jacob Sforno, fifteenth–sixteenth c., Italy) teaches otherwise: that Aaron's silence signals he took comfort in knowing that his sons' deaths actually sanctified God.[3] Because Moses told Aaron in the name of the Eternal, "Through those near to Me I show Myself holy," Aaron is reassured by divine recognition that his sons had only meant to experience nearness to God. As a result, he accepts this heartfelt divine consolation by remaining silent.[4]

Different as these three commentaries may be, they each teach the value of remaining silent as a means to help us move through grieving a loved one. Beyond this, as we will see, cultivating the *middah* of remaining silent at times may have a powerful effect on our souls.

A Deeper Dive

The Hebrew verb *vayidom*, meaning "was silent" in "and Aaron was silent," and the Hebrew noun *domaim* share the same root, *dalet-mem-mem*. Like *vayidom*, *domaim* conveys being quiet, but additionally refers to the inanimate realm of physical existence: minerals, soil, water, metals, and stones, all of which share a defining characteristic of being silent in their natural state.

For human beings, by contrast, being quiet is not usually our natural state. We connect with other people through speech. In fact the Hebrew word for communication, *tikshoret*, literally means "connection." Even so, we know that speech can also distance us from other people. After receiving unsolicited advice, hearing someone's antithetical views, or feeling verbally attacked, for example, adding our voice to the conversation might result in the very opposite of a nurtured connection.

As a parent of adult children who have their own ideas and ways and a resident of a community that runs the gamut of political, economic, and religious perspectives, there are times when, in discussion, remaining silent really does seem to be the wisest response. The alternative of responding instinctively often leads to distancing and regret.

Even at times when we feel warm connections with the people around us, remaining silent may enhance the qualitative experience of our moments together. Specifically, because we do sense closeness, verbal expressions may diminish rather than enhance. Simply being present, without speaking, in this tranquil moment with its calming energy may express everyone's feelings best.

For many of us, silence may be difficult or even counterintuitive. When I am challenged to choose silence, I draw inspiration from a multitude of teachings. A Mishnaic teaching in *Avot* emphasizes the value of remaining quiet: "Shimeon used to say, 'All my life I grew up among the sages, and I have found nothing better for a person than silence.'"[5] This proclamation aligns with the verse in Proverbs 18:28: "Even fools who keep silent are deemed wise."

Developing this value, the Maggid of Nadvorna (Rabbi Tzvi Hirsch Ressler, eighteenth–nineteenth c., Ukraine) teaches that cultivating verbal silence can also satisfy our spiritual hunger to experience hearing the Divine Voice. Jewish traditions view this hunger for direct guidance from the Divine, possibly best expressed in the prophecy of Amos ("A time is coming—declares the Sovereign GOD—when I will send a famine upon the land: not a hunger for bread or a thirst for water, but for hearing the words of GOD"—Amos 8:11), as innate to the human condition. The Maggid counsels:

It is written, "It is good to wait patiently [and quietly] till rescue comes from God" (Lam. 3:26). There are four realms of creation: the *domaim* (inanimate), the vegetative, the animal, and the speaker (human). However, at certain times, a person needs to adopt the posture of the *domaim*, as the Talmud teaches, "May my soul be as dust."[6] Rashi comments that [Aaron] received a reward for his silence: the Eternal spoke with him privately. The key lesson lies in Aaron's action: by lowering himself from the realm of the speaker to that of the silent inanimate, his action caused the usual silence of the Divine presence to now be raised to that of the Speaker. We now can better understand the verse, "It is good to wait patiently [and quietly] till rescue comes from God." By the human being remaining silent vis-à-vis transforming oneself to *domaim* when troubled or questioning God, this elicits the merit of the Eternal's salvation. What may that be? The hitherto silent and hidden Divine now speaks to the person directly.[7]

The Maggid is suggesting that when we monopolize conversations with our chatter, or when two (or more) of us are talking over each other, we leave little room to hear the Divine's "soft murmuring sound" (1 Kings 19:12). To truly listen, we need to humble ourselves and create space within our inner being. Once I as the speaker "lower" myself to that of the silent *domaim*, the silent Divine Voice now "rises" to that of the Speaker. And as we dance back and forth, my silence redeems the Divine's "soft murmuring sound" from concealment to revelation. "The hitherto silent and hidden Divine" may "now speak" to me "directly."

Aaron models for us the importance of remaining silent before the Creator when his instinct may have inclined him otherwise. This requires diligence, inner fortitude, and a recognition of the good silence may bring to our relationships — and to the world.

Even more, Aaron can be said to teach us that one of the best ways to be in alignment with the divine energy within us is to humble and "lower" ourselves to the realm of *domaim*. When we undergo a self-transformative practice to become a more intentional and mindful listener, we too may experience the reward of hearing the Divine Voice speaking to us alone.

Remaining quiet at intentional times can be a potent resource to nurture healthy relationships — and may even open the door of sensing the Divine Presence enveloping our human connections.

The Practice

1. Begin with breath awareness.

2. Then, reflect on the text.
3. Move to quieting down your mind.

These three steps are explained in detail in the introduction.

4. Visualize the following scenario: You are at a dinner table, at home with your family, at a restaurant with friends, or at a celebratory meal with your community. Almost everyone besides you seems to be speaking at the same time, and the cross conversation continues to increase in volume and intensity. What comes up for you? Hold this for a moment. Let your feelings move through you. Allow them to be as they are.

What do you do in this instance?

Now refocus your awareness to your breathing cycles. Imagine through each inhalation that the Creator is giving you the potential for handling this situation as your best self would. As you exhale, visualize what that is.

Now imagine a conversation you are having with another person, perhaps in your home, in nature, or at a café. Direct your awareness to your breath cycles. Inhale fresh and cleansing breaths of the possibility of deeply connecting with this person. Exhale the imagery that this comes to be. Each of you is compassionately, mindfully, and silently listening to the other. Each of you pays attention to each other's words as well as your own.

How does it feel to remain quiet while the other person speaks?

In between this gentle back and forth, do you sense each pause somehow creating a shared silence?

Tazria' / Metsora'

Spiritual Self-Care

> On the seventh day the Priest shall again conduct an examination: if
> the affection has faded and has not spread on the skin, the Priest shall
> pronounce the person pure.
>
> Lev. 13:6

Where We Are

After detailing the dietary laws, the text introduces how to proceed
if a person incurs *tzara'at*, a skin ailment with symptoms resembling
modern-day psoriasis.

At First Glance

Rashi (Shlomo Yitzhaki, eleventh c., France) explains that the word
kei'hah (faded) in the verse means "it appears dimmer than its former
color," and continues: "If however it retains its color or if it has spread,
the priest declares that the individual has *tzara'at*."[1] Chizkuni (Hezekiah ben Manoah, thirteenth c., France) adds: "The examining priest,
upon deciding that the person does not have *tzara'at*, must declare his
decision out loud."[2]

We may suspect the gravity of this ailment by the seemingly overpar-
ticular examination of the color of the infected skin. Still, the ritual of the
examining Priest proclaiming "a clean bill of health" aloud seems to add
to the mystery. Might there be deeper significance inherent in *tzara'at*?

A Deeper Dive

Maimonides (Moses ben Maimon, twelfth–thirteenth c., Spain and
Egypt) suggests: "This is not a natural phenomenon, but was deemed
a sign and a wonder among the people of Israel to warn them against

evil gossip."[3] If Maimonides is correct that speaking gossip or slander about another person causes *tzara'at*, then indecent speech would be the real issue meant to draw our attention.

The Talmud testifies to the gravity of this sin: "One who utters malicious speech with his mouth is a more severe sinner than one who performs a [sinful] action."[4] The biblical account of Miriam's sudden affliction with *tzara'at* after she slanders her brother Moses (Num. 12:1–10) illustrates this explicitly.

Yet, we might question: if the text means to caution us against slander, why doesn't it convey this in more straightforward language? And actually, the Torah does prohibit this directly some six verses later. Leviticus 19:16 reads: "Do not deal basely [via slander] with members of your people." Perhaps, then, there are other, less apparent understandings to be gleaned from our verse.

Let us prepare for a circuitous journey.

Interpreting our verse, Yissakhar Dov Ber of Zloczow (eighteenth c., Ukraine and Safed) begins by relying on the talmudic precept that during the Sabbath, we possess an "extra soul" — a "Shabbat soul" of sorts. "As in the Talmud, Rabbi Shimon ben Lakish said: 'The Blessed Holy One gives a person an additional soul on Shabbat eve, and at the conclusion of Shabbat removes it from him.'"[5] We might understand this "extra soul" as "extra spiritual energy" giving us a keener sense of time on Shabbat. Rabbi Yissakhar further teaches, "This soul that is given to a person on Shabbat is actually called 'Shabbat.'"[6]

He then reinterprets the traditional phrase *shomer* (observe) *Shabbat*, which typically refers to people who observe the ritual laws (*halakhot*) of the Sabbath primarily by abstaining from creative work. Since the word *shomer* also means "to protect, guard" and the word *halakhot* also means "the ways of walking," he teaches:

A person needs to protect or guard their Shabbat soul according to how it "walks" in the upper worlds, longing only to cleave to God. In this way a person needs to conduct themselves on Shabbat and not bring upon themselves any worldly concerns that deviate from this "upper world" awareness of the Divine. Hence this is the spiritual meaning of the phrase "observing Shabbat according to its laws" — protecting this Shabbat soul as it walks [moves about] in the upper worlds.[7]

He is saying the spiritual practice of observing the laws of Shabbat entails safeguarding a Shabbat-like consciousness — an awareness on Shabbat that mirrors in the lower physical world the way this soul always exists within the upper spiritual realm: in an ideal state of oneness with the Creator. This extra Sabbath soul facilitates experiencing increased closeness with the Divine on Shabbat. And this is why on Shabbat we may experience a keener sense of the sacred component in time: because we can experience time through the lens of this other soul.

Rabbi Yissakhar's understanding of how we keep the Sabbath spiritually — an emphasis on our internal experience of Shabbat over and above our external acts — can speak both to Jews who punctiliously observe the rabbinically defined laws and those who honor Shabbat in singularly creative ways. He encourages us to view how we live (i.e., "walk") during Shabbat as a means to protect our own sensitivity to the more ethereal aspects of our lives.

Here, he applies these insights to our verse:

"The Priest shall see" refers to God, the holy blessed One, the Supernal Priest. "[H]im on the seventh day again — *sheinit*" means that the Supernal Priest sees us on Shabbat changed [*sheinit* means both "again" and "changed"]. The Creator sees us behaving differently on Shabbat than during the weekday where we now follow the ways of our extra soul that is called Shabbat. "If his sore has dimmed — *kei'hah* — and has not spread in the skin of his flesh," means that on the Shabbat we do not continue [as during the weekdays] to bring upon ourselves any worldly concerns that distract us [from this "upper world" sensitivity to the Divine]. The distractions actually recede rather than "spread." "[T]he Priest shall declare him pure" means that we are forgiven for our sins.[8]

We might now weave together all three themes: the skin ailment, the prohibition of slander, and the protection of Shabbat soul consciousness.

As we've seen, the *Kohen* (Priest) is required to perform several repetitive examinations, confirming whether the color of the infected area is deepening or fading and also if it is spreading. Hence the *Kohen* can give an accurate diagnosis—physical *and*, I would add, moral, as these inspections will also reveal whether the afflicted person has continued or ceased to slander.

Delving deeper, the degree that the ailment advances or recedes may reflect the integrity of the person's relationship with God. Perhaps the more we protect our Shabbat soul, the higher the consciousness of closeness with the Divine Presence within us (both on the Sabbath day and, on the other six, in form of its spiritual message), the less likely we may be to perpetrate the serious transgression of slandering a fellow human being.

And if the examining *Kohen* does declare a person (or several people) as having contracted *tzara'at*, we may understand the Torah's mandate that these individuals now self-isolate for one week to convey spiritual significance as well. On a core level, enforced solitude seems an effective way of containing the personal and communal harm caused by slander. Afflicted individuals are at least temporarily unable to continue to slander. Meanwhile, a period of isolation would afford them time to contemplate their hurtful actions, repent, and prepare to make amends.

It may also be that the Torah's mandated seven-day seclusion period is meant to guarantee that each individual afflicted with *tzara'at* will be in solitude over a Shabbat. Since the person's connection to God is considered compromised by uttering slander, and given Rabbi Yissakhar's teaching that God as "the Supernal Priest sees us on Shabbat changed," the implied instruction to spend a Shabbat in solitude may be intended to help restore the person's Shabbat soul consciousness, which in turn might strengthen the person's resolve not to sin when returning to the community. In essence, if used properly, mandated self-isolation may be a potent spiritual healing remedy.

All the while, beyond the context of *tzara'at*, Rabbi Yissakhar's teaching that God as "the Supernal Priest sees us on Shabbat changed" seems deeply meaningful. Contemporary rabbi Art Green comments: "A Jew who observes Shabbat in a truly spiritual way looks different on Shabbat than on weekdays. The 'extra soul' of Shabbat is visible as a glowing presence. Here we are told that God too, in the role of cosmic Priest, sees the difference."[9]

Thus God's role as the cosmic Priest can be seen to parallel the role of the human Priest conducting repetitive examinations. Both the cosmic and human Priests are in service to the spiritual well-being of others. Human appearance is a partial indicator of our spiritual health—what I believe God, as the cosmic Priest, is examining in each of us, especially on Shabbat, as an essential component of divine spiritual care.

In my life, I have come to anticipate the arrival of Shabbat long before the sun sets on Friday. On Thursday evening, my body already begins to anticipate the sense of relaxation and serenity that awaits me in under twenty-four hours. The extra illumination of Divine Presence brings with it an inner calmness, a letting go and renewed spirit seldom even imaginable during the busy work week with all its tumult.

As mind, body, heart, and soul holistically unite with each other, I become aware of a visceral encounter with my personal Shabbat soul. When lighting the Shabbat candles shortly before sunset on Friday, I sense an energetic shift in my consciousness. Throughout the Sabbath I am not as distracted by this-worldly concerns—current events, work obligations, and so on. By mindfully protecting my Shabbat soul consciousness through both external actions and internal spiritual practice, I remain immersed in sensing the Divine Presence. I treasure time with my children and grandchildren, togetherness we as a family do not have during the week. I can sense the Shabbat soul consciousness in my family (and among friends when I host Shabbat meditation gatherings as well). Actually, spending time with my grandchildren is my nearly guaranteed way to sense increased awareness of the Divine—a splendid way of protecting my Shabbat soul. Altogether, the energy of connection with the Divine Presence within each one of us becomes remarkably palpable.

By cultivating the practice of *shomer Shabbat*, we can protect this invaluable part of ourselves. Shabbat soul consciousness affords us a weekly spiritual vacation, as if we are on our own internal sacred island of time within an external sea of turbulence. It is a marvel how one-seventh of the week at a spiritual spa for our spiritual health disproportionately and profoundly affects the remaining six days—a true modern-day wonder of a way to cultivate spiritual self-care.

The Practice

1. Begin with breath awareness.
2. Then, reflect on the text.
3. Move to quieting down your mind.

These three steps are explained in detail in the introduction.

4. Visualize moments during your week when you felt overwhelmed, stressed, uncentered, spent. What does this feel like: in your mind, in your body, in your soul?

Now imagine adding a new, time-centered dimension to your life for spiritual self-care.

Pause for a moment and direct your awareness to your breath. As you deeply inhale your breath's life-giving energies, visualize yourself receiving the gift of this new time-centered dimension. As you fully exhale, imagine you are using this gift for spiritual self-care.

You choose how to honor this sacred time. Explore within yourself what will bring you a sense of calmness, joy, relaxation, renewal. Do you walk in nature—along the sea, up a mountain trail, on a path deep in the woods? Do you sit in a comfy chair with your favorite beverage, reading that book you've been waiting to get to? Do you connect with people you love or welcome the chance to be alone? Are there other ways of being that might help you honor your spiritual side?

Explore your own understanding of spiritual self-care.

'Aḥarei Mot / Kedoshim

Letting Go of the Me to Be with the We

> When he goes in to make expiation in the Shrine, nobody else shall be in
> the Tent of Meeting until he comes out.

Lev. 16:17

Where We Are

Having detailed the many examinations a Priest must conduct before
declaring that a person is contaminated with *tzara'at* (a skin ailment
with symptoms resembling modern-day psoriasis) and, from there, the
rituals the afflicted person must undergo in order to return to health,
the text explains the prohibition against intimate relations during a
wife's menstrual cycle.

The Torah now introduces Aaron's unique service as the High Priest
for Yom Kippur. His mindful attention to every detail invokes forgiveness from the Eternal for all Israel's transgressions.

At First Glance

Our verse prohibits any person from entering the Tent of Meeting (the
inner courtyard) when the High Priest enters the sacred "shrine" (or
Holy of Holies, the innermost sanctum of the *mishkan*). This annual
encounter between the Eternal and the High Priest on Yom Kippur is
to remain intimate and private—one person, in one place, at only one
time, with the One.

Chizkuni (Hezekiah ben Manoah, thirteenth c., France) explains the
injunction, "Nobody else shall be in the Tent of Meeting," as meaning,
"Not just any human being, as non-priests are never allowed into those
areas, but this is a warning to other priests not to be in this designated
space during the period that the High Priest performs these functions."[1]

While this may be obvious to some—since non-Priests are always forbidden from entering this inner courtyard—Chizkuni's interpretation posits that the real concern behind the prohibition is to ensure that the other Priests, who would customarily go into the inner courtyard, do not enter at this time. But why state this in such an ostensibly convoluted way? Why wouldn't the text simply state, "No other Priests shall be in the Tent of Meeting"?

The Bekhor Shor (Joseph ben Isaac Bekhor Shor, twelfth c., France) alternatively holds that the verse prohibits exactly what it states. The textual wording of "nobody else" means "all people" in order "to emphasize the exceptional solemnness of this time and place."[2] This is the Torah's way of accentuating the intense holiness of this moment. The High Priest's unique service and responsibilities require such exceptional spiritual sensitivity that only the High Priest is qualified to be present in this sacred space at this solemn moment.

However, logically the Bekhor Shor's answer to one question now raises even more questions. If the verse prohibits "all people" from entering the Tent of Meeting, wouldn't this exclude the High Priest too? In the beginning of our verse, "when he goes into" refers to the High Priest entering the sacred Shrine. However, he must first pass through the Tent of Meeting, which "all people" are prohibited from doing. How could it be possible that the High Priest is not included in "all people?" And yet how *could* he be included with "all people"? All these questions would not arise had the verse explicitly stated that only the High Priest can enter both the Tent of Meeting and the sacred shrine. Might the ambiguities be inviting us to seek another way of understanding?

A Deeper Dive

Returning to our quandary: How does the Torah expect the High Priest to engage in the expected Yom Kippur rituals in the holy shrine when, as a "person," he appears to be prohibited to pass through the Tent of Meeting—which he must pass through enroute to the holy shrine?

The Hasidic masters attempt to resolve this quandary through quite a radical and creative approach. Somehow, as strange as many of us may find this interpretation, the High Priest spiritually sheds his shared state of "being a person" before entering the Tent of Meeting. This enables him to pass through the area prohibited to "all people," ensuring him safe passage into the sacred shrine without transgression. How may we understand this unorthodox idea?

The Mei Ha'Shiloach (Moredechai Yosef Leiner of Ishbitz, nineteenth c., Poland) teaches: "During the Yom Kippur service with its influx of sacred energies that flow into the world from the Blessed's realm above, there is no place for a person's limited consciousness of sense of self."[3] He adds: "When entering the sacred Shrine on Yom Kippur, the High Priest must nullify any independent sense of self before the Divine."[4] Before the High Priest can even begin to approach the Tent of Meeting, he has to leave behind his identity as a separate self. The shedding of ego as a spiritual practice becomes the focal point of the High Priest's preparation for this solemn moment of entering the sacred shrine — which Jewish tradition believes to be the closest a human being can come to experiencing the Divine and still remaining alive in a physical body. Only by letting go of the "me" can the High Priest then lean into the deepest experience of union between a human being and the Divine, a transcendental state of one with the One understood as "We."

This shedding of the "me" to become the "we" remains mysterious, in part because the Mei HaShiloach never explains how the High Priest would have prepared himself spiritually to realize what sounds like an otherworldly state. And yet we still may glean from this spiritual practice of shedding ego a way for us too to experience deep union with the Divine.

The Piaseczner Rebbe (Kalonymus Kalmish Shapira, twentieth c., Poland) offers guidance:

> It is taught from the Ba'al Shem Tov [Israel ben Eliezer, eighteenth c., Ukraine] concerning the verse, "And I stand between GOD and you." (Deut. 5:5) that the sense of I-ness that a person feels within themselves — whereby a person is concerned with and pursues only their own needs — is what obstructs and precludes a direct encounter between "GOD and you."
>
> A person is able to minimize the sense of "I-ness" through loving one's fellow, and not by being a separate self, remaining aloof. When

I stand by myself, then the barrier exists "between GOD and you." Rather, the essence of the person and their soul, which transcends separateness, can be healed and they will no longer be an entity by themselves—their desires, concerns and joys are shared with others.

They also desire that all will be good for their friends as for themselves, and if their friend needs a favor, they will promptly do it. All this brings a person to feel that their life has a purpose that transcends their own self. Rather they become aware of being a part of the other. This enables one to uproot the "I-ness" from their heart, and together we will be able to become close to the one Creator.[5]

Many of us equate the practice of diminishing our ego with thinking less of ourselves, but we might reconsider it to mean thinking about ourselves less. If we are less "I" focused, we may be more focused on other people's needs. The delightful irony is that the less each of us concentrates on ourselves, the more likely we may feel part of a much larger world. This expanded world, encompassing all kinds of people and all other creations, may then enhance our own personal encounter with the Divine.

In essence, the Piaseczner Rebbe is saying, the spiritual practice of diminishing one's ego and then redirecting ego energy to help others can lead to our connecting with lovingkindness. This soul exchange then advances both "uproot[ing] the 'I-ness' from the . . . heart" and sensing connection with the Divine.

Cultivating the *middah* of "letting go of the me to be with the we" and investing our soul in fulfilling the human need for connection, we may nurture God consciousness in ourselves and the world around us.

The Practice

1. Begin with breath awareness.
2. Then, reflect on the text.
3. Move to quieting down your mind.

These three steps are explained in detail in the introduction.

4. Visualize a moment in your life when you felt almost consumed or governed by your own needs and wants. Without judging this, explore the experience and consequences. What does this look like to you? Does it affect how you see people, and how you imagine you might be seen? What feelings does it manifest?

Pause for a moment and direct your awareness to your breathing cycles. As you inhale, imagine you are breathing in the potential to cultivate connection with someone. Your focal point is no longer "you" but this other person. As you exhale, imagine what this new way of connecting would be like.

How are you engaging differently with this person?

Again, pause and direct your awareness to three full breathing cycles. Imagine yourself inhaling the potential to be more and more in the "we" space and less and less in the "me" space. As you exhale, sense what your connection with this other person feels like, and gently lean into these feelings.

Imagine the two of you each exclaiming, "I never realized before how much we have in common!"

What does this encounter feel like right now?

Is your prior focus on personal needs present in the same way?

Do you sense the previous clear line between "me" and "you" blurring a little into "we?"

'Emor

Loving Peace and Pursuing Peace

GOD said to Moses: Speak to the priests, the sons of Aaron, and say to
them: None shall defile himself for any [dead] person among his kin.

Lev. 21:1

Where We Are

We continue to learn about the intricately designed Yom Kippur service.
Historically, the first Yom Kippur occurred when Moses descended
from Mount Sinai with the second set of tablets inscribed with the
Ten Utterances, or Ten Commandments (he had shattered the first set
during the Golden Calf debacle). Yom Kippur literally means the "day
of atonement"—total forgiveness after having indulged in idolatry—
and annually invites us to repent for our mistakes and turn toward our
Creator.

The Torah then defines forbidden sexual relationships. Afterwards,
the Torah repeats several times the importance of being holy and sanctifying oneself in relationship with the Eternal. We then learn about
several laws governing our behavior in society: providing food for the
poor, being honest with others, loving one's fellow, and using proper
weights and measures in business.

This now brings us to the verse under discussion. The Torah prohibits Priests from touching a human corpse, as this would render them
spiritually unfit to continue their priestly duties until they undergo a
purification process.

At First Glance

Rashi (Shlomo Yitzhaki, eleventh c., France) addresses the apparent
redundancy in this verse, "Speak to the Priests . . . and say to them." What

does "say to them" add that "speak to the Priests" does not convey? He relies on a talmudic interpretation that teaches, "The first clause clearly addresses the Priests themselves, while the second clause is intended to exhort the Priests to also teach their children—'them'—to avoid defilement."[1]

This underscores the significant role of the status of spiritual purity in the priesthood—so much so that even now adult Priests must convey this teaching to their minor children who are born into the priestly class but are not yet responsible for priestly duties.

A different apparent redundancy intrigues the Alshich (Moshe Alshich, sixteenth c., Turkey and Safed, the Holy Land) who asks why the verse states "the sons of Aaron" after "say to the Priests," since everyone already knows the Priests are the sons of Aaron.[2] Yet he leaves this question unanswered, possibly in keeping with the talmudic sages' recognition that we don't have an answer for every question. Or perhaps the Alshich is encouraging us to provide our own answer.

One way of responding to the Alshich's unanswered question may be to interpret the meaning of "Priest" more expansively, in a way that includes, but is not limited to, the sons of Aaron. In Hebrew the word for Priest, *Kohen*, literally means a person who is in service. And at Mount Sinai, God refers to the whole nation as "a kingdom of Priests" (Exod. 19:6).If this is the case, what priestly service might be entailed for the general population?

The talmudic sage Hillel counsels: "Be among the students of Aaron [the first Priest]—love peace and pursue peace, love all people and bring them near to the Torah."[3]

Sforno (Obadiah ben Jacob Sforno, fifteenth–sixteenth c., Italy) suggests that being "a kingdom of Priests" articulates the divine mandate for the Israelite nation to instruct all humankind about the existence and awareness of the Creator, and to be in relationship with the Creator.[4]

In this vein, we might now understand the phrase "speak to the Priests" to include the entire Israelite nation, and "the sons of Aaron" to mean the formal Priests, those from the direct lineage of Aaron, the first *Kohen*. Both the formal Priests and the "kingdom of Priests" are to convey the same spiritual message, but in different ways: the formal Priests through specified rituals and rules and the kingdom of Priests likely by cultivating a unique consciousness.

If we view ourselves as Priests, as people in service to humanity, and find meaning in both Hillel and Sforno's interpretations, we might see the two understandings as part of a larger whole. We might cultivate the *middah* of "loving peace and pursuing peace" by "loving all people" and by "bringing them close to the Torah."

What is the connection between these two ideas?

A Deeper Dive

To begin to understand how the Israelite nation is to love and pursue peace through loving and bringing humanity closer to the Torah, we might reinterpret the word "Torah" in a spiritual sense. Rather than specific religious teachings or practices, "Torah" may imply a more nuanced consciousness — specifically, a manifestation of the Torah of awareness of the Divine. The mystics teach, "The Torah and the Blessed Holy One are one and the same."[5] From this spiritual understanding, "bringing people closer to Torah" would involve bringing people — including you and me — closer to the Divine by inspiring us to love and connect with our spiritual selves.

In this vein, the *Me'or Eynayim* (Menachem Nachum Twersky, eighteenth c., Ukraine) writes: "Every Israelite who actively committed themselves to being in service to God is actually referred to as a priest."[6] Then he asks: "What does it mean to love peace and pursue peace? This means that when a person holds on to the Blessed One's Torah and Service, they bring peace to both the heavenly realms and the earthly realms. And how is this done? Hillel answers by loving all people and bringing them near to the Torah."[7] Not to be confused with proselytizing, which Judaism rejects, the Me'or Eynayim is saying that Jews are meant to inspire humanity to become aware of the Infinite Creator — of all human beings.

This awareness may develop into the realization that the Creator's lifegiving energy permeates every crevice of creation. This makes it possible for the entirety of humanity to connect with each other and with all of creation. Service to humanity, then, can facilitate the harmonization of the world. So interpreted, the sacred wisdom of the Torah — often misunderstood to be exclusive and available to only select people—expands into a universal guide for establishing a healed and unified world.

Yet not every Jew is quick to accept this divine mandate. The Me'or Eynayim holds that these individuals "lack awareness of the Blessed One, due to their consciousness being limited. Everyone perceives worldly matters but that awareness is restricted to the physical realm—a lower and smaller awareness. From this less developed consciousness one can expand and raise their awareness to include that of the blessed Creator's existence, a more mature consciousness."[8]

The mystics refer to a limited or child consciousness as *katnut* (smallness), and an expanded or unlimited or adult consciousness that includes awareness of the Divine Presence as *gadlut* (largeness). The Me'or Eynayim speaks strongly about cultivating *gadlut*:

> The adult [in each of us] possesses a "larger and higher" *gadlut* perception of the Eternal. However, the child consciousness [in each of us] perceives the world through *katnut*—a "smaller and lower" awareness, limited to earthly matters. The adult consciousness in us, affording us the awareness of the Divine and spirituality, needs to be cautious of the child in us. If not, even at seventy years old, a person may be considered a [spiritual] child. Therefore, raise yourself above your smallness, inherent within earthly matters alone, until you cultivate an adult awareness and connect with the higher consciousness of being in relationship with the Divine.[9]

Some of us may understandably take issue with the Me'or Eynayim's labeling of people as either adult or child depending on whether they have a developed God concept that guides how they live. To my mind, the most salient question emerging from this teaching is really: Is it true that nurturing a divine consciousness can help us grow in the endeavor to "love peace and pursue it"?

Reflecting on this question from the backdrop of my own life journey, I would say yes, this is true for me, and it may be for others as well. As for myself, I came into traditional Judaism as an adult, and everything I needed to learn was new and foreign. The rudimentary skill set required to engage with the traditional text in both Hebrew and Aramaic—learning how to read in two new languages—brought me back to elementary school. Learning how to participate in communal prayer in synagogue, which also required Hebrew literacy, had the same effect on me. Confronted by a plethora of mitzvot that I was expected to observe almost immediately exacerbated what was already quite a formidable challenge for the adult me as I tried to enter the Jewish religious world. I really did feel like a spiritual child.

What towers over all of this, though, is how my growing God consciousness profoundly and positively affected my capacity to "love peace and pursue it." I credit my adult consciousness with enabling me to lovingly and compassionately connect with people who are very different than I am. My own cultivation of an awareness of the Divine allows me to see the divine spark in others so much more naturally, without the intense challenges I experienced earlier in adulthood, when (by my assessment today) I was spiritually a child. It took me years to understand and internalize this—and I'm still working at it! We generally are not taught, and hence lack both the skill set and experience, to mature our spiritual sensitivities, to develop our awareness of our Creator, and hence be able to more effectively "love peace and pursue it."

But with the aspiration to do so, we might now creatively read the mandate of our verse—cultivating the *middah* of Priest within each of us—in an alternative way. To be in service to both our Creator and to our fellow human beings, the higher consciousness in us might best keep guiding the lower consciousness in us on how to nurture awareness and relationship with the Divine. Then, we just might become ennobled and responsible for honoring the different pieces of who we are—Priest, Israelite, and human being.

The Practice

1. Begin with breath awareness.
2. Then, reflect on the text.
3. Move to quieting down your mind.

These three steps are explained in detail in the introduction.

4. Visualize yourself as a Priest, in the more general sense of being in service to others. What ideas does this conjure up? What is being asked of you? How might you move through this day with "Priest consciousness"?

Pause for three intentional breath cycles. Inhaling, direct your awareness to receiving life and its potential to be in service to others. Returning the breath, imagine actualizing your possibilities.

Now, picture yourself discovering a way to be in service to all of humanity, "loving peace and pursuing peace." What does this teaching mean to you?

How would you approach loving peace and then pursuing it?

To love peace, whom do you love and how do you love?

To pursue peace, whom do you pursue and how do you pursue?

Can you see yourself doing this work of service beyond the borders of this practice?

Be-har / Be-ḥukkotai

Taking a Leap of Faith

> If you walk in My statutes and observe My commandments, to do them,
> I will grant your rains in their season, so that the earth shall yield its
> produce and the trees of the field their fruit.
>
> Lev. 26:3–4[1]

Where We Are

We receive laws to safeguard the Priests' and sacrificial offerings' spiritual purity, a strong reminder never to desecrate God's name, an enumeration of the annual holidays, and a directive to ensure the sacred menorah burns continuously.

Three additional mitzvot are to take effect when the Israelites enter the Land of Israel. *Shemitah*, meaning release, prohibits farming the land every seventh year. On *yovel*, the jubilee year, all Hebrews are to be freed from indentured servitude and released from their debts. *Reebeet*, interest, disallows charging interest when extending a loan. The text then highlights proper real estate transaction practices and the necessity of preventing poverty by providing aid to those who suffer financially.

We now arrive at our conditional verse: "If you walk in My statues and observe My commandments, to do them; [then]. . . ." The promised rewards include abundant material blessings, peace, security, and continuous awareness of the Divine's protection and presence among the Israelite nation.

At First Glance

From our verse the tradition derives the *middah* of taking a leap of faith.

To understand how this follows and what taking a leap of faith entails, we first need to understand the context in which this verse occurs. The

Torah includes 613 mitzvot (divinely ordained commandments). The tradition divides them into two categories: *mishpatim* (rules whose rationale the human mind can grasp, such as those governing societal behavior) and *chukim* (statutes whose reasons are not readily grasped, such as certain ritual laws).

In our verse, the first phrase, "if you walk in My statutes [*chukim*]," might then be understood as referring to divine, suprarational decrees that cannot be understood by the human mind. Meanwhile, the next clause, "and observe My commandments [mitzvot]" might be referencing all 613 commandments—both those laws that can be easily understood and those that cannot. If so, however, why then would the text need to first single out the statutes? And do each of the three verbs, "walk," "observe," and "do" (the text continues, "to do them") suggest three different actions?

Addressing only the second question, Rashi (Shlomo Yitzhaki, eleventh c., France) holds that each clause does indeed teach about a different action, therefore necessitating its inclusion in the verse. He explains that "If you walk in My statutes" conveys a stern warning to intensely engage in Torah study; "observe My commandments" means that learning Torah rests on heeding the teachings one learns; and "to do them" signifies the actual performance of the mitzvot, after which one merits the blessings in the subsequent verses.[2]

By contrast, Sforno (Obadiah ben Jacob Sforno, fifteenth–sixteenth c., Italy) addresses both questions. His interpretation rests upon a person's ideal attitude when observing a mitzvah. First, he explains, statutes are similar to royal decrees: subjects of a king must obey those edicts if they desire prosperous lives, even if they don't understand the king's rationales. The injunction "walk in My statutes" means moving with the statutes as one ideally walks forward in life, not begrudgingly or sluggishly.

Next, he comments, "observe My commandments" indicates the ideal attitude one displays when fulfilling each of the commandments. This means approaching each mitzvah with respectful and mindful precision, rather than mechanically by rote—and, likewise, doing so regardless of one's understanding of the rationale.

Lastly, "to do them" instructs us to cultivate love as the foundational emotion in our observance. When we invest our actions with love (rather than fear of incurring the wrath of God), we demonstrate that we perform the Divine's will as if it were our own.[3]

Sforno is encouraging us to embrace faith, rather than understanding, as the impetus driving a mitzvot-infused life. Whereas the tradition does encourage us to discover the reasons for some of the commandments, we finite humans just cannot grasp the logic of every mitzvah. Instead, we will need to take a leap of faith that all of the commandments equally express the divine will for us.

We may consider that conditionalizing observance on our intellect's capacity to grasp the meaning of each mitzvah limits our opportunity to connect with God, whose will transcends human logic. A leap of faith, a mindset of deep trust, then becomes the cohesive element fortifying a person's spiritual life.

A Deeper Dive

The Maggid of Mezeritch (Dov Ber Friedman, eighteenth c., Poland) takes us on a journey to teach the importance of love in influencing a person's willingness, and desire, to take that leap of faith: "A person who observes a Torah law and knows its reason, fulfills it with passion and great desire. This may not be the case with someone who observes a statute whereby the Torah does not give a clear reason. Although the person does observe the latter it is because it is a Divine-ordained decree. Hence, their experience may lack enthusiasm." This explains "if you walk in My statutes": even though you do not know their reasons, you can always fulfill them with feeling close to the Divine and, hence, with passion. Even more so when to "observe My commandments" involves understanding their reasons.[4]

Psychologically, he is saying, if we understand the reasons inherent in a Torah commandment, we might observe it with greater enthusiasm than we would another commandment for which we lack a similar sense of understanding. From there, the Maggid uses a parable to differentiate between following a royal decree out of obligation and following it out of love:

When a king issues a command to his servants, they obey the command even though they may not know its reason. They are obligated in all cases to follow the royal decree. But this is not the case with the king's son. The prince also obeys his father's royal decrees, whether he grasps the rationale or not, but unlike the servant, he does everything from his great love for his father. Regarding the servants, even though of course they obey every command, their loyalty derives strictly from fear of punishment rather than from passion and loving the king.[5]

The Maggid's teaching can be understood as offering us a new approach to observance. Even when we humans do not understand the "why," we do possess free will to determine the "how." We can observe "royal decrees" out of obligation (as do the servants), or with love (the pathway of the prince). From a legal point of view, the choice has no bearing, since actual performance is what matters. Nonetheless, love may prompt us to embrace even those commandments we do not understand.

In other words, we may be able to integrate our spiritual "inner servant" with our spiritual "inner prince." Our "inner servant" directs us to yield to a Higher Will because our role in our relationship with God requires loyalty through observance of God's commandments. Fidelity to the divine relationship is the driving factor. Our "inner prince" also directs us to yield to the Higher Will, again because fulfilling royal commands as a faithful subject is our role in the relationship. However, we now follow the will of our spiritual Parent, which is quite dissimilar from obeying a king from a place of servitude. We can take—or ready ourselves to take—an additional leap of faith in order to fulfill all the commandments equally because we love each other, child and Parent alike.

This integrative construct can guide us out of a black-and-white binary and into the grey fluidity of many different emotions in religious practice. The fact that the verse uses the word "walking" suggests movement rather than stagnant, emotionally flat observance. The Maggid picks up on this when he writes: "This is the deeper teaching in the verse, 'If you walk in My statutes.' Even though they lack logical reasoning, you can still walk with passion and excitement [as the prince]. Then, concerning

'My commandments', whereby you do grasp their meaning, you 'observe.' This means that you will be precise to perform them according to their prescribed manner. This teaches us that respecting and honoring the Eternal's wishes [as the servant] need to be cultivated in addition to love."[6] The quest to harmonize these two opposing energies—prince observance and servant observance—may make our practice increasingly dynamic, and also sustainable.

Along my own journey into and out of ultra-Orthodoxy, I felt strong community pressure to assume the role of the loyal servant. My teachers emphasized the importance of unwavering blind faith as fundamental to observing the mitzvot, and I became obsessed with "doing it right," fearing divine punishment for any transgressions or being cast out by the community. Love, enthusiasm, and passion did not play key roles in my observance.

Finally, my yearning to sense closeness to the Divine compelled me to give myself permission to ask God the reasons for at least some of the mitzvot. Exercising my own being more (and relying on other people's interpretations less), I found myself in a lively dialogue with God. This exchange did not always provide clear answers—then and now—but something else wonderful happened: I sensed I was an active participant in my relationship with my Creator. And being in an alive intellectual and emotional relationship with God was what my heart was seeking all along.

I began to feel more love from and much closer to the Divine, and, from there, more at ease in not knowing the reasons for all my actions. Oddly enough, by honoring my inquisitive mind, I became increasingly able to embrace both a faith-driven and trust-driven life. I could emotionally trust in God, take that leap of faith, because I felt love from and for my Creator. I started to sense internal harmony: being the "king's servant" together with my new role as the "king's child."

The Practice

1. Begin with breath awareness.
2. Then, reflect on the text.
3. Move to quieting down your mind.

These three steps are explained in detail in the introduction.

4. Visualize a relationship you have with someone, perhaps at work or in community. It is pleasant and cordial but not that close. Imagine now receiving a request that you do not understand, and, even more, believe is unnecessary. Still, your commitment to the group compels you to accede. How do you feel about this?

Now, visualize the same scenario, except that someone you love is asking you to take this action, and your deep love for this person is compelling your response. Do you experience fulfilling the ask as taking a leap of faith? What feelings arise for you now?

4

Numbers (Be-midbar)

Be-midbar

Ascending the Ladder of a Sinai Consciousness

On the first day of the second month, in the second year after the exodus from the land of Egypt, GOD spoke to Moses in the wilderness of Sinai, in the Tent of Meeting.

Num. 1:1

Where We Are

As Leviticus ends, several admonitions warn the Israelites of the negative consequences of not walking in the Eternal's ways, and we learn the practice of tithing produce and animals as gifts to the Temple.

Numbers opens with God speaking to Moses *be-midbar*, "in the wilderness," of Sinai.

At First Glance

Upon close reading, our verse reveals new and even odd wording. In Exodus, the Torah refers to Sinai by its full name, "Mount Sinai." Here in Numbers, for the first time, the text refers to the surrounding desert area as "wilderness of Sinai." Why does the text change the name to "wilderness of Sinai" as the Israelites ready themselves to journey toward the Promised Land, and hence further away from Mount Sinai?

Rashbam (Samuel ben Meir, twelfth c., France) distinguishes between God's communication with Moses atop the actual mountain (Mount Sinai) and all subsequent encounters with Moses once the *mishkan* (Tabernacle) is erected and the Israelites prepare to travel ("in the wilderness of Sinai, in the Tent of Meeting").[1]

We may understand this to mean that until now, Moses' encounters with God have been limited to the top of a stationary mountain. But now that the Israelites are preparing to begin their journey, the Divine Voice will journey with them as well. Instead of on Mount Sinai, Moses will now encounter God in the Tent of Meeting within the *mishkan*, which the Israelites will disassemble and reassemble at each encampment.

In light of this, however, we might ask, what unique idea does "wilderness of Sinai" suggest that "Tent of Meeting" does not? Why doesn't the verse simply state, "GOD spoke to Moses in the Tent of Meeting"?

The midrash responds by proclaiming: "Anyone who does not make themselves ownerless like the wilderness [of Sinai] cannot acquire the wisdom of the Torah."[2] This interpretation invites us to appreciate the value of receiving Torah wisdom specifically "in the wilderness," an understanding the term "Tent of Meeting" does not imply. In essence, the midrash views "wilderness of Sinai" as the *way* (and not where) we learn Torah.

A Deeper Dive

This insight may encourage us to adopt the behavior of a curious explorer when we encounter Torah. To amplify our learning experience, we would ideally be "ownerless" of preconceived notions. We can gently put those aside to be receptive and open-minded—or actually "empty-minded." Just as the desert is bare, our minds are best bared as well. This modality of learning, and even of being, births the *middah* of ascending the ladder of a "Sinai consciousness" to a higher awareness of the Divine.

The mystics teach us that Sinai is the ladder we ascend to acquire wisdom and emotionally experience the divine Torah within us. One of the early Hasidic rebbes in particular, Yaakov Yosef of Ostrog (eighteenth c., Ukraine), expounds on this idea of Sinai as a ladder:

> The Zohar explains that the *gematria* [numerical value of each Hebrew letter] of *sulam*—[*samech-lamed-mem*] "ladder"—equals 130, the same as Sinai—[*samech-yud-nun-yud*].[3] Therefore when the Eternal descended from above to the Mount to give Israel the Torah, the place became known as Mount Sinai. For the Blessed One descends to earth from the highest realms upon the ladder. Similar to [in Jacob's dream] "a stairway [ladder] was set on the ground and its top reached to the sky" (Gen. 28:12). In this vein, we can now refer to Mount Sinai as the Mount of the Ladder.[4]

This act of the Eternal descending upon a ladder to bequeath the Torah as a sacred gift to us may also be teaching us what exactly it is we are learning when we "learn Torah." What occurred at the "mount of the ladder" pierced through the barrier that hitherto divided the spiritual realm (the heavens) from the physical realm (the earth). The ladder of Sinai ("a stairway set on the ground and its top reached to the sky") seamlessly unites these two realms forever. By descending upon the ladder, the Eternal can be understood to concretize nonphysical infinite wisdom—which is beyond human capacity to understand— into a physical sacred document within our cognitive capacity to grasp. We might then infer that by our now climbing up the ladder, we human beings can spiritualize the physical.

Yet, we might also ask, is the opportunity to climb the ladder truly possible for any one of us? In the story about the Giving of the Torah, only Moses ascends the ladder of higher consciousness to receive the Torah. Only he receives the opportunity to transcend his own limitations, and only then.

However, Rabbi Yaakov Yosef alludes to a transition from Moses' exclusive to our own inclusive opportunity:

> At times, this "ladder" is referred to as "wilderness of Sinai," for a person may merit the experience of holy attachment through their speech. For all the letters [in the Torah] derive above from the Blessed Speaker. And when a person speaks below on earth, the life force and energy within the letters ascends, similar to "a stairway set on the ground and its top reached to the sky." For the person's words ascend above before the Blessed Holy One, and therefore this is referred to as the "wilderness of Sinai"—the Sinai consciousness of ascending to higher awareness.[5]

Yaakov Yosef explains the transition of Torah accessibility from restricted access to all-inclusiveness by understanding that the text itself transforms. "Mount Sinai" (for Moses only) becomes "wilderness of Sinai" (for everyone). The "wilderness of Sinai" enables all people to ascend the mount of the ladder.

He accomplishes this by viewing "wilderness of Sinai" through a more nuanced and creative perspective. When vocalized differently, *mem-dalet-beit-reish*, the Hebrew letters that spell *midbar* (wilderness), also form *midaber* (speaking). Hence, the "mount of the ladder," limited to only Moses, transforms into the "wilderness and speech of the ladder," inviting all of us to ascend the ladder of Sinai consciousness through sacred speech.

Even if we tend to view this ladder as a vertical ascension tool, the actual experience may be more of an inward motion. Neo-Hasidic teacher Rabbi Arthur Green (twenty-first c., United States) opines: "We are seeking a more fully *internalized* version of that foot-of-the-mountain experience, one in which *Sinai is a vertical metaphor for an inner event*. The journey 'up the mountain' is in fact a journey to a 'higher' rung of consciousness. That 'higher,' in our contemporary parlance, needs to be rendered as a *deeper* truth than that of ordinary perception or reason. The 'heaven' that is its goal exists within the human soul."[6]

Rabbi Green's perspective has been my own personal experience. When I began my journey into seriously learning about and expressing my Judaism, I imagined that somehow the awareness of God I was seeking was "high up in the clouds." Naïve as I was, I imagined the spiritually sensitive person meditating on the top of a mountain, literally reaching into the heavens to find and encounter our Creator. Eventually, I began to see that I was seeking a paradigm shift of consciousness—not a physical higher space, but a new way of being in the world. The visceral experience of the Divine Presence I hungered for did not lie above me—it lay within me. How overjoyed I was to learn that the Hebrew word for Divine Presence, *Shekhinah*, means "dwelling." The transcendental aspect of the infinite Creator "high up in the clouds" was really dwelling deep within me. Thus I have come to see that we can experience the higher rung of internal consciousness right here on earth.

We can also extend this encounter to others in how we speak with them. With increased sensitivity, open-heartedness, and compassion, we have the potential to elevate everyday speech to a sacred realm wherein awareness of the Divine may be sensed in how we speak. This affords us another way of ascending the ladder of internal consciousness of the Divine.

In the end, though, the success of "ascending the ladder of a Sinai consciousness" may largely rest on cultivating the mindset of conceptual "ownerlessness." The spontaneity of the moment that this mindset allows contributes significantly to cultivating a higher consciousness, as it makes room for the Divine Presence to be encountered.

The Practice

1. Begin with breath awareness.
2. Then, reflect on the text.
3. Move to quieting down your mind.

These three steps are explained in detail in the introduction.

4. Visualize yourself at the bottom of a ladder reaching high up into the sky. You implicitly understand that all through the course of your life you have never experienced what awaits you at the top. Curiosity impels you to ascend and discover your unknown. You further intuit that in order to reach the top, you may not take along any preconceived notions of what to expect. You are being asked to rely on trusting the spontaneity of the moment.

How do you feel about experiencing this sense of being "ownerless"?

Begin to speak to yourself, either out loud or quietly within, as you set out on this new journey. Hear yourself describe what you sense, and what you are thinking and feeling all the while.

Imagine now that what you are really doing is gently burrowing deeper and deeper within yourself. As you inhale, direct your awareness to possessing the potential to explore your internal landscape. Perhaps even pause for a few breath cycles to experience the moment. Then, with each exhalation, take another step into the realm of your inner consciousness, a deep quarry filled with precious jewels of awareness.

Now, in your quarry, you hear a still, small voice teaching you your own Torah.

What does this sound like? What are you hearing?

What are you feeling now?

Naso'

Creating Soul-to-Soul Connections

> GOD spoke to Moses: Speak to Aaron and his sons: Thus shall you bless
> the people of Israel. Say to them....
>
> Num. 6:22–23

Where We Are

The Israelite nation prepares to depart from Mount Sinai toward the Promised Land, where it has encamped for a year since the Exodus from Egypt.
The Eternal commands Moses to take a census of the population, and then
instructs Moses about the four encampments around the central *mishkan*
(Tabernacle) that the twelve tribes of Israel will adopt along their travels.

The Torah addresses the "Nazarite vow" whereby individuals drawn
to ascetic lives vow to abstain from specific physical pleasures defined by
the Torah for at least thirty days. The "Priestly Blessing" section begins
with our verse under discussion. Earlier, in Exodus (9:22), Aaron, the first
Kohen (Priest), had blessed the people when the *mishkan* was completed.
Now, the words of that blessing are revealed.

At First Glance

The custom of blessing the people with this thirty-four-hundred-year-
old biblical invocation has become a more inclusive and heartwarming
tradition. At designated times, today's *Kohanim*, those who trace their
lineage to the ancient priestly class during the Holy Temple period, bless
the congregation as part of the synagogue prayer service. Before beginning the Friday evening Shabbat meal, many parents place their hands
on their children's heads and bless them with this same Priestly Blessing,
adopting the practice of the *Kohanim*, who spread their hands over the
congregation when they bless.

More recently the tradition encourages everyone to bless anyone, with words of their choosing, for any reason at all. For example, sometimes at weddings the bride and groom bless their family members and friends. Many Jews bless family and friends on their birthdays. Blessing each other is a way to cultivate the *middah* of creating soul-to-soul connections.

Our traditional commentaries open the door for us to better understand this practice. In our verse, the Hebrew word that means "say" in "Thus shall you bless the people of Israel. Say to them . . ." contains one extra letter: the *vav*. Could the Torah contain a typo? Might this have been some sort of editorial oversight? While over the past few centuries biblical critics have come to accept such possibilities, for the most part Jewish tradition responds with a resounding "absolutely not." Since the Torah is a divinely authored—or inspired—body of sacred wisdom, Jewish theology would equate the notion of an error with heresy. However, the commentators do address apparent textual oddities or inconsistencies. In this case, Rashi (Shlomo Yitzhaki, eleventh c., France) believes the extra letter cautions the priest "not to bless the people hurriedly with haste; rather taking the extra time [as symbolized by the extra letter] to bless them mindfully and wholeheartedly."[1]

Emphasizing that the blessing is a sacred and connecting moment, the Malbim (Meir Leibush ben Yehiel Michel Wisser, nineteenth c., Ukraine) points out that God directs Aaron and his sons to bless the Israelites by using the verb "say" rather than "speak" (while God is said to speak to Moses and directs Moses to speak to Aaron, Aaron is directed to "say"). Unlike "speaking," he explains: "'Saying' happens when the person articulating the words is facing the person being addressed, literally 'face to face.' If we were to ask them to whom they are addressing their words, the answer would be 'to the person directly in front of me.' When I say my words to this person, I know that they will hear me."[2]

A Deeper Dive

The Malbim is teaching us that being physically near and attuned to the person we are blessing contributes to the experience of a soul-to-soul connection. Contemporary Hasidic teacher Yitzhak Meyer Morgenstern

(Israel) adds that when blessing someone, "Looking into your friend's eyes is peering into their pure and precious soul."[3]

In this vein, the Orakh Le-Hayyim (Avraham Hayyim of Zloczow, eighteenth–nineteenth c., Ukraine) observes about our verse:

> The Holy Blessed One gave [physical and spiritual] blessings to Abraham our Father, who passed them onto Isaac, and he to Jacob, and then to his sons. However, the Holy Blessed One then gave the act of blessing to the priests, since they manifest Divine kindness and love. When the priests spiritually awaken love within themselves to bless Israel, they simultaneously awaken love far, far above in the uppermost Source, causing goodness and blessings to flow upon Israel and all creatures.[4]

Here the Orakh Le-Hayyim takes us through a multistep process of cultivating the practice of blessing as it relates specifically to Priests. In my view, reflected in this synopsis, since Exodus 19:16 speaks of the Israelites as a "kingdom of Priests," his wisdom is more expansively true for all of us.

He begins with connecting a blessing to love. Love for the Divine can only be nurtured if we intentionally cultivate love for ourselves. Only from self-love can we awaken love in the celestial realm. Why? Because the part of ourselves that we can always love, regardless of external circumstances, is the Divine Presence within each of us. Stirring this innate love, a mode of loving the Divine, affects our lives with other human beings and our connection to the upper world as well.

The mystics speak about two types of Divine-human encounters: ita'ruta' de-ley'la', "an awakening from above," initiated by God, and ita'ruta' de-ltata', "an awakening from below," initiated by humankind. At times, they teach, a sacred action below, such as loving oneself, energetically awakens that same action above in the celestial realm. This spiritual stimulation of love from above then flows back to our lower world, with the energy of love now becoming enclothed in a powerful act of blessing.

I understand this teaching deeply. At earlier times in my life when I experienced self-loathing, I felt like a hypocrite robotically going through the motions when offering an expected blessing, such as to the parents of a newborn child. Of course, I wanted good for others, but I lacked the faith in the wondrous powers of *my* blessing. Fundamentally I faced two challenges of belief: that love really did lie within me and that any blessing I could utter would possess power. During those painful times, I never really considered that spiritually awakening love within me was possible, so at first I did not intentionally seek a life in traditional Judaism that practiced this. But then I began to notice: the power of the blessings given by other people around me seemed to originate from their own internal love. Their blessings embodied love.

Cultivating self-love, then, had to be one of the next steps along my Jewish spiritual journey. But how was I to learn to love myself—or, even more, to discover the love I was told was already within me?

The Orakh Le-Hayyim speaks to this inherent component of the blessing practice: "How were the priests able to attain a state of such total love? Surely, they had to cultivate *teshuvah*—completely turning to God, seeing themselves in an absolutely humble way. [It was] similar to being at Sinai, when all of Israel stood at the level of total love and unity, because they had turned to God."[5] He is saying that the actual experience of connecting with the Divine can awaken this potential. We may then find ourselves able to reach into our inner self and encounter the godly expression of love.

I began to explore texts that speak to the spiritual dimension of *teshuvah*. I learned that this is an actual spiritual practice requiring dedicated intentional time to be with oneself and become more mindful of one's thoughts and feelings. Before this intentional practice I had no idea how emotionally shut down I was. In time, the more I began to sense the Divine's energy of love and aliveness within me, the more my heart began to melt and open.

Eventually, the Divine in me became the pivotal point of my identity, and loving myself grew from loving and sensing closeness to the Source of my life. It was as if the Orakh Le-Hayyim was speaking directly to me. As my own feelings of worthiness grew, my newly discovered self-love catalyzed me into believing that I too possessed the ability to truly bless another person.

When blessing another person, I now invoke the name of the Eternal with *this* love, and *this* defines the moment as sacred. Inherent in the blessing is my appreciation that its power derives from the Creator, the Source of the blessing. I activate the blessing from above to move through me, and in this sense, God, not I, is the spiritual force of the blessing.

Another realization: before I cultivated this intentional practice, my understanding of my place in the world, both as a Jew and a human being, derived almost exclusively from my intellect. Yet the Jewish mystics teach us that our visceral and immanent experience of the Divine is an emotional encounter—through the heart.

Returning to our verse, the Orakh Le-Hayyim speaks likewise to the derivation of the desire to bless:

> The act of "say to them" [in our verse] takes place within the heart, as in "Should you *say* in your heart." (Deut. 7:17) The heart is the place to which we turn in *teshuvah*. They needed to turn to God to come to love all Israel. Reaching [the Source] within themselves enabled them to draw blessings upon Israel from [the Source] high above. And these blessings now flow throughout all existence, establishing them as universal blessings for all creation.[6]

Tradition tells us that the spiritual oxygen giving vitality to blessings and soul-to-soul connections derives from a heart-driven life.

The Practice

1. Begin with breath awareness.
2. Then, reflect on the text.
3. Move to quieting down your mind.

These three steps are explained in detail in the introduction.

4. Visualize a moment in your future when you are filled with feelings of joy, gratitude, and sheer excitement to be alive, propelling you to share this wondrous state of being with someone you love.

Before you begin, pause and direct your awareness to your breath. Imagine it is the Creator's breath of life entering you through your nostrils, moving through your body, and then exiting out of your nostrils. Be with this for a few cycles.

Now, from as connected a place as possible, gaze into your loved one's eyes with a smile and bless this person in whatever way feels meaningful right now. If you are inclined, invoke the Divine to manifest your intentions.

What comes up for you emotionally when you imagine this encounter?

Be-ha'alotekha

Receiving a Second Chance

> But there were some who were impure by reason of a corpse and could
> not offer the Passover sacrifice on that day.... Those affected said to them
> [Moses and Aaron], "Impure though we are ... why must we be debarred
> from presenting GOD's offering at its set time with the rest of the Israelites?"
> Moses said to them, "Stand by, and let me hear what instructions GOD
> gives about you." And GOD spoke to Moses: "Speak to the Israelite people,
> saying: Regarding anyone—whether you or your posterity—shall offer it
> in the second month, on the fourteenth day of the month, at twilight."
> Num. 9:6–11

Where We Are

Aaron confers the Priestly Blessing for the first time. The leaders of
the twelve tribes bring their own personal celebration offerings to the
Tabernacle. The Torah reminds us of the priestly responsibility to light
the menorah.

A year after the Israelites left Egypt, the Eternal legislates an annual
Passover offering in remembrance of the original offering while still in
Egypt. Our verses pick up with a problem arising in light of this divine
directive. One of the newly binding toraitic laws forbids a person from
offering and eating any of the sacrifice while temporarily impure through
contact with a human corpse. The person remains ineligible until under-
going a specific ritual.[1]

The current problem arises because the Passover offering must be
performed specifically on the anniversary date of the original one performed in Egypt. Hence the very people showing honor to Joseph by
carrying his bones from Egypt to Israel are now disqualified from participating in the nation's Passover offering.

This is one of those rare moments in the Bible when people feel so painfully excluded that they challenge the status quo by bringing their case to Moses. As a result, Moses asks the Eternal how to proceed, and the holiday of Pesaḥ Sheni—the second Passover—becomes inscribed in the Bible. More recently the tradition views Pesaḥ Sheni as a modern holiday of second chances.

At First Glance

Rashi (Shlomo Yitzhaki, eleventh c., France) explains that Moses has the confidence to immediately bring this to God because he was "like a pupil who is certain that he will get information from his teacher at any time. Happy, indeed, is a human being who may so confidently [trust] that at any time when they wish to do so they may speak with the *Shechinah!*"[2] Rashi seems to be teaching that God grants every human being direct access in the form of the Divine Presence, the *Shekhinah*, that lives deep within us.

And yet, one has to be open to that access. Interpreting "your posterity" in our verse ("And GOD spoke to Moses: 'Speak to the Israelite people, saying: Regarding anyone—whether you or your posterity—shall offer it in the second month, on the fourteenth day of the month, at twilight'"), Chizkuni (Hezekiah ben Manoah, thirteenth c., France) says this also refers to individuals in future generations who act on a change of heart—those who move from excluding themselves, because they don't feel spiritually connected to their own history, to expressing or inquiring about their Jewish identity. In essence, those who take the initiative to return to their heritage also deserve and receive a second chance.[3]

A Deeper Dive

In biblical times, the touching of a corpse made a person ineligible to experience closeness with the Divine through the sacrificial rituals. In contemporary times, a person may feel excluded and prevented from participating in religious, spiritual, or cultural traditions that also bring closeness with the Divine. Without any ritual impurity, the person may nonetheless for other reasons feel debarred, diminished, and even less alive than others.

I've seen this happen when a Jewish school refused admission to a child because both parents were of the same gender. My own daughter, who was born deaf, felt so painfully diminished by traditional communities that she left a Torah-based religious life. What if, instead, people's cries for inclusion were compassionately met by affirmations that "it's never too late to be included! You absolutely have a second chance!"?

Still, as in the biblical account where the men bring their indignation to Moses, the responsibility to take advantage of this gift of a second chance lies within the excluded people themselves. Contemporary Israeli Torah scholar Rabbi Avraham Arieh Trugman echoes this idea when he comments: "[Pesaḥ Sheni] shows that when the desire is strong enough to draw close to God or to serve Him nothing ultimately stands in the way. This is confirmed by a statement of the Rabbis: 'Nothing stands in the way of will.' Not only did these men succeed in their request, [but] their spiritual passion [also] revealed a new mitzvah in the Torah in response. This incident serves as a great lesson for anyone wanting to sincerely dedicate themselves to spiritual progress and determined action."[4]

While some might view placing the onus on the excluded individual as a kind of victim blaming, the rabbis are teaching instead that this actually grants agency, by honoring the person's power.

Rabbi Yoseph Yitzchak Schneerson of Lubavitch (twentieth c., Russia and United States) additionally teaches that the message of Pesaḥ Sheni is "there's no such thing as 'too late.' One can always rectify things."[5] It is never too late because the Eternal said yes to the Israelites who originally sought a second chance.

If our own spiritual parent tells us "it's never too late," it may lie within each of us to come to the place where we believe in the Pesaḥ Sheni message of second chances. The mere desiring to receive a second chance may itself derive from a deep sense of believing that this is possible. This holiday only became a reality because our ancestors believed that their painful feelings of "being disbarred" could be assuaged.

If this is so, how might we summon faith that exclusion *can* be remedied if we seek its rectification? Trusting in our spiritual parent may provide us with the needed encouragement and support. In my own life journey, up until the day I decided to be honest with my Creator, I sensed the pain of exclusion—a death-like experience of being diminished.

For fifteen years I lived in the ultra-Orthodox world. For me, the very clear expectations of how I was to think and behave eventually felt like they were robbing me of my inner truth. I couldn't express my critical thinking or emotional experiences or honor my yen to experiment and explore. I yearned to live a life that would honor the Jewish tradition, but little by little the energy it took to live what felt like someone else's life whittled away.

In 1991, fifteen years into this way of living, a traumatic realization manifested quickly. As Saddam Hussein began to launch missiles from Iraq to Israel, I, now a Jerusalemite, felt an inner attack—the external war exacerbating my inner war. I had to leave this world, because there was no place there for me to be honest with God, my soul, and my conscience.

For the next ten years I lived outside the traditional Jewish way of life and faced a spiritual existential crisis. I felt stuck in no-man's-land: I couldn't live in the traditional Jewish Israeli world and be honest with both God and me, and yet I couldn't live outside of this world and hope to find inner serenity. I kept hoping that magically God would lead me to a way of honoring my soul, my conscience, *and* the tradition.

On my fiftieth birthday, in 2001, I woke up to the unbearable pain of loneliness and estrangement from my own tradition and gave myself the birthday gift of reaching out to the Eternal. Now, for the first time, I simply and literally begged God with hot tears to help me return to traditional Judaism in a way that felt alive and honest.

Suddenly spiritual ideas I'd learned when I was ultra-Orthodox, that my soul is a part of God dwelling within me, and that God gives each of us second chances, sprung up. I willed to change my relationship with the *Shekhinah* because now I intuitively believed I could. It was as if my soul could talk, and she was asking for a second chance to do this project called living in a better, divinely connected way.

What followed on that very same day was as if the Eternal called out to me and said, "I've been waiting for you for all these years to finally cry out to Me for help. Now I can help you and of course give you a second chance. Hold on to My hand and never let go and you will learn to live a Judaism that you have dreamt for."

"Wow!" I said to myself. And I felt held, heard, and homeward bound for the first time in twenty-five years.

This second chance required me to be really honest with myself, unlike earlier in my life. Now I gave myself permission to think creatively and critically, and to open my heart to feel my true feelings. I began to experiment and to cultivate Jewish spiritual practices to sense the Divine Presence, and I started to realize that I was no longer halakhically (legally) defined but rather informed. Then I saw that I was embracing a radical postdenominational way of being with the Divine, with the Jewish tradition, and with my own soul.

From time to time, I wonder: What would have happened to me if I hadn't pleaded with God for a second chance?

The Practice

1. Begin with breath awareness.
2. Then, reflect on the text.
3. Move to quieting down your mind.

These three steps are explained in detail in the introduction.

4. Visualize a moment in the past when you felt excluded by others, or when you excluded yourself, in any context. Gently allow yourself to settle into your emotional landscape. What do you feel?

Try to experience any difficult feelings with both courage and compassion. Breathe in the feelings, one at a time, pause and hold the feeling, and then release the feeling back into the universe. Remember that the feelings do not define you but rather teach you about you. Continue this cleansing breathing awareness for a few more cycles. Now, gently ask yourself, "Why is this so painful for me? Do I feel unworthy? What else may be contributing to how I feel?" And ask, "Have I concluded I can never be included?"

Pause for a minute and direct your awareness to your breathing as a life-affirming, cleansing experience. Embody the experience of new breath moving through you.

Now gently invoke an opportunity: "What if I can receive a second chance? All I have to do is will it so much that I will request it and even expect it." Make this part of your breathwork. With each inhalation, breathe in the potential to will the change. With each exhalation, visualize yourself actualizing that potential.

What does your second chance look like? What has to happen?

What might you do now to make it happen?

Shelaḥ-Lekha

Cultivating Self-Confidence

This is what they [the ten naysayer scouts] told him [Moses]: "We came
to the land you sent us to; it does indeed flow with milk and honey. . . .
However, the people who inhabit the country are powerful." . . . Caleb
hushed the people before Moses and said, "Let us by all means go up, and
we shall gain possession of it, for we shall surely overcome it." But the
other men who had gone up with him said, "We cannot attack the people,
for it is stronger than we . . . and we looked like grasshoppers to ourselves,
and so we must have looked to them [the Canaanites]." . . . But My servant
Caleb . . . was imbued with a different spirit and remained loyal to Me.
Num. 13:27–28,30–31,33, 14:24

Where We Are

A few days after Pesaḥ Sheni, the Israelites begin what was originally
intended to have been a direct journey into the Land of Israel. Two divine
signs direct them when to move and when to camp: during the day a
pillar of cloud leads the nation and at night it appears as a pillar of fire.

Moses sends the twelve tribal leaders ahead of the nation to scout
out the Promised Land. When they return forty days later, all but two
of the twelve tribal leaders, Caleb and Joshua, bring the devastating
news in our passage.

At First Glance

Caleb seems to possess incredible courage. Along with Joshua, he challenges the dispiriting judgment by the powerful majority of ten not to
proceed and conquer the land. He asserts that this rebellious behavior,
utterly disrespecting the divine plan, demonstrates a lack of the required
faith to undertake this venture.

Or HaHayim (Hayim ibn Attar, eighteenth c., Morocco and Jerusalem) comments that while initially the ten naysaying scouts appear to be speaking only with Moses, this may not be the case. "The trick the scouts played on Moses was that whereas ostensibly they addressed their words to Moses, they ensured that the whole community could hear them at the same time."[1] This suggests the scouts intend to surreptitiously persuade the Israelites not to heed the divine plan to ascend to the land. Indeed, by appearing to speak only with Moses, yet within earshot of the nation, they are able to set their plan into motion. Had they only spoken with Moses, had the entire nation not heard and supported their report, Moses could have quickly rebuffed them for such a rebellious stance.

Rashi (Shlomo Yitzhaki, eleventh c., France) points out that the word *mimennu* (than we) in the scouts' declaration of "for it is stronger than we" can also be understood to mean "than Him," thereby referring to the Omnipresent. Through this understanding, the gravity of the scouts' sin extends far beyond a weakened faith to literally uttering blasphemy.[2]

The scouts' observation, "We looked like grasshoppers to ourselves, and so we must have looked to them," may also point to their own low self-esteem. In line with a sense of inferiority, the Babylonian Talmud renders the scouts' point-of-view: "We heard [the Canaanites] say one to another: 'There are ants in the vineyards that look like human beings.'"[3]

Rabbi Dr. Abraham J. Twerski (twentieth–twenty-first c., United States and Israel) analyzes the impact of degraded self-worth like this: "The principle is clearly stated. The way you feel about yourself is the way you believe that others perceive you. If you feel inadequate, you are certain to conclude that other people have noticed and are discussing your inadequacies."[4]

Caleb, by contrast, possesses the exact opposite of the scouts' self-doubt: his own strong faith. Rashi references a talmudic interpretation in which Caleb fiercely retorts: "We can indeed go up—even to heaven, if He were to say 'Make ladders and go up there' we should listen to Him because we would be successful in all His words that He bids us to do.'"[5]

Might our verse be encouraging us to become more like Caleb, "imbued with a different spirit," as we cultivate the *middah* of self-confidence?

A Deeper Dive

Rabbi Raz Hartman (twentieth–twenty-first c., Israel) points out that this portion teaches that "an essential *middah* that most of the world does not urge us to develop is self-confidence and trusting in oneself. There is something within each of us of intrinsic value and . . . our opinions, thoughts, and deeds are essential to who we are. This self-confidence includes the strength to step forward in the way that appears 'to me' to be correct, without looking behind me and making sure that everyone else is pleased."[6]

Reb Simcha Bunim of Przysucha (eighteenth–nineteenth c., Poland) connects self-knowledge with self-confidence. He teaches that someone who knows herself or himself doesn't need to be anyone else. One can admire another individual without wanting to be that person—one's job is to be oneself.[7] Essentially, the more we know and honor ourselves, the more likely we are to rely on our own self-awareness.

Rabbi Hartman develops this idea:

The root of this self-confidence derives from cultivating faith in the Divine light that dwells within each of us. This Divine light illuminates the awareness of something unique within each of us which we ourselves are surer about than the world in its entirety. In fact, the global community needs and subconsciously longs for each person to reveal this distinctive part of themselves. In order to express this and illuminate the world with this inner part of who we are, a person must believe they possess this. . . .

How ironic that this inner trust is strengthened when we encounter opposition. In these moments of difficulty and struggle, one's spiritual courage and inner self-awareness are being tested. As this struggle becomes deeper, one needs to know when to yield to the opposition and when to say, "better that I am guilty of walking on my own path." If we know how to navigate these moments with a true integration of humility and self-confidence, we will increasingly grow this inner light that dwells within us. We will know in truth that we can in fact depend on ourselves.[8]

Drawing on this understanding of encountering opposition to elucidate our verses, Rabbi Hartman observes that the story of the scouts is, at its core, an argument between Caleb and the other scouts. The ten scouts perceive themselves as small and thus project that the Canaanites must also view them as inconsequential. Caleb, on the other hand, draws on his inner knowledge and self-confidence to proclaim, "We shall surely overcome." The fundamental difference is Caleb's connection to the Divine Presence within him that nurtures his identity, self-confidence, and inner steadfastness.

To be sure that we do not confuse this self-confidence with arrogance, Rabbi Hartman points out:

One may confuse Caleb's "sacred audacity" with blatant insolence. Two points clarify the difference. These factors play an essential role in cultivating the necessary humbled self-confidence in a person's relationship with the Divine. The first point brings the Divine Presence into a person's decision-making process by asking: What is the Divine requiring of me at this moment? Essentially the individual must increase their personal prayer to grasp the particular way that resonates with their faith in the Divine will and wisdom. Especially how this informs each of us in a unique way.

The second point is that in moments that are fundamental to our life path, it is possible to pay attention *only* to our inner self-awareness. With these important and essential matters in life, one's ultimate decision can come only from one's heart and soul. When our very faith stands on the scale, one needs tremendous sacred audacity to say, "Here I am unable to ask anyone else; this is the very root of my life."[9]

The Piaseczner Rebbe, Kalonymus Kalmish Shapira (twentieth c., Poland), sees Caleb's choice not to try to demolish the other scouts' arguments but solely to speak his inner belief in the God within himself ("Let us by all means go up, and we shall gain possession of it, for we shall surely overcome it") as a testament to his divinely infused self-confidence.[10] The Piaseczner uplifts Caleb's response as an inspiring balance between two seemingly incompatible character traits: self-confidence and humility. Caleb is sufficiently humble to know that his confident stance derives only from his faith in God, who is directing the Israelites to enter the Promised Land.

The Piaseczner also suggests a visualization practice to cultivate self-confidence and connection to the Divine within: "Envision yourself as a *tzaddik*—the ideal spiritual person you really can be. Imagine the greatness of your soul, its root and its splendor, as the Eternal comes to joyfully unite with Her. Persist and deeply immerse yourself in this visualization.—Hold these images right before your eyes. It is impossible that this will not awaken within you a higher consciousness."[11]

In this way, I believe our passage is encouraging us to realize that, like Caleb, we can be "imbued with a different spirit." Caleb's humble and self-confident consciousness of the Divine Presence within him *is* what defines him, and he becomes a spiritual model for us of how to be imbued with sacred audacity, by humbly encountering the Divine Presence within.

The higher consciousness the Piaseczner Rebbe is encouraging us to bring forth may yield our own "different spirit" of humble self-confidence. This spirit may in turn allow us to proclaim our truth as an authentic response to what the Divine is asking of us at the very moment.

The Practice

1. Begin with breath awareness.
2. Then, reflect on the text.
3. Move to quieting down your mind.

These three steps are explained in detail in the introduction.

4. Visualize a moment in your life in which you sense you've come closest to possessing a "different spirit." What is the setting? Are you engaged with others or alone? What seems to elicit this "different spirit"?

What does it feel like, physically, emotionally, spiritually?

What would you say are the essential components of your "different spirit"? Is the Divine integral to your experience?

Do you sense humble self-confidence — an inner Caleb energy manifesting itself to you and others?

Koraḥ

Healing an Inflated Sense of Self

> Now Koraḥ . . . betook himself along with Dathan and Abiram . . . to rise up
> against Moses. They combined against Moses and Aaron and said to them,
> "You have gone too far! For all the community are holy . . . and GOD is in
> their midst. Why then do you raise yourselves above GOD's congregation?"
> When Moses heard this, he fell on his face.
>
> Num. 16:1–4

Where We Are

After ten of the twelve scouts report that the Promised Land cannot
be conquered, trauma and fright grip the Israelite nation: "The whole
community broke into loud cries, and the people wept that night" (Num.
14:1). Many wish they would have died, and some even want to return
to Egypt.

The Eternal proclaims that no one from that generation—save Caleb
and Joshua, the two scouts resolute in divine faith—will enter the Promised Land. Instead, they will wander in the wilderness for forty years.

The people now regret their response and want to enter and conquer
the land, but Moses cautions that this would now defy the Eternal's
wishes. Ignoring Moses, they adamantly proceed with their plan—but
"the Amalekites and the Canaanites who dwelt in that hill country came
down and dealt them a shattering blow at Hormah" (Num. 14:45). The
people's plummeting morale and reigning insecurity set the stage for
more rebellion.

In our verse, Moses' cousin Koraḥ attempts to delegitimize Moses'
leadership and usurp his power.

At First Glance

Rashi (Shlomo Yitzhaki, eleventh c., France) cites a midrashic teaching that interprets the phrase "and Korah betook himself... to rise against Moses" to mean that Korah takes himself to a place of opposition. Namely, by questioning "why then do you raise yourselves above GOD's congregation," he challenges Moses' appointment of his brother Aaron to the priesthood as unjust nepotism.[1]

What truly lies behind Korah's opposition? The midrash elaborates Korah's point of view: "Clearly you chose Aaron only because he is your brother, even though it is not only you who was at Sinai and heard God speak."[2] It seems that Korah believes he is more deserving than Aaron. Consequentially, he either forgets or fails to acknowledge that God, not Moses, has appointed Aaron to the priesthood.

On the receiving end of this unjust accusation stands Moses, described as "very humble, more so than any other human being on earth" (Num. 12:3). "When he heard this, he fell on his face" (Num. 16:4). Rashi holds that this incident, following on the heels of several other insurrections, weakens Moses' spirit to such a degree that his first reaction is to simply fall down.[3] Even the strong redeemer Moses can bear no more cumulative rebellions—for a moment he becomes incapable of responding.

In another reading, the Bekhor Shor (Joseph ben Isaac Bekhor Shor, twelfth c., France) comments, "Moses fell on his face *in shame*" for Korah.[4] Moses is embarrassed by Korah's self-demeaning behavior. His falling on his face encapsulates his shame both of Korah and for Korah.

Alternatively, the Netziv (Naftali Zvi Yehuda Berlin, nineteenth c., Poland) suggests that Moses' falling to the ground exemplifies the humble response "of prayer": he was hoping to receive a Divine Revelation on how to confront this challenge.[5] The Jewish tradition views a deferential, humble admission to God, "I do not know what to do. Please guide me," as a sign of inner fortitude, rather than preconceiving it as a weakness.

Expressing a different view, the Or HaHayim (Hayim ibn Attar, eighteenth c., Morocco and Jerusalem) views Moses' lowering himself as a physical response to Korah's wrongful accusation of self-exaltation: "Far from raising himself above the people, he humbles himself and makes himself equal to the dust of the earth."[6]

However we may understand Moses' act of falling upon his face, it does not seem to have any positive effect on Korah. Rather, the tension between Moses and Korah only continues to escalate until God finally quells Korah's uprising.

A Deeper Dive

Our verse may be teaching something deeper: how humility enables Moses to retain dignity and self-respect in a public attack. With Moses as our model, we may recognize humility as the character trait that heals an inflated sense of self.

Each of us likely possesses an inner humble Moses and an inner arrogant Korah. The Netivot Shalom (Sholom Noach Berezovsky, twentieth c., Israel) speaks to the pain arrogance may unleash on others and ourselves, and how humility may provide a soothing balm for its spiritual sting:

> It is taught in the Holy Zohar "that Korah's argumentative behavior breaks down peace and unity. And one who sabotages unity does the same with the Blessed Holy One."[7] The deeper cause and root of Korah's divisive approach with others is excessive self-absorption. This trait can grab such a strong hold on an individual that it defines how a person engages with others. While the symptom is the unfortunate breakdown of peace and unity, the root cause is an obsession with one's ego. This obsession consumes all the energy in a person's mindset and heart. So much so, that everyone else mentally and emotionally stands in the person's way, even though the "other" may not harm the person in any noticeable way.[8]

The Netivot Shalom addresses the inner Korah energy that seems to be part of the human condition—possessing the sense of separateness and fragmentation due to an all-consuming ego. At times, in particular when we face threats to our survival, a concentrated focus on ego may be necessary for us to take the actions that will save our lives. Yet when this way of living becomes a person's modus operandi, the survival instinct loses its role as an asset and becomes a deficit.

There have been times along my life journey when I myself suffered from an exaggerated sense of self. For example, I was not as sensitive to others' needs, including, I painfully admit, my children's needs, as I wish I had been. I was easily distracted by my own inner demons. My survival instinct took over, and that instinct fed into an exaggerated sense of self. This triggered an inner state of painful fragmentation between my integrity and conscience on one hand and how I showed myself to the world, especially to my family and close friends, on the other. I imagine I came across to them as arrogant—self-righteous, impatient, quick to anger.

From this hurting place I repeatedly asked God, "Why is this happening to me?" And finally, as if God were directly answering me, the response came: "To you? That is the problem here. It is not always about *you*. Rather ask the question, 'What is being asked of me through this?'"

I intuitively sensed the truth in this divine response, and it hit me hard. Perhaps as a religious experience, as I began to feel closer to the Divine within me, the door of humility opened for me.

When I reflect on that painful slice of my life compared to how I live my Judaism now, I don't recognize that person as me. I look back at my younger me with both acute sadness and acceptance, but not regret in the sense of brandishing judgment. My faith and trust in God tell me that this was the person I was meant to be then. I was meant to go through, and grow through, that confusing and self-centered period of time, for reasons beyond my understanding. I am confident that I would not have accessed the compassion, patience, and empathy I try to exercise today without that hot crucible from which I was forged.

So it is that I deeply resonate with the Netivot Shalom's guidance on letting go of the overt attention on self:

Peace and unity derive from . . . the trait of humility and a non-exaggerated sense of self. This spiritual disposition does not minimize the worth of a person, but rather minimizes the amount of energy a person needs to feel their self-worth. It really is about gently yielding to that which is more encompassing than the limited self—to the unlimited blessed Divine Presence within each of us. The diminishing sense of an inflated self, expresses humility and naturally defuses the harm an exaggerated ego brings to all of us.[9]

The Netivot Shalom identifies humility as the gelling agent for connection and peace. Cultivating the *middah* of humility by "yielding . . . to the unlimited blessed Divine Presence within each of us" may allow us to thrive. If we can trust enough in the Divine, we may be able to respond compassionately when confronted by divisive forces around us and within us.

In the biblical account, Moses' humility ultimately defeats Korah's arrogance and brings healing to the nation. Our own cultivation of humility may contribute to bring self-healing and healing of the world in our times.

The Practice

1. Begin with breath awareness.
2. Then, reflect on the text.
3. Move to quieting down your mind.

These three steps are explained in detail in the introduction.

4. Visualize a moment in your life where you behaved arrogantly, expressing your inner Korah. If this is difficult, talk to yourself gently. The purpose of the exercise is not to judge yourself, but to reflect on your earlier experience. As you inhale, imagine receiving the awareness and the potential to do this spiritual practice. Pause and hold whatever comes up, and then release the energy of Korah into the universe.

Going deeper, try to observe the event as a curious explorer, with the sole goal of increasing your awareness of the circumstances and its effects. What (real or perceived) threat instigates your response? What feelings emerge? What is your embodied experience—of your heart, face, muscles, posture?

Pause for a few breathing cycles and simply be aware of life moving through you, bringing calm and relaxed energy. From this serene space, begin to sense the possibility of healing any inner brokenness caused by the Koraḥ energy. Imagine you are discovering another part of you—your inner Moses—the humble part of you that gently yields to the Divine's world instead of resisting it.

Now, moving deeper into full belly breathes, begin to visualize activating your inner Moses. Feel your diaphragm contract as you receive your fresh Moses energy. As you exhale, move deeper into fully returning your breath and sense your diaphragm expanding as you activate your Moses energy. What does this activation look and feel like? How does your inner Moses experience and respond to the world?

When you are ready, visualize your inner Moses responding to the original threat. As you inhale, take a pause. The very act of pausing, followed by praying, expresses humility of itself. As you exhale, yield with humility into the moment. Inhaling again, imagine praying, beseeching, seeking in any way that resonates with you for ways to restore unity and peace to the moment. Exhaling, continue yielding with humility into the moment of your response.

What does this response look like now? How does it feel to respond in this way to your own inner Koraḥ?

Ḥukkat / Balak

Using the Power of Speech to Enhance the Quality of Life

> Now Balaam, seeing that it pleased GOD to bless Israel . . . looked up and
> saw Israel encamped tribe by tribe, the spirit of God came upon him . . .
> [and] he said . . . "How fair are your tents, O Jacob, your dwellings, O Israel!"
> Num. 24:1–3,5

Where We Are

The Eternal quashes Koraḥ's insurrection and Aaron is recognized as
High Priest. Thirty-eight years later, the Israelites are approaching the
Promised Land when Miriam, Moses' sister, passes away. Up until now,
they have had access to water through a rock which, due to Miriam's
merit, miraculously yields as much water as they need, but with Miriam's passing, the rock dries up. The people panic and the Eternal directs
Moses to speak to the rock to bring forth more water.

Moses and Aaron gather the people to witness this event, but instead
of speaking to the rock, Moses hits it. Water does pour forth, but since
Moses did not follow God's directive, both he and Aaron are now forbidden from entering the Promised Land. Soon afterwards, Aaron passes
away and his son Elazar becomes High Priest.

Continuing their journey to the Promised Land, the Israelites are
poised to experience the fulfillment of God's original promise to Abraham four hundred years ago. Now we witness another miraculous phenomenon. Balak, king of the Moabites, fears the might of the Israelites,
who have thwarted all attacks along their journey. He asks the prophet
Balaam to curse them. Twice Balaam attempts the curse and both times
he fails: the words pouring forth from his mouth bless Israel instead.
Balaam explains to an infuriated Balak that he has no control over the
words God places in his mouth. Balak replies that he will take Balaam

"to another place. Perhaps God will deem it right that you damn them for me there" (Num. 23:27). Then our verse begins.

At First Glance

Balaam's blessing exemplifies the *middah* of using the power of speech to enhance, instead of diminishing, the quality of life.

Rashi (Shlomo Yitzhaki, eleventh c., France) explains that Balaam's seeing "Israel encamped tribe by tribe" means the prophet takes notice that "each tribe dwelt in their Divine appointed location and did not encamp on other tribes' property; also, the openings of each family's tent never faced the opening of their neighbor's, thus ensuring that one could not peer into their neighbor's tent."[1] Rashi himself notes how the Israelites extended honor to each other's need for privacy.

The Malbim (Meir Leibush ben Yehiel Michel Wisser, nineteenth c., Ukraine) draws attention to the significance of the word "Israel" in our verse, "Balaam looked up and saw Israel encamped tribe by tribe." Pointing to the fact that "Israel" only appears here, and not the two earlier times when Balaam attempted to curse the Israelites, he explains: "Unlike the previous two encounters when Balaam saw only a segment of the nation, he now sees all of Israel together as one unified nation. And because of the nation's unity 'the spirit of God came upon him', which did not occur the previous two times."[2]

What effect does this have on Balaam? Rashi observes that when "the spirit of God came upon him . . . his heart inclined him to comply with the will of the Eternal and immediately bless the Israelites."[3] This contrasts with Balaam's two previous attempts to curse the Israelites, when only God's intervention transformed the intended curses into blessings.

We may now have a clearer picture of what Balaam saw and how this affects his own capacity to bless rather than curse. Unlike the divisiveness and rebellion of Korah's time thirty-eight years earlier, honor and unity now characterize the nation. As much as Balak vehemently wishes to curse the Israelites, their unity prevents him from succeeding. From fertile unified soil, life-affirming speech may blossom.

But why does Balak adopt the strategy of a verbal curse by Balaam rather than a traditional military campaign to defeat the Israelites? The midrash comments that Balak employs this atypical tactic only after reaching out to the "elders of Midian" (Num. 22:4) for counsel. Seeing that "Israel always supernaturally gained victory over those that sought to destroy them," and also knowing that Moses "grew up in Midian," Balak decides to "ask them about his ways." When the Midianites reply, "'[Moses'] power lies only in his mouth [i.e., his prayer]', they [Balak and presumably his ministers] said: 'Then we must come against them with a man whose power also lies in his mouth.'"[4] By summoning Balaam, Balak attempts to build an arsenal of curses to destroy the Israelites. Thus Balak abuses the power of speech by using it as a weapon, and Balaam elevates the power of speech by using it as a blessing.

Proverbs teaches that the power of speech can both support and threaten life: "Death and life are in the power of the tongue" (Prov. 18:21). Perhaps our verse is encouraging us to be more like Balaam: to cultivate the power of speech to enrich ("seeing that it pleased GOD to bless Israel") rather than uglify our lives.

A Deeper Dive

Why do some respectful verbal disagreements devolve into emotionally charged arguments leading to disconnection from others? Why it is that even those of us who bring the best of intentions to a challenging discussion sometimes resort to a default mode of argumentativeness? The Maggid of Mezeritch (Dov Ber Friedman, eighteenth c., Poland) teaches that a shared ethical principle is fundamental to a conversation that enhances its participants' lives, so this negativity may be a result of our not having first shared moral principles to guide our conversation.

The Maggid bases his innovative idea on our verse, "Balaam looked up and saw Israel encamped tribe by tribe, the spirit of God came upon him" (Num. 24:2). To Rashi's explanation that Balaam noticed how "each family's tent never faced the opening of their neighbor's," he points to the talmudic teaching that because of this, "these people are worthy of having the Divine Presence rest on them."[5] To the Maggid, this applies to his generation of Torah scholars where "one person explains the matter from their point of view, and another does the same but from their point of view."[6]

It is not yet clear, and may even seem counterintuitive, how tent openings that do not face each other provide a good model for scholars sharing their viewpoints. As if the Maggid is cautioning us to be patient, he continues: "Now, if Heaven Forbid, their intention is to compete with each other, when one proclaims, 'my interpretation is better than everyone else's', then surely woe to them and to their souls: it would have been better if they were not even born. But if each person intended only to expand the wisdom of the Torah and enhance it, then how fortunate they and their souls are."[7]

We may now appreciate that the Torah scholars' shared value of enhancing Torah wisdom raises the quality of their lives and fosters connection with one another. The paradigm of unification by a common ethical standard establishes a strong foundation whose integrity may readily accommodate diverse and even opposing views.

In conclusion, the Maggid uses the verse "Guard the openings of your mouth" (Mic. 7:5) to affirm that the tent openings that never face each other refer to the people's mouths: "Balaam observed that the Israelites' mouths did not face each other in opposition. Their intentions were not to create conflict. Rather, everyone's intention when voicing their individual perspectives shared the same unified goal — to enhance their relationship with the Divine. For that reason alone, the Talmud acknowledges that 'these people are worthy of having the Divine Presence rest on them.'"[8]

In true Hasidic style, the Maggid overlays a historical narrative onto our present spiritual condition. The Israelites become today's scholars, and by extension all people who might experience the profound effect of a shared ethical value system (such as respect, trust, empathy, creativity, closeness) in harnessing the power of speech for good.

So it is that by intentionally prioritizing common values at the outset when speaking with others in a variety of scenarios, we may experience at least a rudimentary fellowship that anchors and then enables us to express differences more equably. And as the power of our speech progressively enhances our quality of living, we may very well stumble upon the mystery of the Divine Presence dwelling within and around us.

The Practice

1. Begin with breath awareness.
2. Then, reflect on the text.
3. Move to quieting down your mind.

These three steps are explained in detail in the introduction.

4. Visualize yourself sitting down to a discussion with someone you trust and who shares common values. Both of you are enjoying yourselves, learning from one another, feeling warm, open, and connected . . . . and then, suddenly, your divergent views on an issue surface. The two of you continue to share thoughts and ideas on this topic.

What feelings come up for you? What is your embodied experience? Do you sense that the quality of your life benefits from this conversation?

Pause for a moment, and direct your awareness to your breathing cycles. Remaining in the present, experience the flow of life that enters you with each inhalation and departs from you with each exhalation.

Now direct your awareness to internally identifying what you believe to be the shared value(s) providing the foundation for this conversation. Begin to identify them externally with your conversation partner. What do you suggest, and what does your partner offer? Visualize the two of you honoring these values as an anchor for your continuing conversation.

You proceed to share more thoughts and ideas on the polarizing topic. Again, your divergent views surface.

As a storm at sea tests a ship's integrity, do you sense that your difficult conversation may now better weather a spiritual storm?

What feelings come up for you now? What is your embodied experience?

Do you sense that the quality of your life benefits from this conversation?

Pinḥas

Cultivating Shepherd Leadership

> Moses spoke to GOD, saying: "Let GOD, Source of the breath of all flesh, appoint someone over the community, who shall go out before them and come in before them, and who shall take them out and bring them in, so that GOD's community may not be like sheep that have no shepherd."
>
> Num. 27:15–17

Where We Are

Balaam blesses Israel with both physical and spiritual bounty, and a furious Balak orders Balaam to leave.

As the Israelites are poised to enter the Promised Land and the final census is taken, the Torah records the first grassroots feminist protest in Jewish history. A man named Zelophehad dies, leaving behind five daughters and no sons. Since the status quo does not allow women to inherit land, the daughters protest to Moses that their father's allotted portion in the Promised Land will be lost to his descendants: "Give us a holding among our father's kinsmen!" (Num. 27:4). When Moses brings the daughters' heartfelt plea to God, the Eternal responds, "The daughters of Zelophehad speak properly. You shall surely . . . pass the inheritance of their father to them" (Num. 27:6).

The Eternal invites Moses to ascend a nearby mountain to view from afar the Promised Land that the Children of Israel will soon inhabit. After forty years of leading his flock to the Promised Land, he is not allowed to enter. In the past Moses attempted to convince the Eternal to annul the edict, but now he accepts his fate, and asks something else of God.

At First Glance

When the Eternal first appeared to Moses at the burning bush forty years ago, he was shepherding his flock (Exod. 3:1). God called Moses to move from shepherding sheep to shepherding the Israelites. Now Moses beseeches the Divine to continue the tradition. He petitions God to choose a successor who likewise will lead by being in service to others—what Robert K. Greenleaf (twentieth c., United States) refers to as "servant leadership."[1] And God approvingly accepts Moses' request!

Acknowledging that Moses' appeal comes across considerably less than humble (a point several commentators raise), the Or HaHayim (Hayim ibn Attar, eighteenth c., Morocco and Jerusalem) holds that through the lens of the shepherd about to bid farewell to his flock, Moses' concern is fitting: "It seems inappropriate for Moses to have addressed God in such a forward way . . . [but in truth] Moses' entire speech reflected only his love and compassion for his people."[2] Because Moses sees his role as being in service, he feels required to advocate on behalf of his people, regardless of the affront to others, including God.

Rashi (Shlomo Yitzhaki, eleventh c., France) explores an additional requirement of the Torah's understanding of servant leadership by commenting on the word "breath" in the verse, "Source of the breath of all flesh." Rashi suggests: "Moses said to God: 'Master of the Universe, the personality of each person is revealed to you, and no two are alike. Appoint over them a leader who will tolerate each person according to their individual character.'"[3] While we all have relatively similar bodies made of flesh, our personalities are unique. Rashi views Moses' leadership as calibrated to support the very individual people he leads.

Addressing a third component of servant leadership that Moses embodies, Rabbeinu Bahya (Bahya ben Asher ibn Halawa, thirteenth-fourteenth c., Spain) comments on the need for a leader "who shall go out before them and come in before them" (Num. 27:17) as meaning that "the leader personally, and not anyone else, must always be in the front, and not as the way of the kings of the nations who remain at home and send their armies to battle."[4] Moses exemplifies this by leading the Israelite armies during the battles along their journey to the Promised

Land. More broadly, as a shepherd leader he models to the people what is expected of them.

To summarize, these commentators suggest that in the Torah's conception, "shepherd leadership" calls for a leader 1) to honor each person's unique personality, 2) to advocate steadfastly on behalf of one's followers, regardless of the possible imposition of the appeal, and 3) to lead by example. As we will see, shepherd leadership may also speak to our personal inner shepherd—the internal still, small voice that loves and shepherds us along our life path.

A Deeper Dive

In the *Zohar*, the Rabbis usually do not refer to Moses by the customary honorific *Moshe Rabeinu* (Moses our Rabbi) but as *Ra-a`ya Mehemna* (the faithful shepherd). A flock of sheep needs a shepherd to direct them to pasture, and we human beings need our own shepherds to guide and inspire us.

The Piaseczner Rebbe (Kalonymus Kalmish Shapira, 20th c., Poland) opens the window of awareness of our inner shepherd by first directing our attention to a more nuanced understanding of *lifnei-hem* ("before them," or alternatively "within them") in our verse, "who shall go out before them and come in before them":

> This is the meaning of Moses' plea for a leader who can clearly set out *before them* what they need to internally understand in order to actualize their potential awareness from *within them* what they need to know at any given moment. . . . [a leader] who will lead them by role modeling for them how best to use their individual intelligence wisely. The extra emphasis placed on the phrase "for them" [at the end of the verse] means ensuring that each person inside of themselves possesses their own internal shepherd. The [outer] shepherd must enter inside, into the depths of each person, strengthening their faith in the Eternal.[5]

By translating the word *la-hem* at the end of the verse as "for or to them," giving "where there will not be for/to them a shepherd," the Piaseczner captures the elusive quality inherent in shepherd leadership.

One who shepherds one's followers to discover their own inner shepherd has mastered the calling of servant leadership. The leader leads the follower to the follower's own internal leadership!

Developing this idea, I would suggest that the Piaseczner believes we all possess the capacity to discover and encounter our unique internal "shepherd leadership." The leader within us gently, yet clearly, indicates to us how to move along our life journey, with an inner, ephemeral tugging. Some of us experience our internal shepherd through intuition, a sort of sixth sense by which we immediately and mysteriously understand or know something without consciously reasoning. Rav Kook (Avraham Yitzhak HaCohen Kook, nineteenth–twentieth c., Jerusalem) considers "the unique sense of intuition, which derives from the depths of one's personality" as "the spiritual sense . . . through which it is possible to sense God."[6]

Like Moses, our internal shepherd—if we develop it—can lead us in the three ways discussed earlier: 1) to honor our unique personality, rather than adopting a one-size-fits-all approach to living our lives; 2) to advocate on our own behalf regardless of undesirable consequences; and 3) to mindfully model what we sense the Divine Presence is asking specifically of us in all our uniqueness.

The third aspect in particular characterizes this as a spiritual practice, with Moses again as our model. When Moses encounters God at the burning bush (Exod. 3:1–10), the Divine appoints him as the shepherd who will lead his flock out of Egyptian slavery—essentially transforming Moses' responsibility for sheep into the sacred act of shepherding the Jewish people. Before this divine encounter, Moses could honor, and advocate for, himself (the first two of the three components). However, this third element requires him, and by extension us as well, to realize and then act upon the realization that our inner shepherd *is* in fact the Divine shepherding us to sacred action.

Yet to uncover and actualize our inner shepherd seems to require an impetus toward self-agency that is not necessarily natural to all of us. The Piaseczner observes that many of his own disciples (Warsaw Jews during the interwar period) lack this quality: "People are always bemoaning, sighing, 'Where is my freedom of choice? I feel so imprisoned . . .

that it is almost impossible to control myself, to have governance over myself, to choose between what to want and what to deem as repulsive or loathsome.'"[7]

He then suggests the root cause of these symptoms:

For every choice that emerges from an individual's will, rather than reflecting someone else's will [making the choice], there first must be a person who is choosing for themselves [rather than relying on another's choice]. There must be an individuated person—a distinguishable self—, who can decide what they want and need for themselves. But if there is no individuated person—a distinguishable self—, just one among the species, there can be no free choice or personal will. Because, who will choose, if, besides the herd mentality, there is no one there at all?[8]

The Piaseczner now writes his prescription:

So, gaze deep into your soul. Are you bringing forth and expressing your true real self? Are you an individuated person . . . ? Or are you just a member of the species, the human species? . . . A person must individuate and distinguish themselves with the qualitative essence of who they really are: not only must they not remain imprisoned by social rules, cultural customs, or accepted thought without the ability to see beyond them, but they must also have a mind of their own. . . . This means revealing one's own personality and unique sense of self that is within you—that which depicts your very self.[9]

With this understanding, all three phases of internal shepherd leadership may now be seen as planting seeds of the Divine. To "distinguish [ourselves] with the qualitative essence of who [we] really are," the Piaseczner's prescription, we may need to encounter our soul, the Divine Presence within each of us—and, as Rav Kook mentions, to experience this intuitively, meaning we sense this as godly awareness.

Similarly when we advocate on our own behalf we can introduce our godly selves into the world "at all costs." Like Moses commanding in the name of the Eternal, as if the Eternal is moving resound-ingly through him, "Let My people go!" (Exod. 5:1), we might imagine ourselves advocating for a vital objective with nearly commensurate clarity, power, and sense of purpose. When we infuse our intuitive awareness into our actions, led by our internal shepherd, we hallow the moment as godly.

In all, by being faithful to our inner shepherd's leadership, we may model to ourselves and others how to help bring the world to a more redeemed place. Expressing our unique selves and advocating for what we believe the Divine is asking of us, we step forward and try to model it all. The shepherd within seems to be calling us to spiritual activism, to become agents of sacred change.

Part of this spiritual paradigm shift includes recognizing that each of us possesses shepherd leadership, even if this awareness is buried. The shepherd in me hopes to encourage and activate the shepherd in you, as I hope the shepherd in you will do for me.

The Practice

1. Begin with breath awareness.
2. Then, reflect on the text.
3. Move to quieting down your mind.

These three steps are explained in detail in the introduction.

4. Visualize a moment in your life when you felt weak and battered down by life, as if you weren't in charge of your own life. Perhaps you even said to yourself, "If only I could be like so-and-so: strong, energetic, always making things happen!" Breathe in your feelings, letting them move through you, and then gently return your breath to the universe. Stay with whatever unpleasant feelings you may be experiencing.

Now pause for three cleansing and invigorating breath cycles as you move to the next step. Imagine another time in your life when you your-self felt stronger, more energetic, and able to make greater impact. As before, breathe in your feelings, letting them move through you, and gently return your breath to the universe.

Ask yourself: what unique and special aspects of myself are on display here? How do my actions follow from this authentic and valuable me? How do I understand my unique internal shepherd?

What thoughts and feelings does this practice bring up for you?

Mattot / Mase'ei

The Wondrous Journey to Your Soul

These were the marches of the Israelites who started out from the land of Egypt, troop by troop, in the charge of Moses and Aaron.

Num. 33:1

Where We Are

God appoints Joshua to succeed Moses. The Torah details the various Temple offerings, followed by the laws governing vows and oaths. God directs Moses to wage his final war before his death, ensuring safe passage for the nation to enter and settle the Promised Land. The Torah summarizes the forty-two minijourneys comprising Israel's expedition from Egypt to the Promised Land.

At First Glance

Moses the Preacher (eleventh c., France) suggests why every encampment is enumerated here: "To make known God's kindness. Even though God decreed that the Israelites would move about in the wilderness for forty years, do not think that they continuously traveled from place to place for forty years without any rest."[1] In essence, he is saying, the divine plan includes the beneficent gift of time to pause, rejuvenate, experience, and hopefully value much more along the way.

Rashi (Shlomo Yitzhaki, eleventh c., France) alternatively cites a Midrash that compares this detailed enumeration to a "king whose son took ill and he brought him to a distant location to cure him. After they returned home the king began to point out all the various places they encamped during their journey: 'here we slept, here we caught cold, here you had a headache, etc.'"[2] In other words, this may very well be the first travel diary ever recorded in history. Rashi does not elucidate why he believes the Torah's accounting is necessary, though he may be intimating that remembering our stops along the way both honors the journey and ensures these indispensable memories remain alive.

For Maimonides (Moses ben Maimon, twelfth c., Spain and Egypt), the detailing of the stages along the journey provides needed proof for future cynics and naysayers. At the same time, his commentary speaks to what Abraham Joshua Heschel (twentieth c., United States) calls "radical amazement"—experiencing the wonder in our people's journey to the Promised Land:[3]

> Although to those who witnessed them, all the miracles and wonders that were done on their behalf were true. In the future, those that would hear about them would think they were just hearsay and may even deny them as actually having occurred. One of the greatest wonders in the Torah is Israel's survival in the wilderness for forty years and by listing their journey in great detail, future generations would read about them and acknowledge the great wonders entailed in keeping people alive in such places for forty years.[4]

Sforno (Obadiah ben Jacob Sforno, fifteenth–sixteenth c., Italy) offers another explanation. All the journeys are listed "as a way of honoring [the Israelites], for . . . it was only fitting as a reward for their faith [in following God through the wilderness] that they would enter the Land of Israel."[5]

A Deeper Dive

The detailed list of "the marches of the Israelites" seems to convey meaning beyond the descriptive plot of the people leaving Egypt as newly emancipated slaves and arriving at the Land of Israel, now as individuals born into, and able to act upon, freedom. Some of the stages along the forty-year trek are stressful and confusing, while others are unifying and celebratory—and, the Torah seems to be saying, all are necessary. Each one matters and needs to be recorded.

Delving deeper, into each of the people's individual stages of life, the Degel Mahaneh Ephraim (Moshe Chaim Ephraim, eighteenth c.,

Ukraine) recounts an insight he received from his grandfather, the Ba'al Shem Tov (Israel ben Eliezer, eighteenth c., Ukraine):

> These forty-two journeys [of the Israelites] exist in everyone's life, from the moment of their birth until the day of their death. We can understand this as follows: A person's birth, going forth from the mother's womb, corresponds to leaving Egypt. And afterwards, a person sojourns from one encampment to the next, until they reach the [postdeath realm of] "Supernal Land of Eternal Life," corresponding to the spiritual Land of Israel. . . . This comprises a person's journey from constricted consciousness to an expansive consciousness.[6]

In the name of his grandfather, the Degel presents the innovative idea that each of us is on a forty-two-step journey of our soul. Since the Exodus from Egypt is considered the birthing of the Israelite nation, then prior to leaving, we were in the womb. In keeping with this, the Hebrew name for Egypt, Mitzrayim, conveys a place of narrowness and restriction. The Degel suggests that the mother's womb shares those descriptive qualities, but its purpose is completely different: to nurture life rather than diminish it. So, too, the Land of Israel is the antithesis of Egypt: "I have come down to rescue them from the Egyptians and to bring them out of that land to a *good and spacious* land" (Exod. 3:8). For the Degel the parallel in our soul's experience—the ultimate space of expansiveness that is represented by the Land of Israel—is the afterlife. He assumes the truth of a future utopian reality awaiting each of us in the world to come.

In essence, the Degel is encouraging us to view our souls as taking a parallel journey from Egypt to the Land of Israel—journeying from a constricted place of concealed awareness at birth to an expansive revealed awareness upon death, and then into the afterlife.

Here, I would suggest two alternative, spiritual understandings of the afterlife. Perhaps the afterlife represents the soul's homecoming as it reaches its ultimate destination—meaning the ultimate state of consciousness after we have exhausted all our potentials to grow in this life. The utopian idea of reaching perfection may very well not exist in this realm of life, but rather only after life as we know it. Or, possibly, the afterlife may be what lies ahead or after life today—the yet-to-be fresh and unchartered territory along our journeys.

However we may (or may not) understand the afterlife, the Degel's teaching speaks to appreciating and honoring the wondrous process of moving from one "encampment" to the next in the midst of a dynamic life journey to discover our soul.

The Lubavitcher Rebbe (Menachem Mendel Schneerson, twentieth c., United States) offers another spiritual way to understand the Israelites' journey to a "good and expansive land":

> When we cultivate the practice of spiritually leaving Egypt, we must realize that this one step is not sufficient in relation to the next step. Wherever we may find ourselves on our journey, at that moment, we are able to experience it as a "going forth from Egypt" to a "good and expansive land." However, relative to the next step as we move ahead on our soul journey, this liberated place now transforms into our new "Egypt." And for this reason, 1) if we cultivate the practice of journeying to our inner core, each step both liberates us from our past and becomes a new place of narrowness and limitation to transcend towards our future, and 2) each time we journey out of our personal Egypt we do move into a "good and expansive land." However, as this also becomes relative to the next step, it no longer assumes that reality.[7]

Through the Lubavitcher Rebbe's lens, we are each on a spiritual journey from a consciousness that limits us to an increasingly "good and expansive" consciousness that opens us to the infinite potential of our lives. Whatever limitations we last transcended define our current norm, our new personal Egypt, from which we try to arrive at the next "good and expansive" stage of our soul's potential. We might otherwise understand this as a personal growth process wherein whatever challenges we face that promote inner growth become relegated to our personal history. We possess the potential to grow from there.

Not only are we capable, as the Lubavitcher Rebbe sees it, of continuously realizing our potentials; it is incumbent on us to do so. He concludes: "The purpose of a human being is to continuously raise ourselves, higher and higher, acquiring greater awareness of the Divine that does not allow for standing still. Pausing yes, but remaining stationary, no."[8]

We may then appreciate that our soul never quite reaches its destination. To repeat the rebbe's teaching, "The purpose of a human being is to continuously raise ourselves, higher and higher."

This sentiment has become a defining factor in my own spiritual journey. It speaks to me deeply because, sadly, I sense much of our contemporary culture seeming to promote mediocrity as an acceptable and even desirable way of living. Pushing back on that construct, the Degel and the Lubavitcher encourage us to undertake a journey of "radically amazing" proportions, always reaching beyond how we are now to become our even better selves, especially by continuously nurturing our relationship with the Divine.

As we saw earlier, journeying to reach the Promised Land does necessitate pausing at times. So, too, a pause in our own spiritual journey may help reveal the wonder in our lives. I have found it a powerful practice to dedicate time to reflect on where I am on the way to encountering my soul. I try to honor each of my earlier steps, and to recognize each one as "radically amazing." This spiritual pause renews and readies me to embark on the next stage of moving from my inner Egypt toward my inner Promised Land. With gratitude, I forge ahead into the unknown and never ending journey.

Might you join me in this practice?

The Practice

1. Begin with breath awareness.
2. Then, reflect on the text.
3. Move to quieting down your mind.

These three steps are explained in detail in the introduction.

4. Visualize yourself on a path. This path is your life journey. Where are you?

Do you have an end destination, or are you focused on the immediate steps in front of you?

What is your sense of being on this life path? Are you standing still? Resting? Moving? What do you see in front of you? Are you bored? Excited? Bound to other people's expectations of you?

Do you sense wonder in your life journey? Do you sense the potential for wonder in the future?

Pause for a moment, directing your awareness to your breathing cycles. Experience each inhalation as more potential to move along your life journey. Experience each exhalation as manifesting this potential.

Now visualize yourself at a fork on the path. Choosing one of the paths will bring you closer to your true, authentic self. The journey will not always be smooth, but it's your own personal one. It will not always feel good, but it's yours. Despite the challenges, you will move from a more constricted to more expansive space, gaining increasing glimpses of your true self.

Pause for a moment and direct your awareness to your breathing cycles. Imagine the Creator and Source of all life breathing into you the potential of sensing wonder in your journey. Gently receive this gift through your deep inhalation.

As you exhale and return your breath to its Source, imagine you are actually experiencing this moment—this step—along your life journey, as "radically amazing."

What do you sense now? What does this mean to you?

5

Deuteronomy (Devarim)

Devarim

Discovering Our Inner Moral Compass

Turn and journey for yourselves.

Deut. 1:7[1]

Where We Are

God establishes the borders of the land of Canaan that the Israelites will soon inhabit. Numbers concludes, leaving the Israelites preparing to enter the Promised Land.

The fifth book, Deuteronomy, adds very little narratively. The etymology of the word itself derives from the Greek word *Deuteronomion*, meaning "second law," since Moses now reviews the narratives and laws he taught during the forty years after the Exodus from Egypt. Its Hebrew name, Devarim, means "words" ("These are the *words* that Moses addressed to all Israel" [Deut. 1:1]). Moses himself is now the speaker, rather than the transmitter, of God's words.

At First Glance

The Jewish tradition understands Deuteronomy as Moses' farewell address—the faithful shepherd speaking his last will and testament to his beloved flock. In this beginning section, Moses reminds everyone that thirty-nine years earlier, the Eternal gave the directive to turn away from Mount Sinai and begin the journey to the land of Canaan.

Ibn Ezra (Abraham ibn Ezra, eleventh–twelfth c., Spain) explains that the word *p'nu*—"turn"—in our verse implies "leave this place," and that *u-se'u` la'khem*—"and journey for yourselves"—means, "and journey to yourselves."[2] He may be proposing two different yet compatible ideas here: that Moses is reminding the Israelites that thirty-nine years earlier, God directed them 1) to physically leave Mount Sinai (after having encamped there for a year) and, simultaneously, 2) to spiritually "turn and travel to yourselves, within you." In line with this, the word *p'nu* means both "turning away from" and "turning within to." By this second meaning, the text may be understood as "turn and travel within to you."

Just as the Israelites need a compass to direct them on their journey to the Promised Land ("GOD went before them in a pillar of cloud by day, to guide them along the way, and in a pillar of fire by night, to give them light, that they might travel day and night" [Exod. 13:21]), perhaps they equally need a moral compass ("turn and travel within to you") to guide them spiritually to the land of the soul: the Divine Presence within.

The Jewish tradition construes ethical and moral behavior as alignment with God, resulting in sensing closeness to God. Viewed through the lens of the biblical tradition it is God's Voice that determines whether one's behavior is ethically right or wrong. In this light, discovering our inner moral compass might be seen as an essential practice when planting seeds of God consciousness.

A Deeper Dive

Defining *p'nu* even more deeply as an "inner readying," Rabbi Cindy Enger (twenty-first c., United States) encourages us to view it an essential beginning, both for the Israelites to journey to the Promised Land and for each of us to travel inwardly to our deeper selves: "*P'nu* . . . is this turning inward and facing the interior landscape with all of its texture and truths—fear and doubt, compassion and forgiveness, excitement and joy—that prepares our Israelites to take their next step. . . . And Moses is speaking to each of us, as inheritors of the tradition and contemporary readers of the Torah text."[3]

As with a physical journey, when we spiritually turn and travel within ourselves, we traverse a terrain that contains spiritual peaks and valleys, lush forests and arid deserts. Rabbi Eger depicts these as "fear and doubt, compassion and forgiveness, excitement and joy."

Several verses from the book of Isaiah (traditionally read on the Shabbat prior to the holiday of Tisha B'Av) offer insight on why we as a people seem called to "turn and travel within" to discover our inner moral compass.[4] The prophet Isaiah begins by proclaiming:

"My people takes no thought [reflect, observe]." . . . "What need have I of all your sacrifices?" Says GOD. "I am sated [with them] . . . and I have no delight. . . . Trample My courts no more. . . . Your new moons and fixed seasons fill Me with loathing; They are become a burden to Me, I cannot endure them. And when you lift up your hands [in prayer], I will turn My eyes away from you; Though you pray at length, I will not listen. Your hands are stained with crime." (Isa. 1:3,11–15)

Isaiah's quite harsh words seem directed at the very ritual behavior the Israelites adopt based on the Torah's own directives for the Temple practice. Why does God, who commanded these rituals, now reject the people's adherence to the expected behavior—and so much so that later, Isaiah warns this may lead to the Temple's destruction?

Perhaps the prophet's outcry is less about what the Israelites are doing and more about what they are *not* doing. Isaiah exhorts: "'Wash yourselves clean, put your evil doings away from My sight. Cease to do evil. Learn to do good, devote yourselves to justice; aid the wronged. Uphold the rights of the orphan; defend the cause of the widow. Come, let us reach an understanding', says God" (Isa. 1:16–18).

First, Isaiah chastises the people for not "taking thought" ("My people takes no thought"). Then he intimates that the Israelites have degraded themselves ("Wash yourselves clean"). Next, he articulates what the Israelites are *not* doing ("Learn to do good"). In all, God seems to be instructing us that the practice of contemplation ("taking thought") is requisite for developing the moral sense that will direct us to perform the acts of goodness expected of us.

Notably, the Malbim (Meir Leibush ben Yehiel Michel Wisser, nineteenth c., Ukraine) understands the expression *lo hitbonein* (not taking thought) as "not wanting to understand."[5] *Lo hitbonein* also shares the same root (*beit-yud-nun*) with the word *hitbonenut*, the practice of contemplative reflection on our lives at any given time. From this perspective, beyond not thinking about their moral compass, the people do not even *want* to contemplate it. Perhaps they know if they seriously reflected on their behavior (taking thought) they would be forced to confront their immoral behavior. Most likely, as with many people today, they shied away from this personal reckoning of truthfully realizing the need to recalibrate their moral compass to be in alignment with God.

Against this, God makes clear that moral action—"Devote yourselves to justice; aid the wronged. Uphold the rights of the orphan; [and] defend the cause of the widow"—equates with being godly. We may now hear the prophet cautioning us that being religious is less about our behavior being ritually right (and not wrong), and more about our moral behavior revealing the Divine Presence. Rather than limiting our focus to external, ritually based actions, we may need to "turn and travel within to you." If we dedicate time to be with our deeper selves, we may be more likely to discover that inner moral sense lying dormant within—similar to a seed waiting to be planted, to then blossom in our garden of God consciousness. With cultivation of an internal God consciousness, we may open ourselves, in time, to being transformed into how the Divine sees us at our best. From a kind, equable, and empathetic place within, we may naturally enact externally the goodness God expects of each of us.

This, I believe, is why God then invites us, "Come, let us reach an understanding." We are being urged to do this work *with the Divine*. As an agent of change, Isaiah insists that we turn away from the status quo to advance the betterment of the world as a collaborative effort with God.

This is part of a paradigm shift away from an action-driven self toward a heart-driven self that prioritizes being morally right over being ritually right. Orienting ourselves morally, we may realize that infusing goodness, kindness, and compassion into the world is the understanding *and* the doing of what God is asking of us, in Divine-human partnership.

The Practice

1. Begin with breath awareness.
2. Then, reflect on the text.
3. Move to quieting down your mind.

These three steps are explained in detail in the introduction.

4. Visualize yourself moving along on a hiking trail. Where are you right now? What are the sights and scents and sounds?

You reach an intersection. Multiple trails are possible for the taking. Hear yourself asking, "What is my next step?"

Do you need a compass to help you choose the right path? You sense you have one, perhaps in your back pocket. What feelings arise just knowing you have one?

Pause for a few breath cycles. Inhale gently the awareness of needing to have clarity on the hiking trail. As you exhale, breathe into finding your compass to point you in the right direction.

Now, direct your awareness inwardly, as you imagine traveling along your inner spiritual path. What is this path like? What types of terrain do you encounter? What are the sights and sounds, the thoughts and feelings?

What do you need to continue traveling on this pathway? Is discovering your inner moral compass part of what you may need?

Again, pause and direct your awareness to your breath cycles. Inhale new life with all of its new possibilities and discoveries—and imagine actively manifesting them with your exhalations. With these fresh breaths moving through you, imagine now asking the Divine—or your own sense of a higher being—to help you in this practice of discovering your inner moral compass. Imagine yourself accepting the Eternal's invitation to "come let us reach an understanding."

What sensations accompany you as you move into new unchartered waters?

Conclude your practice by deeply experiencing your next inhalation and exhalation as cleansing, invigorating, and encouraging.

Va-'ethannan

Loving Life with All Our Heart, Soul, and Might

> Hear O Israel! The ETERNAL is our God, the ETERNAL alone. And you
> shall love the ETERNAL your God with all your heart and with all your soul
> and with all your might.
>
> Deut. 6:4–5[1]

Where We Are

Moses reviews the establishment of a multitiered justice system with
appointed judges, and then recounts the fiasco involving the scouts. He
reminds the people that they have reached this moment in their lives
solely because they cleave to the Divine Presence and adjures them to
remember that their strength lies in their capacity to sense closeness
with their Creator. This partnership with God alone distinguishes the
nation from the various idol-worshiping cultures surrounding it. He
reviews the Ten Utterances (Ten Commandments) revealed at Mount
Sinai forty years earlier.

We now reach our two verses that the tradition refers to, in part,
as the *Shema* (Hear). The first verse proclaims the unique oneness
of the Eternal and the following verse commands the Israelites to
love God with all "your heart, soul and might." The complete *Shema*
includes three additional biblical paragraphs that are recited with our
two verses.

At First Glance

Sforno (Obadiah ben Jacob Sforno, fifteenth–sixteenth c., Italy) calls
attention to the four components of the *Shema*—"Hear O Israel!"—
"The ETERNAL"—"is our God"—"the ETERNAL alone."

He explains "Hear O Israel!" to mean "Contemplate, reflect and understand this." We are charged to comprehend and ponder the significance of the remainder of the text.

"The ETERNAL," he says, refers to "The One Who brings and continues to bring everything into existence." This teaches that the name ETERNAL refers to our own awareness of the infinite nature of the Creator. We as finite creatures also depend on being kept alive by the infinite Creator — as if the phrase "Let there be" in Genesis, describing the ETERNAL bringing everything into being, was not a one-time event but continues to be uttered throughout the generations.

"Is our God" is *the* One Force "to Whom, as the Supernal Being possessing all the potential to create, it is fitting to direct our devotion, hopes, prayers and service without any intermediary." The first-person possessive ("our God") intimates that God directs all of creation by being "in it," and not only "outside of it." Hence, we can be in a direct relationship with "our God."

Lastly, he understands "the ETERNAL alone" as God being inclusive and unified with everything. "Being that the Eternal created everything from absolutely nothing — giving existence to the universe out of a total void, it is logically impossible that any phenomenon representing an existence independent of the Creator can be true."[2]

Sforno offers a more radical and innovative understanding of the Jewish people's essential proclamation. We might now alternatively read this proclamation as, "Israel, pay attention and reflect that our Creator, being the only infinite One, continuously infuses life into all of creation and yet, while allowing us to be in relationship, simultaneously, remains beyond the limited physical realm." It is not that we believe in only one God, as a monotheistic theology would opine. Rather, the One in whom we believe *is* the only One, unified with everything. Nothing exists outside of the One's existence.

But how are we to understand the subsequent command to "love" God ("You shall love the ETERNAL your God with all your heart and with all your soul and with all your might")? How can the Creator command us to feel anything? While human beings are created with free will to choose how to *behave*, we are not given the ability to decide how to *feel*.

Rashi (Shlomo ben Yitzhaki, eleventh c., France) cites a midrash that understands this command as teaching us how we are to emotionally approach fulfilling all the commandments.[3] "When a servant fulfills the command of their master out of fear, then when the master overburdens him, he leaves him. This cannot compare to a person who serves from love."[4] Here, loving God means loving to fulfill God's commandments, too.

Along this approach to loving God, the Talmud explains what initially seems like a misspelling of the word *levavecha* ("your heart").[5] Normally in Hebrew, "heart" is spelled with two letters: *lamed-veit*, but in our text the second letter is doubled: *lamed-veit-veit*. The Talmud interprets this to mean, "Love the Omnipresent with both of your inclinations" (the two *veits*)—which is to say with a "wholehearted" love. At times our heart inclines us to want to actively be in service to God's world, with all the endless possibilities this brings. However, at other times, our heart inclines us to want to actively be in service to our own comforts and desires. These inclinations compete for our attention. Instead of allowing the two inclinations to pull in opposite directions, the command to love the Eternal asks us to harness them together. For example, I enjoy eating all different kinds of food simply because my heart inclines me to do so. The mitzvah of keeping kosher invites me to continue eating, but now within prescribed rules that also nurture my connection with my Creator. By observing kashrut (the prescribed dietary laws), I am able to love eating without compromising my love of experiencing closeness with the Divine.

Still, the question remains: How can the Eternal command us to experience a specific feeling when human beings do not possess the capacity to will how to feel?

A Deeper Dive

The key to opening the door of this conundrum may lie within one Hebrew letter: the *vav*, translated in our verse as "and" ("And you shall love"). However, the *vav* can also introduce the idea of a cause-and-effect relationship, thereby conveying "*Then* you will love." Rabbi Arthur Green (twenty-first c., United States) explains: "The realization that all is one, that there is nothing that is not filled with the presence of the One, will cause you to be overwhelmed with love. Love is the only possible reaction to this great discovery, one that transforms your perception of all that is."[6]

While human beings cannot be expected to feel a specific feeling, Rabbi Green is teaching us that we *are* able to choose what we *think* about. The *Shema* legislates that we intentionally reflect upon the eternity and ubiquity of the ETERNAL God. And, Rabbi Green says, if we fulfill this command by opening ourselves to the realization that the One lives everywhere in the universe, *then* this mindful practice naturally births the emotion of love. When we choose to fulfill the command *Shema* by contemplation, we are propelled to love.

Drawing from the kabbalistic tradition, the Alter Rebbe (Shneur Zalman of Liadi, eighteenth c., Belarus) delves deeper into this cause-and-effect relationship:

> When the intellect deeply contemplates and immerses itself in the greatness of the Eternal, [such as] 1) how the Creator permeates all of creation, 2) how the Creator encompasses all of creation, and 3) how in the Creator's presence, creation cannot exist as a separate entity, then . . . the *middah* of love is born, and the heart glows with a strong love as fiery coals, with craving, desire, passion, and a yearning soul towards the Infinite Blessed One.[7]

We can transpose the four sections of the *Shema* onto the four stages laid out by the Alter Rebbe: 1) Hear O Israel = deeply contemplate, 2) the ETERNAL = encompassing all of Creation, 3) is our God = permeating all of Creation, and 4) the ETERNAL alone = creation cannot exist as a separate entity. From all this and what follows, "Then you will love," the *middah* of loving God is born.

I, and perhaps you as well, can marvel at the psychological and spiritual insights embedded in these teaching. The Eternal's deeper request may be for each of us to cultivate an expanded consciousness that includes the awareness of the Creator breathing life into every crevice of existence, including our own. We may come to realize that the Creator's continuous breathing into us is the only reason we are alive. Then, perhaps, the desire to stay connected to our own lifeline may also manifest as love.

And yet the etymology of the second word in the *Shema* ("Israel") means "to struggle." Living spiritually in a physical world does not come without effort. For some of us, loving the Creator means that we agree to wholeheartedly love ourselves and all of creation, even when we struggle with this, or perhaps because we struggle with this. We may very well struggle to love people whose values and actions are repugnant to us. Recognizing this possibility, the Hasidic masters teach that it is a mistake to understand loving all of life as a subjective experience. Rather, as spiritual practice, the deeper challenge is to love the Creator's presence imbued in all life as both the reason I love me and the hope that I could somehow transpose this level of love onto you, even if I find your behavior distasteful in the extreme. Cultivating this awareness forces me to struggle within myself rather than with anyone else.

To cultivate the *middah* of loving life "with all of your heart, soul, and might" may be the single most challenging struggle of any human being

The Practice

1. Begin with breath awareness.
2. Then, reflect on the text.
3. Move to quieting down your mind.

These three steps are explained in detail in the introduction.

4. Visualize yourself preparing to recite the *Shema* as a proclamation. What feelings does this bring up?

Inhale deeply before you say the first phrase, *Hear O Israel!*, and direct your attention to its meaning. Imagine you are inhaling the potential of what the words mean. Say the words mindfully out loud through your exhalation. Repeat this with the remaining three phrases: The ETERNAL, is our God, the ETERNAL alone.

Pause for a moment and direct your awareness to your breath for a few cycles. Now gently recite: "And you shall love the ETERNAL your God with all your heart and with all your soul and with all your might."

Again, pause for a moment. Direct your awareness to your breath as a constant reminder of being alive, and of being kept alive.

Reflect on what you are feeling now. Do you sense this experience as different from your previous experiences of reciting the *Shema*?

What do you sense about your relationship with the Divine?

What does loving God with all your heart and with all your soul and with all your might mean to you, emotionally and spiritually?

How might loving God affect loving life itself?

'Ekev

Reimagining Mitzvot as a Source to Shine Our Inner Light

> And if you do obey these rules and observe them carefully, the ETERNAL
> your God will maintain faithfully for you the covenant made on oath
> with your fathers.
>
> Deut. 7:12

Where We Are

After bequeathing the Israelites their proclamation of faith (the *Shema*),
Moses cautions them to always remember that the Divine is the true
source of their prosperity. He reminds them to teach their children
that observing the mitzvot is essential for cultivating a relationship
with the Divine. This emphasis on observance leads the reader directly
into our verses.

At First Glance

Weighing the phrase, "And if you do obey these rules and observe
them carefully," Rashi (Shlomo Yitzhaki, eleventh c., France) points
out that the biblical text does not usually use the word shown here,
eikev (and if), to express the idea of "if, because of, when." Therefore,
he says, *eikev* must convey something that the more common words
do not. Relying on a midrash that adopts the literal meaning of *eikev*
(heel) and understands this "heel" to symbolize "the 'easy/light' mitzvot
that one tends to trample on with their heels," he suggests a different
implication: Although one may be inclined to pay less attention when
observing a light or easy command than to a heavier or more difficult one, one nonetheless needs to pay as much attention. Only then
will God "maintain faithfully for you the covenant made on oath with
your fathers."[1]

But what determines whether a mitzvah is easy or difficult? The Me'am Lo'ez (Yitzchak ben Moshe Magriso, eighteenth c., Turkey) explains that this refers to "their frequency in performance." The "light" commandments "can be observed at any hour of the day," whereas the "heavy" commandments "can only be observed at a specific time, sometimes only once in many years."[2] He continues:

> The Mishnah is therefore speaking of the case when one is performing a common commandment, and then finds themselves with the rare opportunity to perform a less common one. They should not say, "I will forgo the common commandment, since I can do it at any time, and I will do the uncommon one, since later I may not be able to do it." With such logic, one may neglect the common [light] commandments entirely, since one can always find "more important" things to do.[3]

By the Me'am Lo'ez's reasoning, eating matzah at the Passover seder is a "difficult" mitzvah because it occurs only once a year, whereas the prohibition against uttering slander is ever present and thus "easy." Yet for some of us, and for some mitzvot like these, the reverse seems truer: we find it easy to eat matzah at a Passover service and much harder to never defame another human being. Essentially, the Me'am Lo'ez's interpretation limits the Mishnah to a one-size-fits-all approach that doesn't give weight to each person's subjective encounter with a mitzvah.

In contrast, Maimonides (Moses ben Maimon, twelfth c., Spain and Egypt) values a person's subjective experience as *the* key variable determining if the mitzvah is easy or difficult. He writes: "A person must be careful with a mitzvah that *they* perceive to be easy ... as with a mitzvah that *they* consider to be difficult."[4] By this approach, we are to observe the mitzvot we consider easy along with those we view as difficult with equal care and dedication.

But even this view may lead us to ask: Why would anyone who regards ritual practice as meaningful negligently trample on a "light" mitzvah but not on a "heavy" one? Echoing the Me'am Lo'ez, the likelihood of always finding something of greater importance than fulfilling the "light" mitzvot could eventually convince us not to observe the tradition at all.

Uncovering a spiritual *middah* ensconced within this teaching may radically transform our understanding.

A Deeper Dive

The Ba'al Shem Tov (Israel ben Eliezer, eighteenth c., Ukraine) understands the Mishnah to focus on the potential spiritual experience that the person may sense vis-à-vis the mitzvah. Whereas the previous commentaries understand the Mishnah's word *zahir* to mean "be careful," the Ba'al Shem Tov suggests that the Mishnah's intention relies on *zahir*'s other meaning: "to shine or to illuminate." He teaches:

> [Do] not let a day go by without doing a *mitzvah*, be it a light *mitzvah* or a heavy one. Your sign to always remember this is the verse [in *Mishnah Avot* 2:1], "Be as *zahir*—"radiant"—from a light *mitzvah* as from a heavy one." The word *zahir*, which is usually translated as "careful," is related in its root to *zohar*—"radiance." This is to say that the soul can shine and illuminate as much by the performance of a light *mitzvah* as it can from a heavy one.[5]

In true Hasidic spirit, this commentary transforms the Mishnah's wisdom from cautionary advice to an invitation to a spiritually charged expansive experience. The Ba'al Shem Tov teaches that every mitzvah provides an equal opportunity to be a source of spiritual light. All mitzvot afford the practitioner the same potential to "shine forth" through their observance, because all mitzvot open the same gate to our internal selves—and specifically to our Creator, who created light and is the source of our inner light.

In a sense, this interpretation dismisses the relevancy of any given mitzvah's "weight." This mitzvah may feel "light" for me and "heavy" for you, or vice versa, but more importantly, both of us can equally experience our inner light through its observance.

For example, in my own practice, I connect deeply with the mitzvah of welcoming guests into my home. Granted, my parents modeled this practice for my siblings and me beyond what I have experienced in most other homes. They were dedicated to ensuring their guests would be comfortable, relaxed, and well fed. And their energy made plain their love for being incredibly generous in their hospitality.

As I entered the world of traditional practice, thus well trained in cultivating hospitality, I learned that this is also a mitzvah. Because welcoming guests into my home is a means to connect with the Divine Presence dwelling within me and my guests, this mitzvah "lights me up." I feel more alive—and my guests recognize this too.

Equally so, when I refrain from participating in slanderous gossip, another mitzvah, I also sense my inner light shining forth. As if the slander darkens the world with its negative power to divide people, God affords me an opportunity to illuminate the darkness by refraining from adding to it and instead contributing words that enhance a connection with people.

In practice, I experience the mitzvah of hospitality as easy and the mitzvah of avoiding slander as more difficult. Yet both equally afford me the opportunity to connect to my Creator and receive the light that shines forth from this connection.

The lack of this deeper awareness may help us understand the tendency to trample on easy or light mitzvot with one's heels. The Ba'al Shem Tov is transforming mitzvot from a checklist of required ritual obligations to an abundance of exhilarating opportunities to connect with the Source of our potential to shine forth our inner light. Yet if those who observe mitzvot do so solely to fulfill a religious obligation, the more frequently and easily observed commandments in particular may lose their sense of wonder and potential to elicit spiritual awakenings.

If we reenvision the aim of the mitzvot as affording each of us a deeper connection with the Divine—an experiential rather than performative approach—perhaps then *this* (and not the ritual observance itself) is the determining factor that defines the moment as religious. Rather than see ourselves as "being religious," we can cultivate "religious experiences" through which the Eternal's Light may shine brightly within us. This imbues new meaning to "for a commandment is a lamp and the Torah is light" (Prov. 6:23), as the lamp and the light may mean a perception and awareness of the Divine through the Torah's mitzvot.

This is a paradigm shift of consciousness. The spirit-driven life invites each of us to search along our path for sacred practices that cause us to shine. The Jewish tradition enables us to do this through performing mitzvot that kindle the inner light embedded in our souls. Over five decades of experiencing these teachings as truth, I have witnessed countless Jews, crossing all religious denominational lines, including myself, shine in different ways through their performance of different mitzvot, but never all the mitzvot. Scholar Michael Rosen (twentieth c., England and Israel) clarifies this further when he teaches that choosing which mitzvot we will observe requires courageous honesty about how we relate to the mitzvot in general: "If authenticity means to touch some point of personal reality, then one's relationship with the commandments must be refracted through the prism of one's own soul."[6] This metaphor becomes our compass, and points us toward the path of discovering mitzvot deeply meaningful to us as a source from which to shine our inner light.

The Practice

1. Begin with breath awareness.
2. Then, reflect on the text.
3. Move to quieting down your mind.

These three steps are explained in detail in the introduction.

4. Visualize this scenario: You enter a restaurant, you are hungry, you need to eat, and you are able to choose what appeals to you most. You review the menu and the owner of the restaurant suggests trying one of the specials. Ultimately you decide what to order. The waiter brings your meal, you eat, you're delighted with your choices, you feel satiated and happy and full of life. Hold that feeling for a few breath awareness cycles.

Now, imagine yourself repeating this but the restaurant you enter is a spiritual one. You are hungry and thirsty to connect with the Divine, with your soul, with your internal self. Direct your breathing cycles to this spiritual appetite. As you inhale, imagine receiving the awareness of needing to sustain yourself spiritually. As you exhale, imagine being ready to respond to this need.

You view the menu: a list of mitzvot, ethical principles or sacred rituals, seeking out those that seem most likely to shine forth your inner light. Might you choose, for example: infusing more kindness and compassion into your engagement with other people, ensuring not to inflict pain on animals, protecting the natural environment, being honest in your business transactions, experimenting with practicing Shabbat rituals, dedicating time to knowing the Divine Presence within you, or intentionally transmitting to your children your core values. (For a more comprehensive list of mitzvah options, the Sefaria website is a useful resource.)

You cannot possibly do everything right now, so what do you choose? Which mitzvot are most likely to "light you up"? What does that mean to you?

What would you choose first as your appetizer? Your main course? Your dessert?

What do you do now?

Re'eh

Seeing the Potential Blessing in Each Moment

> See, this day I set before you blessing and curse: blessing, if you obey the
> commandments of the ETERNAL your God that I enjoin upon you this
> day; and curse, if you do not obey the commandments of the ETERNAL
> your God, but turn away from the path that I enjoin upon you this day and
> follow other gods.
>
> Deut. 11:26–28

Where We Are

Moses reminds the nation that over the past forty years, God never ceased
to provide for their needs. Furthermore, when they enter the Promised
Land, they will see its goodness, reap its bounty, and lack for nothing.
They are to always remember their Exodus from Egyptian slavery.

At First Glance

The choice driving our passage underscores the Torah's understanding
of human free will.

Ibn Ezra (Abraham ibn Ezra, eleventh–twelfth c., Spain) singles out
as an oddity that the word *re'eh*, translated as "see" ("See, this day I set
before you blessing and a curse"), appears in the singular, whereas all
of the "you"s that follow (for example, *lifnei'hem*—"before you [all]")
are in the plural.[1] He is bothered by a seemingly improper conjugation,
so to speak, on God's part. If all that follows is in the plural, shouldn't
the command to see also be in the plural, addressed to many? Ibn Ezra
doesn't suggest what this may mean, but the attention he draws to it
encourages us to conjecture that the text, and the tradition, may be
balancing the need to honor each individual's own unique experience

of "seeing" and the need for each person to share that personal vision with the community.

The Malbim (Meir Leibush ben Yehiel Michel Wisser, nineteenth c., Ukraine) construes the choice to view the moment as a blessing or a curse in the context of what is actually being asked of us "to see." Alternatively interpreting *tish'meh'u* ("if you obey" or, more commonly, "if you observe, follow") to mean "if you understand," he comments: "When a person themselves chooses to understand that the mitzvot are Godly, *this* is the blessing."[2] He seems to be implying, further, that if a person does not understand the mitzvot as Godly, *this* is the curse.

If we combine these teachings, we may see ourselves individually and collectively as possessing the free will to choose how we see — understand — what a mitzvah truly is.

A Deeper Dive

Have you ever wondered why one person experiences a particular occurrence as a blessing and another person experiences the same or similar event as a curse? Or, why one person absolutely sees God in a given moment and another person absolutely does not?

Responding to these questions, Rabbi Alan Lew (twenty-first c., United States) believes the secret lies within the first word in our verse, "see," which he understands to mean "pay attention to." He enjoins us: pay attention to "your life. Every moment in it is profoundly mixed. Every moment contains a blessing and a curse. Everything depends on our seeing our lives with clear eyes, seeing the potential blessing in each moment as well as the potential curse, choosing the former, forswearing the latter. *Parshat* [the Torah portion] *Re'eh* begins with a concretization of this spiritual reality, a ritual that renders this invisible reality visible."[3]

Rabbi Lew is entreating us to dedicate time to training ourselves to become increasingly aware of what is already occurring at any given moment in our lives. Our capacity to see and then to respond mindfully to whatever occurs around us is the spiritual practice that "renders this invisible reality [the potential blessing in every moment] visible."

Rabbi Lew goes on to explain what it is we need to realize in order to appreciate the moment as a blessing:

The will of God is present every moment. Every moment contains the capacity for good and evil, life and death, a blessing and a curse, and everything depends on our choice. . . . We learn that it is a matter of consciousness. . . . We have to come to see our life very clearly, clearly enough so that we can discern the will of God in it, so that we can tell the difference between the blessings and the curses, so that these things are arrayed before us . . . that sliver of eternity on which we stand and that we call the present moment.[4]

Many years ago I was far from sensing "the will of God in every moment." I felt more spiritually cursed than I care to remember. Even though I dressed the part of an Orthodox Jew, I did not feel a connection to God. To the never-ending and demanding observance of rabbinically legislated laws, yes, but not to God.

One early morning during this time, shortly before sunrise, I found myself perched on the top of the Masada archaeological site in Israel with a group of students. Facing east, high up on its top, we positioned ourselves to witness the sun rise up from the Jordanian horizon on the other side of the Dead Sea, and I sought out a space of solitude. A sliver of the sun emerged, radiating its illuminating light to the world, proclaiming the arrival of a new day. After gazing at this unfolding wonder, I began to write in my journal—and suddenly realized that it was so quiet, all I could hear was my pen moving along on the page. I stopped writing as I felt called to sit in silence. In this moment, experiencing the sun rising and shining, I sensed the presence of my Creator—the wonder, the love, the protection, the Source of life. I whispered to myself, "Wow, what a blessing!" For me it was not a blessing because it was magnificent, but rather because in the stunning quietude I actually sensed the Divine Presence which had long eluded me.

Like a game of hide and seek, even those of us who find God at times in our lives may not at other times. Grappling with this, Rabbi Joseph B. Soloveitchik (twentieth c., United States) concluded that the religious experience of faith "oscillates between ecstasy in God's companionship and despair when [one] feels abandoned by God."[5] This insight may be in keeping with the idea that "every moment contains the capacity for a blessing and a curse."

The Piaseczner Rebbe (Kalonymus Kalmish Shapira, twentieth c., Poland) encourages us to actively choose to go after this blessing by always seeking out the Divine Presence: "We exhort you in the strongest terms: teach yourself to observe. In general, become a person who seeks out the Divine Presence everywhere. Perhaps in your looking you will uncover God's subtle presence and sense the holiness of His glory. And when you seek Him out, you will indeed find Him. Where will you find Him? In yourself and in everything around you."[6]

The Piaseczner teaches that intentional observation of any given moment can afford us a keener awareness of the blessing that is the Divine Presence already present in that moment. And in support of this he offers a radical reinterpretation of our verse. The "I" in "See, this day I set before you blessing and curse" means "It is the Holy Blessed One who places 'I' before us and this becomes the revelation of the Eternal Itself."[7] In other words, what is being set before us is not the blessing or the curse, but the "I" of the Eternal.

This innovative conception sidesteps the typical postmodern construct that makes value dependent on our feelings, in particular on whether we are experiencing pleasure or pain at any given moment. By the Piaseczner's understanding, feeling good about a situation or feeling pain in it is not the point. Rather, seeing the Divine in it is the blessing and not seeing the Divine in it is the curse. The aspiration here is consciousness, not an emotion.

In this light, with practice we might subjectively experience a paradox. If we hone the capacity to readily sense the blessing of the Divine Presence, we may experience this blessing even at a moment when we feel cursed by the particulars of the situation. This is the heart of the Piaseczner's *Aish Kodesh*, which he wrote from Rosh Hashanah in 1939 to Tisha b'Av 1942 in Warsaw, prior to his deportation to the Trawniki death camp. In the middle of the curse, he counterintuitively did see and experience the blessing of God's Presence.

Some of us might ask: What, then, is the first step? How do I actively seek out the Eternal in any given external moment? In my experience, whether or not we sense the Divine Presence in an external moment may depend significantly on whether we have already cultivated an awareness of the Divine Presence within our internal being, which we can then project onto the moment. If we do not sense God within us, it can be much harder for us to sense God outside of us.

If we open ourselves to seeing that in any given moment the Eternal places the Divine Presence before us, we may be able to change our relationship to that moment. If we exercise our free will to *choose* to see it in this way, to try to see the Divine Presence in every moment, we may uncover and reveal the blessing in that moment—a matter of subjective perception that is, in fact, the only possible ground of personal relationship.

This consciousness redeems us from the delusion that we are mere victims of our own life's circumstances. And that is a true blessing.

The Practice

1. Begin with breath awareness.
2. Then, reflect on the text.
3. Move to quieting down your mind.

These three steps are explained in detail in the introduction.

4. Visualize a moment in your life when you felt blessed. Feel yourself back in the moment. What other feelings come up for you when you feel blessed?

Hold that as you pause for a few mindful breathing cycles—breathing in the blessing and exhaling your feelings into the universe.

Now, imagine a moment in your life when you felt cursed. What other feelings does this provoke?

Hold this as you pause for a few mindful breathing cycles—breathing in the sense of being cursed and exhaling those feelings into the universe.

Now, from this place, imagine that you reach a fork. You need to decide: Do I choose 1) to continue the path of experiencing this moment solely as a curse or 2) the other fork that leads me to also see the Divine Presence in this same scenario.

Which fork do you choose?

If you are able to choose the second fork, what is your consciousness of the blessing in this dark moment?

Conclude your practice with one deep cleansing breath cycle. Feel life-giving breath moving through you: deeply inhale, pause, fully exhale, and pause.

How are you feeling now?

Shofetim

Cultivating Wholeheartedness

You must be wholehearted with the ETERNAL, your God.

Deut. 18:13

Where We Are

Moses instructs the Israelites that all traces of idol worship must be destroyed upon entering the Promised Land. He cautions everyone to be wary of false prophets and those who may entice the people to stray from Israelite culture.

The Torah enumerates the permitted animals and fowl for consumption. It is obligatory to help any poor or needy kindred in the land. Moses reviews the three annual pilgrimage festivals to Jerusalem's Holy Temple and reminds everyone never to arrive empty-handed. He specifies that the court system must exist in every city and that God will appoint a king. Seeking advice from fortune tellers is prohibited. Immediately following this prohibition, Moses conveys, "You must be wholehearted with the ETERNAL, your God."

At First Glance

Rashi (Shlomo Yitzhaki, eleventh c., France) comments (in relation to a midrash) that being wholehearted means "to walk with God completely and honestly, putting your hope in the Eternal and not inquiring about the future. Rather, accept completely whatever occurs. In that way you will be with God."[1]

His interpretation takes cues from the preceding biblical prohibition against inquiring into one's future ("Let no one be found among you . . . who is an augur, a soothsayer, a diviner, a sorcerer" [Deut. 18:10]). Rashi is intimating that relying on another human being to predict, interpret, or manipulate the unknown future distracts a person from being fully present with whatever occurs at the moment. Even worse, it can breed a misleading illusion of being able to control events, detracting and distracting from the sacred experience of being wholly present with God.

Nachmanides (Moses ben Nachman, thirteenth c., Spain and Acre, the Holy Land) translates *tamim* (heretofore rendered as "wholehearted") according to its other meaning, "to be perfect," and hence reads the verse as "You must be perfect with the ETERNAL, your God." He adds: "We should remain faithful in believing that only the Creator knows the future . . . and in this manner we become whole, indicating perfection, meaning this awareness is without blemish and deficiency."[2]

One might question Nachmanides' intent here. The Jewish tradition rarely encourages a person to strive for perfection. To deepen one's faith and be on a path toward our better selves, yes, but to reach a point of perfection whereby there is no room for further growth, no. Pragmatically as well, the human ability to maintain unwavering, perfect faith seems beyond reach.

Perhaps, then, Nachmanides the mystic is speaking aspirationally of the *potential* of our souls to be perfect. At minimum, he seems to expect us to exert significant effort to cultivate the *middah* of wholeheartedness as perfectly as possible. And we humans may even sense our own perfected wholeheartedness at times, even if this state of being is far from the norm.

By contrast, Chizkuni (Hezekiah ben Manoah, thirteenth c., France) treats this verse independently of the preceding verses. For him, "to be wholehearted with the ETERNAL your God" means "[to] be exclusively faithful in your relationship with the Divine."[3] He compares this to an intimate and exclusive relationship between two people which disallows either of the partners to entertain, or worse to actualize, intimacy with another person. Being wholehearted with God thus means not worshiping other gods as well.

I do wonder, though, whether Chizkuni might also be suggesting, "When you are wholeheartedly dedicated and faithful to God, then you will experience what it means to be completely intimate with the Eternal."

A Deeper Dive

I recall having a wonderful discussion with a Protestant theologian on the path to becoming a minister. As we were ending our chat, he exclaimed in astonishment, "You talk about God as if you are in a real relationship with God, far beyond believing in a theology of God's existence!" I replied that "I hope to always talk with my fellow human beings as if I am in a godly relationship with them as well." We both smiled at each other, wished each other well, and bid our goodbyes.

As I reflect back on that encounter, and this passage, I see the Eternal beneficently prescribing a remedy for each of us to help heal the world: "Be wholehearted with Me so you can then be wholehearted with My creations." We might each understand "Be wholehearted with Me" as teaching us to "Be wholehearted with the Divine in me." Then, from this healing way of being with ourselves, we may increasingly sense the Divine Presence in all of creation.

Noting that the Hebrew letters in the words for the nature (*ha-teva*) and God (*Elohim*) share the same numerical value of eighty six, the Orakh Le-Hayyim (Avraham Hayyim of Zloczow, eighteenth–nineteenth c., Ukraine) writes that "nature is not something separate from God, but rather God dwells within the natural world, always guiding it along."[4] He teaches that when we see nature, we see God. Nature is itself a sacred vessel for the Divine Presence. In fact, the Creator's guiding immanence in the world is its wholeness.

The Orakh Le-Hayyim encourages us to "endeavor to emulate the Creator" by cultivating wholeness within ourselves:

> A person's soul and body be completely unified without any sense of separation; whereby the soul leads the body. And not when the soul pulls in one direction and the body in the other. This is the meaning of "You must be wholehearted with the ETERNAL, your God." (Deut. 18:13). If you are whole within yourself, when your soul and body are in harmony as one entity without any separation and the soul is leading the body, *then* you will be with the Eternal your God. Just as God dwells within the natural world without any separation, whose

Presence permeates all the world and leads it, likewise, you be whole, where your soul leads your body in the natural world. And then, you will experience attachment to the Eternal your God.[5]

For the Orakh Le-Hayyim, just as the Creator dwells within a natural ecosystem "without any separation," we can too, by cultivating our own internal ecosystem. The spiritual aim is to bring our souls and bodies together in harmony, always with the soul at the helm leading the body. This state of inner wholeness overflows to being in harmony with the Eternal and allows the same for everyone and everything else in the Creator's world.

The Piaseczner Rebbe (Kalonymus Kalmish Shapira, twentieth c., Poland) provides practical advice on how to cultivate the *middah* of wholeheartedness: "Guard against those things that distance [your soul] and bury her in [y]our lowly and chaotic side. . . . [Instead] conduct [yourself] with simplicity and wholeheartedness in all of [your] affairs. . . . Speak from your heart, with wholeheartedness and simplicity."[6]

First, the Piaseczner describes what sabotages the spiritual practice of being wholehearted. Our yielding (even unintentionally and unconsciously) to the ego's default behavior of basic survival causes our souls to recede into a concealed and dormant state, "buried" in the midst of our doing everything possible (read: "chaos") to stay alive. This is the opposite of the Orakh Le-Hayyim's aspiration for us: "You are whole within yourself, . . . your soul and body are in harmony as one entity without any separation and the soul is leading the body." Without intentional spiritual practice, the body leads the soul and buries it as the default practice to remain alive. Intentional attention to our spiritual side allows instead our soul to lead the body.

Second, the Piaseczner teaches us how to fulfill the Orakh Le-Hayyim's vision: "Conduct [yourself] with simplicity and wholeheartedness in all of [your] affairs." He encourages us to be honest with ourselves so we can be truthful with others. Behaving transparently is "simple" because it lacks the complex manipulations that often accompany deceit of oneself and others. And for the Piaseczner, machinations thwart our efforts to cultivate wholeheartedness with God—putting up a barrier between our deceptive conduct and our spiritual awareness of the truth. If we are not wholehearted and authentic when we engage with another person, we rob ourselves of the opportunity offered us to be with God as part of this relationship.

At times, though, full candor may be challenging, may not be what the other person wants of us, and may lead to hurt feelings. At times like these, the Piaseczner advises: "If you find that responding in this [truthful] way will be harmful to you or you have some other obstacle to speaking truthfully, simply say, as our sages advise, 'I do not know' (*Berachot* 4a). But do not twist and bend things to produce a convoluted response that lacks sincerity and simplicity."[7]

I have found this "simple" advice to work remarkably well in many if not most of the challenging interpersonal situations I encounter. Many times, I truly do not know the best recourse. By saying, "I do not know," I cannot be more honest.

The Piaseczner concludes: "If you make [conducting yourself with simplicity and wholeheartedness] a regular practice, your heart and soul will become revealed. Your deeds, words, perspectives, and all your interactions with others will be filled with your soul and her power, as [the soul] emanates from your innermost self, directing you: 'grow, behave and be in continuous relationship with God in all of your affairs.'"[8]

Here the Piaseczner reminds us that the practice of being wholehearted and simply truthful helps to restore the exquisite balance of our spiritual ecosystem. Cultivating the *middah* of wholeheartedness allows our soul to emerge from her state of dormancy and hiddenness and assume her role as the leading energy in our inner being. When our spiritual garden blossoms and our inner ecosystem's balance is restored, *then* we are living with God.

The Practice

1. Begin with breath awareness.
2. Then, reflect on the text.
3. Move to quieting down your mind.

These three steps are explained in detail in the introduction.

4. Visualize a time in your life when you sensed equanimity and whole-heartedness within yourself, or the closest you have ever experienced being in this state.

Direct your awareness to your breath and sense the simple and complete nature of your inhalations and exhalations. We simply are being breathed into. Be in that live affirming state. Try to bring this sense of wholeheartedness into the present. If you can, try to feel your mind, body, heart, and soul in sync with one another.

What feelings come up for you when you experience being aligned (or more aligned)? Is an intuitive awareness of the Divine Presence part of this moment?

Again, direct your awareness to your breathing cycles. Breathe in the energy of potential inner harmony and, as you exhale, feel yourself leaning into that space. Now imagine you will be able to cultivate and nurture a more harmonious inner garden just by adding one important, secret ingredient. What will your spiritual fertilizer be?

Ki Tetse'

Eliciting Compassion to Flow from Above

> If, along the road, you chance upon a bird's nest, in any tree or on the
> ground, with fledglings or eggs and the mother sitting over the fledglings
> or on the eggs, do not take the mother together with her young. Let the
> mother go, and take only the young, in order that you may fare well and
> have a long life.
>
> Deut. 22:6–7

Where We Are

Moses announces that God will send prophets to convey God's word.
Upon entering the Promised Land the people must extend peace offerings before waging war with any existing populations. Extending honor
to one's parents is of extreme importance. The text now introduces the
verses under discussion.

At First Glance

Notably, the reward of long life for sending away the mother bird before
taking her young is shared with only one other mitzvah: honoring one's
parents, which seems significantly more difficult to perform. The Talmud
comments on the seemingly overly generous reward: "If in the case of an
easy command which involves no monetary loss, Scripture states 'you
may fare well and have a long life', it follows so much more that this at
least will be the reward for the fulfillment of more difficult commands."[1]

   Ibn Ezra (Abraham ibn Ezra, eleventh–twelfth c., Spain) interprets
"in order that you may fare well" innovatively as meaning "God will
have compassion on you and do good things for you."[2] Even though
the verse does not state outright that sending away the mother bird
is a compassionate act, Ibn Ezra is teaching that this mitzvah requires

us to show compassion—and, by cause-and-effect, when we do, God responds in kind.

Maimonides (Moses ben Maimon, twelfth c., Spain and Egypt) comments as well on how this mitzvah demonstrates compassion:

> The Torah does not want the mother bird to experience the pain she will endure when seeing her chicks being taken away. The situation is analogous to the prohibition of not slaughtering the calf and its mother on the same day (Lev. 22:28), so that the cow does not watch the death of her calf. Human logic cannot understand the love of a mother animal for the fruit of her womb. Rather, through the power of our imagination we can assume this response to be embedded in the psyche of the animal. If the Torah is so concerned with the feelings of birds and four-legged domesticated animals, how much more is it concerned with the feelings of human beings![3]

For Maimonides, the mitzvah of sending away the mother is not about reward or cause-and-effect. He stresses the paramount value the Torah places on behaving with compassion to birds and animals and suggests that this legislation is designed to teach us to distance ourselves from acts of cruelty. By becoming more sensitive to the quality of life of God's creations (with the mother bird and the cow as examples), we may become increasingly sensitive to the quality of life of our fellow human beings.

A Deeper Dive

The mystics go deeper. The fellow human beings to whom we show compassion include ourselves, each of us being one of God's creations. And cultivating compassion within each of us is a vital spiritual practice in the human-Divine partnership.

The Kedushat Levi (Levi Yitzchak of Berditchev, eighteenth c., Poland and Ukraine) begins by quoting from the Talmud: "The Talmud teaches that one who says in prayer, 'Your compassion reaches even to a bird's nest! Be as compassionate with us' is to be silenced.[4] This person applies the trait of compassion to God, when actually this is a 'command of the King to His servants.'"[5]

The Kedushat Levi says it is a mistake to attribute human ethical traits to God. Then we fall into the common trap of creating God in our human image, rather than seeing ourselves as created in God's image. The Talmud objects to the assumption that this mitzvah exemplifies God's compassion, especially since the verses commanding this action make no mention of compassion. Rather, the verse is instructing us that it is the divine will for each of us to extend random acts of compassion and kindness in the Creator's world. The broader principle is to always ask oneself, "What is God asking of me by this mitzvah?" In this verse, we are taught to be kind and compassionate.

The Kedushat Levi continues: "A person who demonstrates compassion towards creation causes an awakening of compassion Above, and the Supernal One demonstrates compassion to that person as well."[6] This teaching, rooted in the Zohar, reflects that we are in partnership with the Divine.[7] Spiritually, I have found this to be deeply true. When I want something from God, such as manifesting the blessing of peace in the world, instead of asking for it (or in addition to praying for peace), I turn inward to discover that I myself possess the capacity to help bring peace to the world by mindfully behaving in a more peaceful way with my fellow human beings. I model toward others what I am seeking from my Creator. This in effect opens the channel above to bless me with a deeper sense of peace—affording me a glance, even just for a fleeting moment, of a world blessed with peace. This understanding echoes the well-known quote attributed to Mahatma Gandhi (twentieth c., India): "Be the change you want to see in the world."

At heart, the Kedushat Levi is inspiring us to fulfill the Torah's broader mandate for the Jewish people—and, by extension, all human beings: that each of us embody the godly. As the Creator and Sustainer of life, God has bequeathed human beings both the privilege and responsibility to share this sacred endeavor in partnership. When we realize the need for God to bless the world—with more compassion, with more peace—to support this vision, we ourselves act in divine partnership.

The Kedushat Levi further explains this collaborative partnership:

The Blessed Holy One is continuously causing compassion to flow upon us. However, if at times we lack exhibiting compassion towards others, this results in us creating an obstacle, precluding us from receiving this flow of compassion. However, the Blessed Holy One as the Source of great compassion and kindness transforms our hearts, giving us the strength and courage of heart to be more in service to our Creator—and the Creator's creations. Thus, we pray, "You, the Eternal, do not hold back Your compassion from me." (Ps. 40:12) Meaning, may I not be the cause of the blockage that prevents me from receiving Your compassion.[8]

To me, this is one of the Jewish tradition's strongest and clearest articulations of how we are meant to be in this world. Against the backdrop of postmodern culture, where a sense of entitlement and a "what's in it for me" attitude often seem to prevail, we can propel ourselves "to be more in service to our Creator—and the Creator's creations." From this place, we can infuse the world with more kindness and compassion. Before we receive, we must take the initiative to give.

The Kedushat Levi assures us that God's treasure chest of compassion with which to bless human beings remains constant and endless. We ourselves need to remove our own blockages preventing us—and the world—from receiving it. In this light, the Kedushat Levi concludes:

God's commandment that "You may not take the mother along with her offspring" does not reflect God's compassion upon the bird. If God "wanted" to be compassionate, He would not have had to command us to do so. God could protect the bird without us, for God surely possesses the capacity to do so. God's intent here was rather that we stir and awaken our inner quality of compassion by expressing this compassion toward the bird. You gave us this commandment so we would behave with compassion, which then arouses Your compassion toward us.[9]

This insight into our inner dimension echoes a teaching from the Dalai Lama (twentieth–twenty-first c., Tibet and India): "From my own limited experience, I have found that the greatest degree of inner tranquility comes from the development of love and compassion. The more we care for the happiness of others, the greater our own sense of well-being becomes. . . . It is the ultimate source of success in life."[10]

For me, experiencing inner tranquility and enhanced well-being in the Jewish sense equates to my experiencing an encounter with the Divine within me. Cultivating the *middah* of compassion "below" contributes to my own higher awareness of who I essentially am—the manifestation of godliness in the world. I experience eliciting compassion from above through my actions that set it in motion.

Compassion is a seed that can be planted in anyone's garden. May we all plant this seed in our inner garden of divine consciousness so we can draw more compassion flowing from above.

The Practice

1. Begin with breath awareness.
2. Then, reflect on the text.
3. Move to quieting down your mind.

These three steps are explained in detail in the introduction.

4. Visualize a time when you yearned to experience self-compassion or kindness or a reprieve from self-judgment, but despite your best efforts, you could not attain this. Bring this into your present. How does not having this need fulfilled feel right now? Is your inner voice weighing in? If so, how? Might you be inclined to turn to God to bless you with compassion?

Mindfully receive a deep inhalation, imagining it as the breath of limitless possibilities. Now, fully exhale, imagining it as opening your awareness to your capacity to perform an act of random kindness and compassion. What would this look like? Visualize your action and observe what feelings arise from your heart.

Pause for a moment and, experiencing your breath entering you, moving through you and exiting, simply remain in the energy of compassion. As you desire this channel of compassion from above to remain open, now visualize yourself sharing this gift with others around you. What would you do? What would this feel like?

Again, pause, and with the embodied sensations of receiving and returning your life-infusing breath, imagine that by sharing this gift of your inner compassion with others, you begin to sense increased compassion within you and around you.

Remaining in this expanded energy of compassion, ask yourself: Is there a seed in this practice that I might cultivate?

Ki Tavo'

Dynamically Walking in the Eternal's Ways

> You have affirmed this day that the ETERNAL is your God—in whose ways
> you will walk, whose laws and commandments and rules you will observe,
> and whom you will obey. . . . You will be established as a holy people if
> you keep the commandments of the ETERNAL your God, walking in those
> ways.
>
> Deut. 26:17, 28:9

Where We Are

Moses recounts the laws governing marriage, as well as several mitzvot
that address ethical behavior such as not embarrassing people in public, giving gifts to the poor, and taking care of orphans and widows. In
business transactions, honest weights and measures must prevail. The
first fruits of each year are to be brought to Jerusalem and given to the
priests. The text now conveys one of the final 613 mitzvot in the Torah
(originally introduced in Deuteronomy 11:22): becoming a holy people
by walking in the Eternal's ways.

At First Glance

The midrash interprets the mitzvah of "walking" in God's ways (when
it is first introduced) to mean imitating the Divine's behavior: "Just as
the Blessed Holy One manifests compassion, lovingkindness, and righ-
teousness, so should you."[1] *Sefer HaHinuch* (published anonymously,
thirteenth c., Spain) suggests that this commandment means: "A person must choose for themselves in all of their matters and in all of their
actions—whether in eating, drinking, business, words of Torah, prayer,
conversation or in any other thing—the good path of integrity and never

to distance themselves to the extremes."[2] By this understanding, acting with integrity and walking along a balanced, middle path in life are also essential components of emulating God.

Approaching the verse from the negative side, the Chofetz Chaim (Yisrael Meir Kagan, nineteenth–twentieth c., Russia and Poland) cautions us: "We have been commanded to emulate the traits of the Holy One. . . . One who habituates himself to this evil trait [slanderous speech] does not walk in the ways of the Eternal, which is only to do good to others, and he does the opposite—wherefore the Torah designated [slanderous speech] as 'evil'—so that he also transgresses this positive commandment [i.e., 'walking in those ways']."[3]

A Deeper Dive

All three commentaries share a common thread: that the mitzvah of "walking in the ETERNAL's ways" requires us to emulate God's behavior in ways that manifest goodness. I would also suggest that there is no one specific way to dynamically walk with the Eternal while expressing our authentic selves. Our pathway to dynamically walk with God, if we choose it, is uniquely personal to each of us.

A deeper meaning of our passage hence addresses each of our souls. The Lubavitcher Rebbe (Menachem Mendel Schneerson, twentieth c., New York) observes: "A person may observe the legal requirements of the *mitzvot* without ascending to the higher awareness of the Divine afforded by the mitzvah. Spiritually, they merely remain in one place; their spiritual status is no different than it was before they observed the *mitzvah*."[4]

For the Lubavitcher Rebbe, the objective of *mitzvot* observance is experiencing attachment with the Divine. The word "walk" in our passage ("You have affirmed this day that the ETERNAL is your God—in whose ways you will walk") conveys the progression and movement essential for moving the mitzvah practitioner closer to God. If one does not observe this mitzvah "without ascending to the higher awareness of the Divine afforded by [it]," the result is spiritual stagnancy.

He develops this idea:

This *mitzvah* teaches that a person should observe the [other] *mitzvot* in a manner that moves them forward. The spur for this spiritual progress is the fact that the *mitzvot* are "G-d's ways," and so by "walking in them," one emulates Him. This invests the *mitzvot* with the potential to lift a person to a higher or deeper level of Divine service. When a person observes the *mitzvah* of "walking in G-d's ways," their Divine service brings overt spiritual progress. The potential for progress which souls are granted . . . is unlimited.[5]

The Lubavitcher Rebbe understands the mitzvah of walking in God's ways as cultivating an approach to observing all the other mitzvot — with movement, by infusing our observance with vitality and dynamism. The requirement of this specific mitzvah, unlike the others, legislates the desired *attitude* toward observing all the other action-centered mitzvot.

For example, I observe several mitzvot in my life (lighting Shabbat candles every Friday evening, participating in the annual Passover seder, uttering blessings before eating, for example). Because, externally, the traditional laws governing their observance remain the same, there's an inherent danger of stagnancy, that any of us might practice these mitzvot in mechanical, robotic ways.

Yet the Lubavitcher Rebbe teaches me how to also spiritually observe these same three mitzvot. My own internal awareness of the Divine inherent within the mitzvah is moving all the time. By cultivating mindfulness, paying attention to what already exists, I become emotionally attuned to what is new about the mitzvah experience both within me and around me. And in the novel moments existing in the mitzvah, I am able to experience the Divine Presence also in a new way.

Notably, the Piaseczner Rebbe (Kalonymus Kalmish Shapira, twentieth c., Poland) emphasizes that being mindful of one's emotional terrain when observing a mitzvah is part of what it means to be "walking" in the mitzvah. While the intellectual understanding of what is being required in one mitzvah may be different from another, the emotional experience of fulfilling both may be equally flat and stagnant, as if they were the same. He teaches:

You might think that only fleeting and insignificant feelings pass unnoticed because of this lack of attention [of the emotions]. Rather, complete mitzvot provide us with many opportunities to examine and be self-aware; yet whole mitzvot pass in the same way they came. A person may feel something inside himself and [yet] is unable to . . . describe and know what he is feeling. How is the sense of Yom Kippur different from Rosh HaShanah? What is unique about the emotional quality of Passover, and the rest of the holy times?[6]

Perhaps the Piaseczner Rebbe also means that if we do not cultivate emotional awareness as part of how we walk with the Eternal, we also risk not appreciating the difference each time we observe the same mitzvah, too.

The deep wisdom here has not been lost on me. Returning to one of the mitzvot mentioned above, even in the short span of the past five years I have participated in three very diverse Passover seders. The Covid pandemic allowed me to share a seder with only one other person, a close neighbor. Another year I hosted an all-women's seder in my home. Most recently I observed the seder with some of my children and grandchildren. In each case, the observance of the Passover seder mitzvot—telling the story of the Hebrews' liberation from Egyptian slavery, drinking four cups of wine or grape juice, eating matzah and bitter herbs—remained the same. However, my spiritual and emotional experience of each seder, as I encountered the Divine Presence within me and around me, was anything but stagnant. Instead, I *sensed and experienced* aliveness.

When I was with my neighbor, the pandemic had just begun and the streets of Jerusalem were surrealistically empty. We shared texts and ideas about how to experience spiritual freedom amid uncertainty. Unexpectedly, I sensed the Divine Presence guiding us, as if a sacred energy of awareness that we were doing what we could and were here for each other pierced through the intense foreboding. When I was with the group of women, all highly learned in Torah, my sense of closeness with the Divine emerged from immersion in the varied interpretive texts we shared—as if I came to the seder table spiritually hungry and thirsty and now I felt immensely satiated. When singing the traditional seder songs with my daughter and grandchildren I felt the divine miracle of transmitting our tradition moving through my veins—and, more than once, I felt so close to the Divine, I was brought to tears of gratitude and joy.

Going even deeper, the Lubavitcher Rebbe connects observance of a mitzvah with the essence of one's soul:

> The *mitzvot* become G-d's ways, invested with His unlimited power, when their observance is motivated by the essence of the soul, which is an actual part of G-d. Divine service draws the essence of the soul into a particular *mitzvah*. This is the intent of the words of the *Midrash* above ["*you* should emulate G-d"]: "You" refers to the soul. When a person's Divine service is motivated by these qualities . . . graciousness, mercy, and piety . . . the person's efforts bring about the potential for unlimited progress. This will lead to a heightened spiritual consciousness.[7]

The Rebbe introduces the radical idea that walking in the Eternal's ways infuses the energy of our souls, and not merely our bodies, into the mitzvot. The part of you that is "you," your essence, your soul, is the part with which you imitate the Divine. While your external body goes through the motions of the mitzvah, your soul spiritually walks in the Eternal's ways. And as your soul vivifies your body, the soul does the same to the "body" of the mitzvot.

Dynamically walking in the Eternal's ways through this heart-centered approach becomes a never-ending process—an ongoing consciousness of the Divine in its, and our own, infinite capacity to be alive.

The Practice

1. Begin with breath awareness.
2. Then, reflect on the text.
3. Move to quieting down your mind.

These three steps are explained in detail in the introduction.

4. Visualize what it would be like to walk with the Eternal One. When you hear those words what thoughts move through your mind? What feelings does this image bring up for you?

Pause for a moment and breathe this image into your internal being. Feel its energy move through you as you begin to exhale.

Now imagine emulating a godlike trait that might enhance your experience of walking with the Eternal. What trait would that be?

Again, pause for a moment and breathe this godly trait into your internal being. Feel its energy move through you as you begin to exhale.

Now imagine a mitzvah you could adopt that might bring you even closer to this godlike trait. What mitzvah would that be? Would it allow you to express your authentic self? What would you need to do so that when you practice this mitzvah, you feel alive?

Again, pause for a moment and breathe this mitzvah into your internal being. Feel its energy move through you as you begin to exhale.

Imagine now you are expanding your awareness of the Divine through the mitzvah's practice—as if, through your own actions, you are now walking with the Eternal. Feel the dynamic movement traveling through you, and then gently exhale your breath into the universe.

What are you feeling now?

Nitsavim / Va-yelekh

Connecting in Vulnerability

> And the ETERNAL your God will circumcise your heart, and the hearts of
> your offspring, to love the ETERNAL your God with all your heart, and with
> all thy soul, in order that you may live.
>
> Deut. 30:6[1]

Where We Are

After a rather lengthy account of both the blessings for fulfilling the
commandments and admonitions for disobedience, Moses issues his
final charge to his people. By faithfully observing all the terms of the
covenant, they will succeed in all they do. Now, in our verse, Moses
expresses a divine intention in a rather odd figure: the Eternal will circumcise their hearts and their children's hearts as well.

At First Glance

Our verse echoes an earlier mitzvah: "Circumcise the foreskin of your
hearts" (Deut. 10:16).[2] Although mitzvot are often repeated in the Torah,
this recurrence is unique in one respect.[3] Whereas previously the fulfillment of the requirement falls upon each individual, in our verse God
actually facilitates the obligatory action: "And the ETERNAL your God
will circumcise your heart."

Rashi (Shlomo Yitzhaki, eleventh c., France) explains that the original command to circumcise the foreskin of the heart means "You shall
remove the closure and cover that is on your hearts [which prevent My
words gaining entrance to them]."[4] Sforno (Obadiah ben Jacob Sforno,
fifteenth–sixteenth c., Italy) adds that the foreskin and thickening of
the heart mean "prejudices [in the heart] that afflict your intelligence,"
which therefore must be removed.[5]

266

Rabbeinu Bahya (Bahya ben Asher ibn Halawa, thirteenth–fourteenth c., Spain) teaches that the foreskin of the heart refers to "a negative character trait which inhibits development of a personality to its full potential."[6] And Ibn Ezra (Abraham Ibn Ezra, eleventh–twelfth c., Spain) comments rather cryptically on why this command is repeated differently, with now the Eternal stepping in: "Moses says that unlike the circumcision of the flesh, which you are obligated to execute, God will help you and will circumcise your heart and the heart of your seed."[7]

A Deeper Dive

Reading Ibn Ezra through a spiritual lens, we can see him distinguishing between the emotional, spiritual heart and the flesh. It is arguably the heart, more than the flesh, that is the seat of our human vulnerability. Even if we humans logically understand that becoming more vulnerable is essential for connecting with both the Divine and other human beings, many times we just aren't able to do this sacred work. And so the Eternal, in divine awareness of human limitations, intervenes, helping us, and our children, open up our hearts.

Yet, we might ask, why *should* the Eternal make us more vulnerable? Since vulnerability puts one at risk of attack and harm, isn't being so exposed at odds with a fundamental value, life, and with what the Eternal wants for us?

Contemporary speaker Simone Knego responds: "Through my own experience, I've learned that it is through embracing vulnerability that we can experience authentic connections with others."[8] Humans have been created to yearn for connection—both with our own souls and with our fellows: Gensis (2:18) teaches, "It is not good for the Human to be alone." U.S. Surgeon General Dr. Vivek Murthy notes: "You can feel lonely even if you have a lot of people around you, because loneliness is about the quality of your connections."[9] Writer Anaïs Nin explains, "And then the day came when the risk to remain tight in a bud was more painful than the risk it took to blossom."[10]

In my experience, the risk I had to take to blossom was to be willing to expose my own vulnerability. I finally reached the point when I could no longer resist those "tight as a bud" feelings pressing from my inside out. When at last I pushed past survival mode, opening my heart to express this very vulnerability, I was astounded to find myself connecting more deeply, both with other people and with the Divine. Removing the thick protective covering over my heart, I realized, meant that I not only wanted to survive—I wanted to *thrive*.

A noncircumcised heart is a closed heart—dulled and insensitive. A circumcised heart is an open heart. The choice between them might seem obvious. And yet, we may not be able to experience the possibility of a wondrous connection with our deeper selves and with another person without actually being deeply hurt by that choice. There is no guarantee that we will not suffer from disappointment, disillusionment, and distress.

So, we may find ourselves asking, "Do I even believe in this process? And do I desire this closeness enough to take the risk of it not working out?" Exactly because of the fear of hurt and uncertainty that comes with cultivating vulnerability, we might conclude, "I cannot do this alone without divine intervention and guidance." From there we might take the step of entreating the Divine: "God, I need you to help me cultivate the required vulnerability to sense nearness to You."

This, then, is how I understand the Eternal's circumcision of my heart, and yours. Recognizing that even in our relationship with the Divine we hesitate, the Eternal invites us to become closer with ourselves and others via spiritual circumcision. Knowing our ego's need to survive stands in the way of opening our hearts, the Divine responds to our plea by strengthening our faith and trust to risk being raw and vulnerable for the reward of being ready for connection.

Accentuating the difference between a circumcised and an uncircumcised heart, the Piaseczner Rebbe (Kalonymus Kalmish Shapira, twentieth c., Poland) exhorts: "Awaken within our hearts a spark of desire and awareness . . . [so that] we will know that it is not enough to be like a mere servant, the son of a maidservant. It is true that he too serves and obeys the King, but his work is to grind away at the millstones, far from the King. . . . Rather, this is a service with a closed mind and a dulled heart."[11]

The Piaseczner is teaching that even full service to God can still leave us feeling distant from our Creator, if it lacks the circumcision of the heart. By contrast, he explains: "Whenever we do God's work, whether in learning Torah, prayer or observing any of the *mitzvot*, [we can] sense our closeness to the Divine with an open mind and heart."[12] Unlike in the first scenario, here the divine service *emphasizes* the opening of our heart. This emotional openness, which might be likened to a child's pure and spontaneous outpouring of emotion for a parent, is understood to remove any obstacle that prevents sensing closeness to the Divine. When we bring forth abundant feelings into divine service, these in turn enliven our lives, infusing them with spiritual oxygen and the joy of closeness to our spiritual parent.

As we open our hearts to our feelings, the Piaseczner Rebbe suggests that we trust that each feeling—whether we feel pleasure or pain—is a key to unlock the gateway that connects us with our souls, the Divine Presence within each of us:

> For . . . every awakening, even if derived from within the physical experience, is a key to the soul. Every feeling that is connected to something of "this world" opens a spark of our soul, and with this our soul becomes revealed a little bit. . . . When we experience moments of inspiration and awe during the day . . . use such an occurrence as a key to your soul. Any time we feel deeply—even with business concerns and other physically related matters, whether we are feeling sadness or joy, the feeling contains something of a revelation of the soul. She simply is clothed in this mundane situation. Take advantage of this auspicious moment.[13]

Each feeling, rooted as they all are in vulnerability, provides yet another key for connection. The spiritual work to reveal this wonder lies within the mitzvah of gently extricating the thick membrane barring entry to our hearts.

The Practice

1. Begin with breath awareness.
2. Then, reflect on the text.
3. Move to quieting down your mind.

These three steps are explained in detail in the introduction.

4. Visualize a time when you sensed that a wall separated your mind from your heart or emotions. Revisit this moment. Even if you are thinking clearly and you know your feelings are there, still you sense a distance from any emotional responses, as if a tightly sealed lid covers your heart.

Now, on your next inhalation, imagine accepting that the time has arrived to promote your own holistic well-being. Your desire to connect with your own true self far exceeds the emotional wall erected. As you exhale, release any impediments to taking the next step.

Pause for a moment. Now, on your next inhalation, imagine that you are inhaling the potential to change from being close-hearted to open-hearted. You might also inhale asking God to help support you in removing the thick membrane sealing your heart. Then, when you exhale, picture yourself doing whatever you feel ready and willing to do for this opening to manifest.

And you do it! Your heart is exposed, vulnerable, and naked.

Pause for a moment. On your next inhalation, imagine welcoming any feelings that rush in, whatever they are, with equanimity. Exhale any judgments about not-so-pleasant feelings. Inhale the belief that any not-so-pleasant feelings are your God appointed teachers, too. Exhale all criticisms.

Continue to inhale openness and exhale judgments as you ready yourself to bare your heart, perhaps to another person or to the Divine in you.

What does it feel like to begin to circumcise your heart?

Ha'azinu

Remembering Our Third Parent

> Listen, O heavens, and I will speak; and let the earth hear the words of my mouth. . . . You have forgotten the Rock who begot you; you have forgotten the God who delivered you.
>
> Deut. 32:1,18[1]

Where We Are

Moses proclaims to the people that the Eternal is giving them a choice between life and the good, or death and the evil. He urges everyone to choose life. He gives a blessing to his successor, Joshua, to be strong and courageous. We now arrive at Moses' forty-three stanza poem calling upon heaven and earth to bear witness to both the tragedies and the ultimate joy that will come upon Israel.

At First Glance

Ibn Ezra (Abraham ibn Ezra, eleventh–twelfth c., Spain) explains that Moses chooses the heavens and the earth to bear witness because "they exist forever."[2] In other words, Moses believes the poem's sentiments will endure as long as the heavens and earth exist.

The Netziv (Naftali Zvi Yehuda Berlin, nineteenth c., Poland) suggests what precisely it is that the Israelites have forgotten ("You have forgotten the Rock who begot you"), stating, "You have forgotten the kindness that God has bestowed upon you by birthing you into existence."[3]

Sforno (Obadiah ben Jacob Sforno, fifteenth–sixteenth c., Italy) offers a different reason why the Israelites have "forgotten the Rock." Since the Hebrew word *teh-shee*, commonly translated as "forgotten," literally means "weakened," Sforno makes use of that meaning to comment:

"Turning your attention [from Torah] to earthly pleasures weakens your wisdom and awareness of God's greatness."[4]

Rashi (Shlomo Yitzhaki, eleventh c., France) explains Moses' next utterance, "You have forgotten the God who delivered you," to mean "Who brought you forth from the womb"—essentially a reminder that God is our "Supernal Parent" who birthed (delivered) us into existence.[5]

A Deeper Dive

The Piaseczner Rebbe (Kalonymus Kalmish Shapira, twentieth c., Poland) devoted his life to teaching how we can ensure that our connection with the Divine remains intact—and that we will not forget who brought us forth into the world. His book on cultivating a higher consciousness that perceives the Divine Presence, *B'nei Machshava Tova* (*Conscious Community*), begins by invoking our verse, "You have forgotten the God who delivered you." Forgetting God, he maintains, "is the underlying factor that distances a person from God."[6]

He continues: "Whenever we do God's work, whether in learning Torah, prayer or observing any of the *mitzvot*, we may be able to sense our closeness to God."[7] The Piaseczner is teaching that *if we do not forget God*, we may experience nearness to the Divine through these three traditional Jewish modalities. He elaborates: "Everyone knows that when people envision themselves standing in God's presence and literally sense before Whom they stand, they are not subject to distraction or temptation to wander [away from paying attention]."[8]

Observance by itself—of communal prayer, of Torah study, and of the mitzvot—does not guarantee that any of us will experience connection with the Divine. If our minds wander away from the Divine Presence, our hearts are liable to follow. This in turn may cause us to give into temptations that will only increase our remoteness from God and promote forgetfulness of God.

Therefore, he holds, to deeply connect to the Divine Presence, each of us would best cultivate mindfulness, with focused intentional awareness on what we are experiencing *within* ourselves: "All our work must center on how to strengthen our mindfulness: how to broaden it, empower it, enhance it, so we can sense our connection to God more consistently."[9]

By redirecting our focus to mindfulness, we not only push back on the distractions, but the distractions themselves become weaker. The feeling of distance becomes less prevalent, and we become increasingly more likely to experience spiritual intimacy with our Creator.

This construct largely parallels strength training. Generally speaking, if we gain muscle mass, we can lift heavier weights, and then we can gain even more muscle mass. In the spiritual fitness program, the closer we feel to the Divine, the more likely we are to sense subtle aspects of the Divine Presence and become aware of the depth and breadth of God's Presence. This awareness is the spiritual muscle that can grow with the appropriate mindfulness training.

Unlike the body in a physical fitness regime, though, the soul does receive "bonus" days—moments in time that manifest the Divine Presence through a more pristine lens. For example, some of us may feel the Divine Presence more acutely on a special occasion, such as a wedding, a birth, or a holiday. Yet, the Piaseczner notes, we cannot naturally sustain these spiritually infused moments: "The whole reason we fall away from the intensity of this awareness is: 'You have forgotten the God that delivered you.' A person descends from their mindfulness. One's consciousness is not always as pure, clear and strong as it may be on ... auspicious times."[10] Auspicious times may give us a spiritual jolt, a jump-start of sorts that may easily convince us of the truth of the Divine Presence right now. But once these moments pass, we "descend from our mindfulness," forgetting who we essentially are—a created being kept alive by our Creator.

Many years ago, as a teenager, I experienced a painful moment of "descending from mindfulness." But instead of forgetting my third parent, I forgot my own mother, the main nurturer of my life, who believed in me more than I did myself. It was when I was about sixteen years old: I completely forgot to acknowledge Mother's Day. Waking up that Sunday morning I realized I had forgotten to buy a gift or flowers, or at the very least, a card to show my mother that I remembered her honored status in our family. To make matters worse, rather than accept responsibility for my forgetfulness and apologize, I justified my behavior by belittling the holiday.

My mother seldom requested much of me, but she looked at me that Sunday morning with such obvious hurt that it etched its way into my permanent memory bank. Her disappointed eyes penetrated my soul, and with calm and hurt, which made me feel worse, she said "You can forget my birthday and I will not be hurt. But for my first-born child to forget the day that honors my becoming a mother is almost unforgivable. But because I am your mother, I forgive you. But—never ever forget who brought you into the world again!" I never imagined that many decades later that phrase would echo back to me through sacred words in the Torah.

And, until she passed some fifty-plus years later, I never did forget. I made sure never to allow any distractions to the point where I would forget to celebrate my mother's motherhood. As I reflect back on this incident, what now becomes apparent is that I actually hurt myself more than my mother. The idea of being so strongly distracted to the point of forgetfulness left me feeling regretful, empty, less alive.

Bringing this example to our relationship with God, we could probably spend the rest of our lives in theological discussion over whether in fact God "feels" and if so, how. In a sense, though, that may not matter so much as what *we* feel. By forgetting the importance of our relationship with God, we may well bring hurt and disappointment upon ourselves.

To counter "descent from mindfulness," the Piaseczner argues for cultivating mindfulness as part of our daily lives. I believe some of his words benefit from repetition:

Even if someone would want to strengthen and empower his mind and consciousness, he would be unable to sustain this mindfulness consistently for any significant period of time. Therefore, all our work must center on how to strengthen our mindfulness: how to broaden it, empower it, enhance it, so we can sense our connection to God more consistently. And not only during [the "bonus" days discussed above]. . . . Rather, so that our consciousness will be clearly and strongly connected to holiness at all times.[11]

The key that unlocks the gate to becoming more sensitive to our internal soul-being lies with consistent spiritual practice. The Piaseczner assumes the role of spiritual fitness trainer by coaching us to show up and do the work to cultivate the *middah* of remembering our third parent.

How exactly do we do that? Let us return to, and expand upon, his earlier guidance: "Everyone knows that when people envision themselves standing in God's presence and literally sense before Whom they stand, they are not subject to distraction or temptation to wander [away from paying attention]. [But] the opposite is true: they are moved to pour forth their entire spirit and soul in deep and sincere words to God until they seem to be completely absorbed in [connection with] the Blessed One through their words."[12] Focusing on the moment as an opportunity to stand in God's presence, visualizing or mentally and emotionally imagining a direct encounter with God, and holding this image clearly in our minds may naturally awakens our hearts to sense an intimate divine connection.

I would suggest that the Piaseczner does not mean for us to hold a physical image of God in our minds, for God is beyond physicality. Rather, we can devote ourselves wholeheartedly to try to sense or to reexperience a previous connection with God through a spiritual encounter with our own soul. By doing this, we remember the deeper part of ourselves—the wellspring from which we draw our lives. Cultivating mindfulness ensures that we will always remember our third parent and who we really are.

The Practice

1. Begin with breath awareness.
2. Then, reflect on the text.
3. Move to quieting down your mind.

These three steps are explained in detail in the introduction.

4. Visualize someone in your life with whom you enjoy a close and important relationship. Replay in your mind some of those moments

when you felt so close that even if either of you were to physically move away, the two of you would continue to cherish and nurture the relationship. What does this feel like? Can you even put words to the feelings that come from this special closeness? Sit with this for a few minutes, savoring the feelings that move through you.

Now imagine that one of the two of you does in fact move far away.

Could you imagine ever getting to a place where you experience forgetting the other person? Could this be avoided?

How could you continue ensuring the depth of closeness and affection? Would you cultivate a consistent practice to keep the connection alive?

Ve-zo't ha-berakhah

Touching Immortality

> So Moses the servant of GOD died there, in the land of Moab, at the
> command of GOD. . . . Never again did there arise in Israel a prophet
> like Moses—whom GOD singled out face to face, for the various signs
> and portents that GOD sent him to display in the land of Egypt, against
> Pharaoh and all his courtiers and his whole country, and for all the great
> might and awesome power that Moses displayed before all Israel.
>
> Deut. 34:5,10 12

Where We Are

Upon concluding his poem, Moses cautions the people to exert care and
attention to following the mitzvot because "it is your life" (Deut. 32:47).
God tells Moses to ascend Mount Nebo, where he will die in front of all
the people. Moses blesses each of the tribes individually and then the
entire nation. He ascends the mountain and gazes at the Land as the
Eternal says, "This is the Land which I swore to Abraham, to Isaac, and
to Jacob. . . . I have let you see it with your own eyes" (Deut. 34:4). This
brings us to our verses which conclude the Torah.

At First Glance

In our verse, "So Moses the servant of GOD died there, in the land of
Moab, at the command of GOD," the Hebrew *al pee* is translated as "at the
command of GOD." Yet the Talmud employs its literal translation, "by the
mouth of," understanding Moses' death as a result of "the Divine kiss."[1]

Rashi (Shlomo Yitzhaki, eleventh c., France) interprets "face to face"
("Never again did there arise in Israel a prophet like Moses—whom GOD
singled out face to face") to refer to the intimacy of Moses' relationship

with God. They were so close, Rashi says, Moses "used to speak with [God] at any time he desired."[2]

Nachmanides (Moses ben Nachman, thirteenth c., Spain and Acre, the Holy Land) interprets this as referring to the unique "face to face" way in which Moses received his prophetic visions—in contrast with all other prophets who received their visions from "the hand of God resting upon them."[3] Somehow Moses received his prophetic knowledge from the Divine through more intimate means than all other prophets.

The Torah's final words ("and for all the great might and awesome power that Moses displayed before all Israel") are understood to speak to the all-inclusive relationship Moses cultivated with the Israelites themselves. To the Bekhor Shor (Joseph ben Isaac Bekhor Shor, twelfth c., France) they acknowledge the unique way in which Moses conveyed the words of the Divine. While future prophets "would prophesy to limited groups or individuals . . . , everything that Moses did and said was before everyone, for all of Israel and the future generations."[4] The Chizkuni (Hezekiah ben Manoah, thirteenth c., France) asserts that Moses acted this way so that "everyone would believe him."[5]

A Deeper Dive

Echoing the Bekhor Shor above, the Netziv (Naftali Zvi Yehuda Berlin, nineteenth c., Poland) understands "before all Israel" to teach us that unlike the other prophets,

> Moses effected revelations of the Divine Presence before all of Israel: at the parting of the Sea, at Mount Sinai and [during the forty-year sojourn in the wilderness] in the *Mishkan* (Tabernacle). And through this revelation to all, he also revealed his strong love of God. And through this love he was able to reveal to everyone that it was the Blessed One Who created the world and everything in it. Therefore, at any time the Blessed One has the capacity to end the world's existence. But instead, the Blessed One leads the world and reveals His illuminating Face to all. And this is the purpose of creation: for everyone to know that God creates each of us.[6]

Rabbi Berlin emphasizes that the entirety of Moses' teachings leads to a quintessential realization: we are not random, independent entities existing by chance in the universe, but creations of the Divine. And only through the connective energy of love can we ever hope to truly believe this and internalize its consequences.

The Mevasser Tsedek (Yissakhar Dov of Zloczow, eighteenth c., Ukraine and Safed) pulls from the talmudic dictum "The teacher's lips continue speaking even in the grave" to explain that mitzvot which students of a deceased teacher fulfill allow the teacher to continue "to be in service to God even after death."[7] This is the case with Moses, who

> acquired great merit for himself . . . that he shared . . . with all of Israel. Hence, all our merit derives from Moses. Since he was the one who taught Israel how to be in service to God, whenever one of us worships God or fulfills a *mitzvah*, it is as though Moses is serving God. Thus, even after his death . . . he is still in service to the blessed Creator through the Children of Israel, who are all his disciples.[8]

If we continue to live by Moses' wisdom as transmitted to us through the generations, he remains alive in our spiritual DNA.

I understand these and many other teachings as testaments to an awesome truth ensconced in the Torah's wisdom. Learning Moses' Torah is both an individual and an infinite experience. The Torah is a continuum that outlives us all—we inherited it from previous generations, and it will be our legacy for future generations. Touching the Torah in this way touches immortality.

Every Friday, as the sun begins to dip into the horizon, I light my Shabbat candles, say the traditional blessing welcoming Her Presence into my home, take in a family photograph of myself as an infant with my mother, her mother, and her mother—four generations alive together—and wish each of them a Shabbat Shalom. Then my gaze returns to the dancing flames. I meditate on the wonder that I have merited to experience. I imagine the great-grandmother of my great-grandmother lighting her Shabbat candles in eighteenth-century Poland and tearfully beseeching

God, *Please let me have a descendent who can light Shabbat candles in Jerusalem.* I remain in total awe of this sacred moment of awareness. She is me — or I am her — six generations apart, brought together in Jerusalem through a spiritual time warp. And it does not stop there — for now I am also blessed to light Shabbat candles with my children and grandchildren, as they continue the tradition of touching immortality.

Rabbi David Schuck (twentieth–twenty-first c., United States) invokes a teaching from Rabbi Baruch of Mezhibizh (eighteenth–nineteenth c., Ukraine), who reminds us that as soon as the Torah is completed, we begin again with Genesis:

> Reb Baruch suggests that this is not accidental. He reminds us that when we use the Torah to approach those mysteries, something new emerges, a novel idea, and creation is renewed. This is the power of mindfulness. If we live with our eyes open to what is actually happening, moment to moment, and we allow ourselves to bring our attention to the truth of our experience, something new emerges. . . . The end of the Torah is also its beginning.[9]

The beginning and the end of the Torah can also be seen to reveal that a life of cultivating mindfulness equates with a heart-driven life. The final letter in the final word in the Torah is the *lamed* (in "Israel"), and the first letter that begins the first word is the *bet* (in *bere'shit*, "in the beginning"). In practice, the ending, *lamed*, beautifully flows into the "new" beginning, *bet*. As we finish chanting the Torah scroll in the synagogue with "Israel," we pause, and then immediately begin chanting "Bere'shit." The *lamed* at the end followed by the *bet* in the beginning spells *lev*, which means heart. And this is the heart of the matter. The Torah never ends. It continues ad infinitum through our hearts. Our heart is the exact midpoint, the dot in the present that connects all the Torah that precedes us with all the Torah that will follow us.

This is why a heart-centered life keeps us in the present. For every moment is both the "end of a beginning" and the "beginning of the next end." History pours into our hearts, and from our hearts into our future. This spiritual awareness touches our own immortality.

The Practice

1. Begin with breath awareness.
2. Then, reflect on the text.
3. Move to quieting down your mind.

These three steps are explained in detail in the introduction.

4. Visualize your own sense of touching immortality. What does immortality mean to you? What thoughts wander through you? What feelings does this bring up?

Pause for a moment, and for a few cycles, breathe in your imagined energy of immortality, gently hold it for a moment, and now release this energy back into the universe.

Now direct your attention to touching people who came before you—perhaps beloved family members in your biological or chosen family's lineage, people who have influenced you along your life journey and are no longer alive, or others from centuries ago whose ancient wisdom you embellish with your own. If you are able to, gaze at a picture or listen to a voice recording of any of these people, or reflect on their teachings or stories. What ideas or traditions passed on to you have helped shape you to be who you are? What embodied sensations or feelings does this bring up for you?

Pause for a moment and, for a few cycles, breathe in the energy of being with someone who is no longer living in this world but retains meaning for you in your life today. Gently hold this energy for a moment, and then, through your exhalation, release this sensation back into the universe.

Now direct your attention to someone or some people who will follow you—perhaps children or grandchildren in your biological or chosen family, or students or people you have mentored in your own way. Or, perhaps, imagine you are transmitting whatever gives your life meaning and a sense of purpose, or the values and principles you live by, to someone in the future. What do you imagine your legacy to be? How do you wish to be remembered? What do you want to bequeath to the next generation? And in what forms will these transmissions manifest — images, writings, recordings, oral teachings, art works?

Pause for a moment, and for a few cycles, as you breathe in, visualize yourself giving a piece of your own life — your soul — to the people who will follow you. Gently, hold this energy for a moment, and now release it back into the universe.

Now, for your final practice, a practice of ending and beginning all at once, imagine you are receiving life from those before you and simultaneously giving life to those after you. With one hand, experience yourself reaching back in your history to accept your legacy from those before you — and with your other hand, feel yourself reaching into the unknown future, to bequeath your legacy to those who will follow you. How does it feel to be in the middle of your own history and future at the same time?

Can you sense wonder in a tradition that affords you immortality?

NOTES

Introduction

1. Ariel Goldberg, "Leonard Cohen Speaks about G-d Consciousness and Judaism," 7:29. Recording of "Jewish Public Library of Montreal" panel, 1964. Youtube, December 6, 2016, www.youtube.com/watch?v=cFMm_x1qlPY.
2. Shapira, *B'nei Machshavah Tovah*, 7.
3. *Zohar*, 3:225.
4. Every Sabbath, it is customary to chant aloud in the synagogue a portion of the Five Books of Moses: the first five books of the Bible, Genesis through Deuteronomy. Each weekly portion is called *parashat ha-shavua*, the Torah portion of the week. While there are fifty-four portions altogether, when these are recited on the Sabbath, seven are combined—hence the forty-seven weekly portions.
5. Idel, "Rebbe of Piaseczno," 66.
6. See both Green and Mayse, *New Hasidism: Roots* and Green and Mayse, *New Hasidism: Branches*.
7. Maisels, "Self and Self-Transformation," 84.
8. See Maisels, "Self and Self-Transformation," 84–135.
9. Feigelson, *Eternal Questions*, xvii.
10. Kook, *Shmoneh Kvatzim*, 8:213.
11. Pinson, *Breathing and Quieting the Mind*, 108–9, 169.
12. Shapira, *Derekh haMelekh*, 654–55.
13. Mitchell, foreword to Boorstein, *That's Funny, You Don't Look Buddhist*, xi.
14. *Kohelet Rabbah*, chap. 7. Author's translation.
15. Rav Yaakov HaLevi Filber, "Bringing Fire from the Ordinary Person" [in Hebrew], *Arutz Sheva*, 2012, www.inn.co.il/news/523283.
16. Rabbi Moshe Alshich, *Alshich HaKadosh, Parshat Shemini*, in Magriso, *MeAm Lo'Ez: Avoth*, 8.
17. Nachman of Breslov, *Likutey Moharan*, vol. 5, 65:2.

Bere'shit

1. *Mishnah Sanhedrin* 4:5.
2. Rashi on Babylonian Talmud *Sanhedrin* 37a.
3. Rosen, *Quest for Authenticity*, 140n11.
4. *Mishnah Avot* 2:1.
5. Rosen, *Quest for Authenticity*, 140–41.

6. Kook, *Pinkas Yerushalayim*, entry 4.

7. Kook, *Olat Ra'ayah*, vol. 1, 330–31.

8. Rosen, *Quest for Authenticity*, 137.

9. Although this sentiment is often said to originate with Nechama Leibovitz, no specific source was located.

Noaḥ

1. Rashi on Gen. 6:14.

2. Rashi on Gen. 6:16.

3. Ibn Ezra on Gen. 6:16.

4. Israel ben Eliezer, *Keter Shem Tov*, 283.

5. Menachem Mendel Schneerson, "*Mayim Rabim, Shabbat Parshat Noach 1965*" [in Hebrew], Chabad, 2014, www.chabad.org/therebbe/article_cdo/aid/4313262 /jewish/page.htm.

6. Shapira, *B'nei Machshava Tovah*, 23.

7. Zev Wolf of Zhitomir, *Or Ha-Me'ir*, in Green, Leader, and Mayse, *Speaking Torah*, vol. 1, 472.

8. Shapira, *B'nei Machshava Tovah*, 24.

Lekh Lekha

1. Rashi on Gen. 12:1.

2. Rashi on Gen. 12:1.

3. Berezovsky, *Netivot Shalom, Bere'shit*, 66–67.

4. *Mishnah Avot* 5:3.

5. Maimonides on *Avot* 5:3.

6. *Bereshit Rabbah* 39, 2.

7. *Bereshit Rabbah* 39, 2.

8. Menachem Mendel Schneerson, adapted by Yanki Tauber, "The Three Journeys of Abraham," Chabad, 2017, www.chabad.org/parshah/article_cdo/aid/2613/jewish /The-Three-Journeys-of-Abraham.htm.

9. Jonathan Sacks, "The Courage Not to Conform," Parasha Lekh Lekha 2013, Rabbi Sacks Legacy, www.rabbisacks.org/covenant-conversation/lech-lecha/the-courage -not-to-conform/.

10. Adapted from Rosen, *Quest for Authenticity*, 23.

11. Rosen, *Quest for Authenticity*, 22–23.

12. Buber, *Tales of the Hasidim*, book 1, 251.

Va-yera'

1. Author's translation.

2. *Shavuot* 35b.

3. Rashi on Gen. 18:3. Note that according to the original Hebrew, Rashi explains that Abraham is speaking to *Adonai*, literally "my L/lord/Eternal/Sovereign." Rashi also points out that while Abraham invites all three strangers to stay, he actually

directs his remarks to the leader of the three, although it remains unclear how Abraham would have known who the leader was.

4. *Shabbat* 127a.
5. Jonathan Sacks, "Even Higher Than Angels," 2010, Rabbi Sacks Legacy, www .rabbisacks.org/covenant-conversation/vayera/even-higher-than-angels/.
6. Menachem Mendel Schneerson, "Erev Rosh HaShanah," 1962, translated by Eliyahu Tauger, Chabad, 2013, www.chabad.org/parshah/article_cdo/aid/2529658 /jewish/Likkutei-Sichot-Vayeira.htm.
7. I heard this teaching from Rabbi Sholom Brodt at a class in Jerusalem in 2013.

Ḥayyei Sarah

1. Author's translation.
2. Rashi on Gen. 23:2.
3. Rashi on Gen. 23:1.
4. *Berachot* 5a.
5. Shapira, *Drashot M'Shanot Ha'Za'am*, 91.
6. Shapira, *Drashot M'Shanot Ha'Za'am*, 91.
7. Shapira, *Drashot M'Shanot Ha'Za'am*, 91.
8. Shapira, *Drashot M'Shanot Ha'Za'am*, 91.
9. Abramson, *Torah from the Years of Wrath*, 82.
10. Reiser, "Sarah Our Rebbe," 16.

Toledot

1. Wineberg, *Lessons in Tanya*, vol. 1, 138.
2. Shapira, *B'nei Machshava Tovah*, 7.

Va-yetse'

1. *Tikkunei Zohar*, 17a.
2. Rashi on Gen. 28:21–22.
3. Nachmanides on Gen. 28:20.
4. Menachem Mendel Schneerson, *Likkutei Sichot*, vol. 25, 243–51, adapted by Yanki Tauber, "Home of Stone," Chabad, 2015, www.chabad.org/parshah/article_cdo /aid/2656/jewish/Home-of-Stone.htm.
5. *Eruvin* 13b.

Va-yishlaḥ

1. Rashi on Gen. 32:25.
2. Rashi on Gen. 32:25.
3. Menachem ben Sorek on Gen. 32:25.
4. Jonathan Sacks, "Jacob Wrestling," 2007, Rabbi Sacks Legacy, www.rabbisacks .org/covenant-conversation/vayishlach/jacob-wrestling.
5. "Vayislach," adapted by Rabbi Yael Levy, Nov. 30, 2017, A Way In, www.awayin .org/teachings-archive/2017/11/30/vayishlach.

6. Sacks, "Jacob Wrestling."
7. Hayyim on Gen. 33:3.

Va-yeshev

1. Rashi on Gen. 37:13.
2. Rashi on Gen. 37:15.
3. Rashi on Gen. 37:17.
4. Menachem Mendel Schneerson, "A Rift Extending across History," adapted by Yanki Tauber, Chabad, 2014, www.chabad.org/parshah/article_cdo/aid/1122 /jewish/A-Rift-Extending-Across-History.htm.
5. Schneerson, "A Rift Extending across History."
6. Schneerson, "A Rift Extending across History."

Mikkets

1. Ibn Ezra on Gen. 42:7.
2. Rashi on Gen. 42:7.
3. Sforno on Gen. 42:7.
4. Jonathan Sacks, "Disguise," 2006, Rabbi Sacks Legacy, www.rabbisacks.org /covenant-conversation/mikketz/disguise.
5. Shapira, B'nei Machshava Tovah, 36.
6. Shapira, B'nei Machshava Tovah, 36–37.

Va-yiggash

1. Rashi on Gen. 44:18.
2. Sforno on Gen. 44:18.
3. Sforno on Gen. 44:17–18.
4. Rambam, Mishneh Torah, hilchot ha'tshuva, halakhah 2, Sefaria, www.sefaria.org /Mishneh_Torah,_Repentance.2.1.
5. Dov Ber Friedman, Or Torah, in Green, Leader, and Mayse, Speaking Torah, vol. 1, 431.
6. Jonathan Sacks, "Vayigash: The Birth of Forgiveness," 2011, www.rabbisacks.org /covenant-conversation/vayigash/the-birth-of-forgiveness/.
7. Rashi on Gen. 47:28.

Va-yeḥi

1. Author's translation.
2. Rashi on Gen. 47:29.
3. Onkelos on Gen. 47:29.
4. Nachman of Breslov, Likutey Moharan, 55.
5. Shmuel Weiss's article "Talk Ain't Cheap" appeared on the "Torah from Dixie" website in July 2010 but is no longer available online.
6. This popularly quoted teaching is variously attributed to Rebbe Nachman and the Lubavitcher Rebbe; I was unable to locate the source.

Shemot

1. Rashi on Exod. 3:2.
2. Nachmanides on Exod. 3:5.
3. I learned this teaching from Rabbi Shalom Brodt at an in-person class in Jerusalem in 2013.
4. Gematria refers to the practice of assigning numerical values to the letters of the Hebrew alphabet. As used in biblical interpretation, when two different words or phrases share the same gematria, it means they are related to each other.
5. Adapted from Rabbi Shalom Brodt's teaching at an in-person class in Jerusalem in 2013.
6. Jonathan Sacks, "Of What Was Moses Afraid," 2008, Rabbi Sacks Legacy, www .rabbisacks.org/covenant-conversation/shemot/of-what-was-moses-afraid.
7. Shapira, *B'nei Machshava Tovah*, 16.

Va-'era'

1. *Shemot Rabbah*, 86.
2. Kook, *Rav Kook Hagadah*, 171–74.
3. Twersky, *Me'or Eynayim*, vol. 1, 261.
4. Green, Leader, and Mayse, *Speaking Torah*, vol.1, 177.
5. This is a well-known reading in Hasidism, but I do not have a specific source for it.

Bo'

1. Rashi on Exod. 12:2.
2. Sforno on Exod. 12:2.
3. The author translated and adapted this teaching from Berezovsky, *Netivot Shalom*, vol. *Shemot*, 85–88.
4. *Sanhedrin* 45a.
5. *Sanhedrin* 42a.

Be-shallaḥ

1. Sforno on Exod. 14:30.
2. *Pesikta de-Rav Kahana*, ed. S. Buber, 189a.
3. *Mekhilta d'Rabbi Yishmael, Vayehi Beshalach* 5:17 on Exod. 14:21.
4. Menachem Mendel Schneerson, "The Muddy Path," adapted by Yanki Tauber, Chabad, 2011, www.chabad.org/holidays/passover/pesach_cdo/aid/2851/jewish /The-Muddy-Path.htm.
5. Schneerson, "The Muddy Path."

Yitro

1. Author's translation.
2. *Mekhilta d'Rabbi Yishmael, Shira* 8:10, on Exod. 20:1.

3. *Makkot* 24a.

4. *Mekhilta d'Rabbi Yishmael, Bachodesh* 9:8, on Exod. 20:15.

5. Ibn Ezra on Exod. 20:15.

6. Sforno on Exod. 20:15.

7. *Tanḥuma, Nitzavim* 3:1.

8. *Tanḥuma, Nitzavim* 3:1.

9. *Ta'anit* 26b.

10. *Shabbat* 105a.

11. Shapira, *Drashot M'Shanot Ha'Za'am*, 139–40.

12. Shapira, *Derekh haMelekh*, 257.

13. Shapira, *Derekh haMelekh*, 258, 260.

Mishpatim

1. Author's translation.

2. Rashbam on Exod. 24:7.

3. *Aggadat Bereshit* 74:2.

4. Shapira, *Derekh haMelekh*, 540.

5. Shneur Zalman of Liadi, *Likkutei Amarim Tanya*, 11–13.

6. Maimonides, *Hilchot Yesodei HaTorah*, 2:10.

7. *Tikunei Zohar*, Introduction.

8. *Tikunei Zohar* 92a.

9. Twersky, *Me'or Eynayim*, 313–15.

10. Twersky, *Me'or Eynayim*, 313–15.

11. Green, Leader, and Mayse, *Speaking Torah*, vol. 1, 212.

Terumah

1. Ibn Ezra on Exod. 25:8.

2. Or HaHayim on Exod. 25:8.

3. Rashi on Exod. 15:2.

4. Kotzker Rebbe's and Samson Raphael Hirsch's comments in *Stone Chumash*, 377.

5. Steinsaltz, *Psalms with Commentary*, 107.

6. Berezovsky, *Netivot Shalom: Shemot*, 196.

7. Yisroel Hopstein, "Avodat Yisrael," in Feigelson, *Eternal Questions*, 109.

8. Feigelson, *Eternal Questions*, 109.

Tetsavveh

1. *Kitzur Baal HaTurim* on Exod. 27:20.

2. Nachmanides on Exod. 19:6.

3. YaShaR on Exod. 19:6.

4. Sforno on Exod. 19:6.

5. Adam Jacobs, "Reincarnation in Judaism," Jan. 2011, www.huffpost.com/entry/reincarnation-in-judaism_b_811379.

6. *Makkot* 11a.

7. Rabbeinu Bahya on Exod. 32:32.

Ki Tissa'

1. Rashi on Num. 1:1.
2. Rashi on Exod. 30:12.
3. Berezovsky, *Netivot Shalom: Shemot*, 230.
4. Maimonides, *Mishneh Torah*, Zemanim, "The Laws of Shekalim," 1:1, Sefaria, 2021, www.sefaria.org/Mishneh_Torah%2C_Sheqel_Dues.1?lang=en .
5. Leiner, *Mei HaShiloach*, vol. 1, 149.
6. Jonathan Sacks, "Counting the Contributions," 2010, Rabbi Sacks Legacy, www .rabbisacks.org/covenant-conversation/ki-tissa/counting-the-contributions.
7. Twerski, *Let Us Make Man*, 4.

Va-yak'hel / Pekudei

1. Rashi on Exod. 35:2.
2. Heschel, *Sabbath*, 6.
3. Twersky, *Me'or Eynayim*, 598.
4. Twersky, *Me'or Eynayim*, 598.
5. Twersky, *Me'or Eynayim*, 599.
6. *Shabbat* 118b; Shapira, *Drashot M'Shanot Ha'Za'am*, 108–9.

Va-yikra'

1. Rashi on Lev. 1:1.
2. *Sanhedrin* 37a.
3. Shapira, *Derekh haMelekh*, 131.
4. Abramson, *Torah from the Years of Wrath*, 30, 54.
5. Shapira, *B'nei Machshava Tovah*, 28.
6. Twersky, *Me'or Eynayim*, 361.
7. Green, *Speaking Torah*, vol. 1, 250.
8. Or HaHayim on Exod. 3:8.

Tsav

1. Chizkuni on Lev. 6:6.
2. Chizkuni on Lev. 6:6.
3. Ibn Ezra on Prov. 20:27.
4. Kook, *Orot HaKodesh*, vol. 3, 3:1:11.
5. Kook, *Orot HaKodesh*, vol. 3, 3:1:11.
6. Rav Yaakov HaLevi Filber, "Bringing Fire from the Ordinary Person" [in Hebrew], 2018, Arutz Sheva, www.inn.co.il/news/523283. Author's translation.

Shemini

1. Rashi on Lev. 10:3.
2. Nachmanides on Lev. 10:3.

3. Sforno on Lev. 10:3.

4. Understanding when and how the Jewish tradition theologically understands death as a sanctification of the Eternal is of extreme importance, but beyond the scope of this book.

5. *Mishnah Avot* 1:17.

6. *Berakhot* 17a.

7. Tzvi Hirsch Ressler, "Tzemach HaShem L'Tzvi," in Green, Leader, and Mayse, *Speaking Torah*, vol. 1, 347–48.

Tazria' / Metsora'

1. Rashi on Lev. 13:6.

2. Chizkuni on Lev. 13:6.

3. Maimonides, *Mishneh Torah*, "Defilmenet by Tza'ra'at" 16:10, Sefaria, 2020, www.sefaria.org/Mishneh_Torah%2C_Defilement_by_Leprosy.16.10?lang=bi.

4. *Arakhin* 15a.

5. *Beitzah* 16a.

6. Yissakhar Dov Ber of Zloczow, "Mevasser Tzedek," in Green, Leader, and Mayse, *Speaking Torah*, vol. 1, 341–42.

7. Yissakhar Dov Ber of Zloczow, "Mevasser Tzedek," 341–42.

8. Yissakhar Dov Ber of Zloczow, "Mevasser Tzedek," 341–42.

9. Green's comments in Green, Leader, and Mayse, *Speaking Torah*, vol. 1, 278.

'Aḥarei Mot / Kedoshim

1. Chizkuni on Lev. 16:17.

2. *Bekhor Shor* on Lev. 16:17.

3. Leiner, *Mei HaShiloach*, vol. 1, 122.

4. Leiner, *Mei HaShiloach*, vol. 2, 85.

5. Shapira, *Tzav V'Ziruz*, 384–86.

'Emor

1. *Yevamot* 114a; Rashi on Lev. 21:1.

2. Alshich on Lev. 21:1.

3. *Mishnah Avot*, 1:12.

4. Sforno on Exod. 19:6.

5. Zohar, vol. 2, 90b.

6. Twersky, *Me'or Eynayim*, 406.

7. Twersky, *Me'or Eynayim*, 406.

8. Twersky, *Me'or Eynayim*, 406.

9. Twersky, *Me'or Eynayim*, 406.

Be-har / Be-ḥukkotai

1. Author's translation.

2. Rashi on Lev. 26:3.

3. Sforno on Lev. 26:3.
4. Dov Ber Friedman, "Ohr Torah," in Green, Leader, and Mayse, *Speaking Torah*, vol. 1, 319–20.
5. Friedman, "Ohr Torah," 319–20.
6. Friedman, "Ohr Torah," 319–20.

Be-midbar

1. Rashbam on Num. 1:1.
2. *Bemidbar Rabbah* 1:7.
3. Zohar 1:149a.
4. Yaakov Yosef of Ostreg, "Rav Yeevi," in Green, Leader, and Mayse, *Speaking Torah*, vol. 2, 415.
5. Yaakov Yosef of Ostreg, "Rav Yeevi," 415.
6. Green, *Judaism for the World*, 172.

Naso'

1. Rashi on Num. 6:23.
2. Malbim, on Num. 6:23.
3. Morgenstern, *Sefer B'Yam Darkecha*, 18. Translation by Jonah Gelfand.
4. Avraham Hayyim of Zloczow, "Orakh Le-Hayyim," in Green, Leader, and Mayse, *Speaking Torah*, vol. 2, 411–12.
5. Avraham Hayyim of Zloczow, "Orakh Le-Hayyim," 411–12.
6. Avraham Hayyim of Zloczow, "Orakh Le-Hayyim," 411–12.

Be-ha'alotekha

1. This is because the ritual offering in Hebrew is *korban*, which derives from *karov*, closeness. Spiritually, bringing the *korban* provides a means to feel closer to God, and ideally the person experiences a greater sense of aliveness through this ritual. By contrast, death is equated energetically with "turning off" the Creator's life-giving energies. A person who touches a corpse spiritually absorbs this "no longer alive" energy and needs to undergo a ritual to once again "turn on" the life-giving energies.
2. Rashi on Num. 9:7.
3. Chizkuni on Num. 9:10.
4. Avraham Arieh Trugman, "Pesach Sheni," 2021, *Ohr Chadash*, www.thetrugmans .com/pesach-sheni-2/.
5. Yosef Yitzhak Schneersohn, "Pesach Sheni: Still Time to Connect," translated by Uri Kaploun, 2014, www.chabad.org/therebbe/article_cdo/aid/96070/jewish /Pesach-Sheni-Still-Time-to-Connect.htm.

Shelaḥ-Lekha

1. Or HaHayim on Num. 13:27.
2. Rashi on Num. 13:31.

3. *Sotah* 35a.

4. Twerski, *Let Us Make Man*, 10.

5. Rashi on Num. 13:30, referencing *Sotah* 35a.

6. Raz Hartman, "Parshat Shelach" [in Hebrew], *Kehillat V'Ani Tefillah* (weekly newsletter), 2014.

7. Rosen, *Quest for Authenticity*, 141.

8. Hartman, "Parshat Shelach."

9. Hartman, "Parshat Shelach."

10. Shapira, *Drashot M'Shanot Ha'Za'am*, 144–45.

11. Shapira, *Tzav V'Ziruz*, 340.

Koraḥ

1. *Tanḥuma, Korach* 1; Rashi on Num. 16:1.

2. *Tanḥuma, Korach* 4.

3. Rashi on Num. 16:4.

4. Bekhor Shor on Num. 16:4. Emphasis added.

5. Netziv, *Ha'Amek Dvar*, on Num. 16:4.

6. Or HaHayim on Num. 16:4.

7. *Zohar*, vol. 3, 176a.

8. Berezovsky, *Netivot Shalom: Be-midbar*, 97–98.

9. Berezovsky, *Netivot Shalom: Be-midbar*, 97–98.

Ḥukkat / Balak

1. Rashi on Num. 24:2.

2. Malbim, on Num. 24:2.

3. Rashi on Num. 24:2.

4. *Tanḥuma*, Balak 3.

5. Rashi on Num. 24:2; *Baba Batra* 60a.

6. Dov Ber Friedman, "Or Torah," in Green, Leader, and Mayse, *Speaking Torah*, vol. 2, 381.

7. Friedman, "Or Torah," 381.

8. Author's translation; Friedman, "Or Torah," 381.

Pinḥas

1. Robert K. Greenleaf, "What Is Servant Leadership?," 2021, Robert K. Greenleaf Center for Servant Leadership, www.greenleaf.org/what-is-servant-leadership.

2. Or HaHayim on Num. 27:15.

3. Rashi on Num. 27:15, pulling from *Midrash Tanḥuma, Pinchas* 10.

4. Rabbeinu Bahya on Num. 27:17.

5. Shapira, *Drashot M'Shanot Ha'Za'am*, 148.

6. Kook, *Shemoneh Kvatzim*, 3:81.

7. Shapira, *Tzav V'Ziruz*, 331.

8. Shapira, *Tzav V'Ziruz*, 331.

9. Shapira, *Tzav V'Ziruz*, 331–32.

Mattot / Maseʿei

1. Moses the Preacher on Num. 33:1, in Rashi on Num. 33:1.
2. *Midrash Tanḥuma* 4:10:3, in Rashi on Num. 33:1.
3. Heschel, *God in Search of Man*, 45–46.
4. Maimonides, *Guide to the Perplexed* 3, 50.
5. Sforno on Num. 33:1.
6. Ephraim, *Degel Mahaneh Ephraim*, 284.
7. Schneerson, *Likutei Sichot*, 353–54.
8. Schneerson, *Likutei Sichot*, 354.

Devarim

1. Author's translation.
2. Ibn Ezra on Deut. 1:7.
3. Enger, "To Take the Next Step," in *Torah Without End.*
4. Tisha b'Av is the ninth of the summer month of Av and the anniversary of the destruction of both of Israel's holy Temples in Jerusalem, the first in 425 BCE by the ancient Babylonians and the second in 70 CE by the Roman Empire. Tisha b'Av has become the saddest day in the Jewish calendar. Over the past two thousand years, this is when the Jewish people's sense of living in the Diaspora, in exile, peaks and is most acute. The establishment of the State of Israel in 1948 has profoundly tempered this sentiment. Because the first word in the Book of Isaiah is *hazon* — "vision" — the tradition refers to the Shabbat prior to Tisha b'Av as "*Shabbat Hazon.*"
5. Malbim, on Isa. 1:3.

Va-'etḥannan

1. This translation is faithful to THE JPS TANAKH: Gender-Sensitive Edition except for the author's inclusion of the word "and" to begin the final sentence, which appears in other translations and is essential to this commentary.
2. Sforno on Deut. 6:4.
3. *Sifrei Devarim* 32:1.
4. Rashi on Deut. 6:5.
5. *Berakhot 54a.*
6. Green, *Well of Living Insight*, 105.
7. Shneur Zalman of Liadi, *Likkutei Amarim Tanya*, 14.

ʿEkev

1. *Tanḥuma, Eikev* 1; Rashi on Deut. 7:12.
2. Magriso, *Me'Am Lo'ez: Avoth*, 70–71.
3. Magriso, *Me'Am Lo'ez: Avoth*, 70–71.
4. Maimonides on *Mishnah Avot* 2:1.

5. Israel ben Eliezer, *Tza'va'ot M'Rivash Tov*, 35.

6. Rosen, *Quest for Authenticity*, 139.

Re'eh

1. Ibn Ezra on Deut. 11:26.

2. Malbim, on Deut. 11:26–28.

3. Lew, *This Is Real*, 65–66.

4. Lew, *This is Real*, 66–67.

5. Soloveitchik, *Lonely Man of Faith*, 2.

6. Shapira, *B'nei Machshava Tovah*, 28.

7. Shapira, *Drashot M'Shanot Ha'Za'am*, 213.

Shofetim

1. *Sifrei Devarim* 173:3; Rashi on Deut. 18:13.

2. Nachmanides on Deut. 18:13.

3. Chizkuni on Deut. 18:13.

4. Avraham Hayyim of Zloczow, *Orakh Le-Hayyim*, in Green, Leader, and Mayse, *Speaking Torah*, vol. 2, 338–39.

5. Avraham Hayyim of Zloczow, *Orakh Le-Hayyim*, 338–39.

6. Shapira, *B'nei Machshava Tovah*, 36–37.

7. Shapira, *B'nei Machshava Tovah*, 38.

8. Shapira, *B'nei Machshava Tovah*, 38.

Ki Tetse'

1. *Chullin* 142a.

2. Ibn Ezra on Deut. 22:7.

3. Maimonides, *Moreh Nevuhim* 3, 48.

4. *Berakhot* 33b.

5. Levi Yitzchak of Berditchev, *Kedushat Levi*, in Green, Leader, and Mayse, *Speaking Torah*, vol. 2, 333–34.

6. Levi Yitzchak of Berditchev, *Kedushat Levi*, 333–34.

7. Zohar 1:77b.

8. Levi Yitzchak of Berditchev, *Kedushat Levi*, 333–34.

9. Levi Yitzchak of Berditchev, *Kedushat Levi*, 333–34.

10. Tenzin Gyatso, the Dalai Lama, "Compassion and the Individual," Office of His Holiness the Dalai Lama, 2022, www.dalailama.com/messages/compassion-and-human-values/compassion.

Ki Tavo'

1. *Sifrei Dvarim*, 49:1 on Deut. 11:22.

2. *Sefer HaHinuch*, 485.

3. Yisrael Meir Kagen, "Introduction to the Laws of the Prohibition of Lashon Hara and Rechilut," Positive Commandment 14, *Chofetz Chaim*, Sefaria, 2011, www

.sefaria.org/Chafetz_Chaim%2C_Introduction_to_the_Laws_of_the_Prohibition
_of_Lashon_Hara_and_Rechilut%2C_Positive_Commandments.14?lang=bi&
with=About&lang2=en.

4. Menachem Mendel Schneerson, *Likkutei Sichot*, vol. 4, 1130–35, adapted from
Eliyahu Touger's translation of the original Yiddish, Chabad, 2017, www.chabad
.org/therebbe/article_cdo/aid/2613867/jewish/Likkutei-Sichot-Ki-Savo.htm.

5. Menachem Mendel Schneerson, *Likkutei Sichot*, vol. 4, 1130–35.

6. Shapira, *B'nei Machshava Tovah*, 27–28.

7. Menachem Mendel Schneerson, *Likkutei Sichot*, vol. 4, 1130–35.

Nitsavim / Va-yelekh

1. Author's translation.

2. Author's translation.

3. For example, the Ten Utterances (Commandments) originally given at Mount
Sinai (Exod. 20:1–14) recurs in Deuteronomy (5:6–18).

4. Rashi on Deut. 10:16.

5. Sforno on Deut. 10:16.

6. Rabbeinu Bahya on Deut. 10:16.

7. Ibn Ezra on Deut. 30:6.

8. Simone Knego, "Vulnerability Is the Key to Authentic Connection and Growth,"
May 26, 2023, www.simoneknego.com/vulnerability-is-the-path-to-authentic
-connection-and-growth/.

9. Dr. Vivek Murthy's remarks were recorded in the NPR news show "All Things
Considered," May 2, 2023, www.npr.org/2023/05/02/1173418268/loneliness
-connection-mental-health-dementia-surgeon-general.

10. This quote is popularly attributed to Anaïs Nin but I was unable to locate a particular source.

11. Shapira, *B'nei Machshava Tovah*, 7.

12. Shapira, *B'nei Machshava Tovah*, 7.

13. Shapira, *B'nei Machshava Tovah*, 21–23.

Ha'azinu

1. Author's translation.

2. Ibn Ezra on Deut. 32:1.

3. *Netziv, Haamek Dvar*, Deut. 32:18.

4. Sforno on Deut. 32:18.

5. Rashi on Deut. 32:18.

6. Shapira, *B'nei Machshava Tovah*, 11.

7. Shapira, *B'nei Machshava Tovah*, 9.

8. Shapira, *B'nei Machshava Tovah*, 11.

9. Shapira, *B'nei Machshava Tovah*, 11.

10. Shapira, *B'nei Machshava Tovah*, 11.

11. Shapira, *B'nei Machshava Tovah*, 11.

12. Shapira, *B'nei Machshava Tovah*, 11.

Ve-zo't ha-berakhah

1. *Moed Katan* 28a.
2. Rashi on Deut. 34:10.
3. Nachmanides on Deut. 34:10.
4. Bekhor Shor on Deut. 34:12.
5. Chizkuni on Deut. 34:12.
6. Netziv, *Ha'amek Davar*, Deut. 34:12.
7. *Yevamot* 97a.
8. Yissakhar Dov Ber, *Mevasser Tsedek*, in Green, Leader, and Mayse, *Speaking Torah*, vol. 2, 314–15.
9. Schuck, "Eye See the End and It's the Beginning."

BIBLIOGRAPHY

Abramson, Henry. *Torah from the Years of Wrath 1939–1943: The Historical Context of the Aish Kodesh*. N.p.: CreateSpace, 2017.

Berezovsky, Sholom Noach. *Netivot Shalom: Be-midbar*. Jerusalem: Yeshivat Beit Avraham Slonim, 2000.

———. *Netivot Shalom: Bere'shit*. Jerusalem: Yeshivat Beit Avraham Slonim, 2000.

———. *Netivot Shalom: Shemot*. Jerusalem: Yeshivat Beit Avraham Slonim, 2000.

Bonhardt, Simcha Bunim. *Ramatayim Zofim*. Warsaw: n.p., 1882.

Boorstein, Sylvia. *That's Funny, You Don't Look Buddhist: On Being a Faithful Jew and a Passionate Buddhist*. San Francisco: Harper Collins, 1997.

Buber, Martin. *Tales of the Hasidim*. Book 1, *The Early Masters*. Book 2, *The Later Masters*. New York: Schocken Books, 1947.

Dessler, Elijah Eliezer. *Michtav Me'Eliyahu*. Edited by Arych Carmel. Jerusalem: Feldheim, 1994.

Eliezer, Israel ben. *Keter Shem Tov haShalem*. New York: Kehot Publication Society, 2004.

———. *Tza'va'ot M'Rivash Tov*. Jerusalem: Beit Ha'Ba'al Shem Tov, 2013.

Enger, Cindy. "To Take the Next Step." In *Torah without End: Neo-Hasidic Teachings and Practices in Honor of Rabbi Jonathan Slater*, edited by Michael Strassfeld, 88–89. Teaneck NJ: Ben Yehuda Press, 2022.

Ephraim, Moshe Chaim. *Degel Mahaneh Ephraim*. Jerusalem: Ohr HaHayim, 2011.

Feigelson, Josh. *Eternal Questions: Reflections, Conversations, and Jewish Mindfulness Practices for the Weekly Torah Portion*. Teaneck NJ: Ben Yehuda Press, 2022.

Ginsburgh, Yitzchak. *Rectifying the State of Israel: A Political Platform Based on Kabbalah*. 2nd ed. Jerusalem: Gal Einai, 2003.

Green, Arthur, ed. *Hasidic Spirituality for a New Era: The Religious Writings of Hillel Zeitlin*. Mahwah NJ: Paulist Press, 2012.

———. *Judaism for the World: Reflections on God, Life, and Love*. New Haven CT: Yale University Press, 2020.

———. *Well of Living Insight: Comments on the Siddur*. Monee IL: Be'er Press. 2023.

Green, Arthur, Ebn Leader, Ariel Evan Mayse, and Or N. Rose, eds. *Speaking Torah: Spiritual Teachings from around the Maggid's Table*. 2 vols. Woodstock VT: Jewish Lights, 2013.

Green, Arthur, and Ariel Evan Mayse, eds. *A New Hasidism: Branches*. Philadelphia: The Jewish Publication Society, 2019.

———. *A New Hasidism: Roots*. Philadelphia: The Jewish Publication Society, 2019.

Greenleaf, Robert K. *The Servant as Leader*. South Orange NJ: Greenleaf Center for Servant Leadership, 2015.

Held, Shai. *Abraham Joshua Heschel: The Call of Transcendence*. Bloomington, IN: Indiana University Press, 2013.

Heschel, Abraham Joshua. *God in Search of Man*. New York: Farrar, Straus, and Giroux, 1955.

————. *The Sabbath: Its Meaning for Modern Man*. New York: Harper & Row, 1966.

Idel, Moshe. "The Rebbe of Piaseczno: Between Two Trends in Hasidism." In *Hasidism, Suffering and Renewal: The Prewar and Holocaust Legacy of Rabbi Kalonymus Kalman Shapira*, edited by Don Seeman, Daniel Reiser, and Ariel Evan Mayse, 29–53. Albany NY: SUNY Press, 2021.

Jacobs, Louis. *The Doctrine of the Zaddik in the Thought of Elimelech of Lizensk*. Cincinnati OH: Judaic Studies Program, University of Cincinnati, 1978.

THE JPS TANAKH: Gender-Sensitive Edition. Philadelphia: The Jewish Publication Society, 2023.

Kahane, Meir. *Beyond Words: Selected Writings of Rabbi Meir Kahane, 1960–1990*. Edited by David Fein. 7 vols. Brooklyn NY: Institute for Publication of the Writings of Rabbi Meir Kahane, 2010.

Kook, Abraham Isaac. *The Lights of Penitence, the Moral Principles, Lights of Holiness, Essays, Letters, and Poems*. Translated by Ben Zion Bokser. New York: Paulist Press, 1978.

————. *Olat Ra'ayah*. Jerusalem: Mossad HaRav Kook, 1948.

————. *Orot HaKodesh*. Jerusalem: Mossad HaRav Kook, 2022.

————. *Orot: Orot HaTchiya*. Jerusalem: Maggid Books, 2015.

————. "Pinkas Yerushalayim." Unpublished manuscript, 1933.

————. *The Rav Kook Hagadah: Springtime of the World*. Trans Bezalel Naor. Spring Valley NY: Orot, 2012.

————. *Shmoneh Kvatzim*. Jerusalem: Mossad HaRav Kook, 2020.

The Koren Siddur. Jerusalem: Koren, 2016.

Kushner, Harold S. *When Bad Things Happen to Good People*. 20th anniversary edition. New York: Schocken Books, 2001.

Leiner, Mordechai Yosef. *Mei HaShiloach*. 2 vols. Bnei Brak: Elchanan Reuven Goldhaver and Yehuda Yosef Spieglman, 2021.

Levinas, Emmanuel. *Ethics and Infinity*. Translated by Richard A. Cohen. Pittsburgh: Duquesne University Press, 1985.

Lew, Alan. *This Is Real and You Are Completely Unprepared*. Boston: Little, Brown, 2003.

Luzzatto, Moses Hayyim. *Mesillat Yesharim: The Path of the Upright*. Translated by Mordecai Menahem Kaplan. Commentary by Ira F. Stone. Philadelphia: The Jewish Publication Society, 2010.

Magriso, Yitzchak ben Moshe. *MeAm Lo'Ez: Avoth*. Edited by Aryeh Kaplan. Translated by David N. Barocas. New York and Jerusalem: Moznaim, 1990.

Maisels, James. "The Self and Self-Transformation in the Thought and Practice of Rabbi Kalonymus Kalmish Shapira." PhD diss., University of Chicago, 2014.

Malbim, Meir Leibush ben Yehiel Michal Wisser. *Peirush HaMalbim Ha-me-nukad HaShalem*. Jerusalem: Chorev, 2011.

Morgenstern, Yitzchok Myer. *Sefer B'Yam Darkecha: Darkhei Avodah L'Ma'aseh*. 8th ed. Bnei Brak: n.p., 2022.

Morinis, Alan. *Everyday Holiness: The Jewish Spiritual Path of Mussar*. Boston: Trumpeter, 2007.

Nachman of Breslov. *Likutey Moharan*. Vol. 5, *Lessons 33–48*. Edited by Ozer Bergman. Translated by Moshe Mykoff. Jerusalem and New York: Breslov Research Institute, 1997.

Pinson, DovBer. *Breathing and Quieting the Mind*. New York: Iyyun, 2014.

Rabinowicz, Yaakov Yitzchak. *Nifla'ot ha-Yehudi*. Jerusalem: Yo'etz Kim Kadesh Rakatz, 1992.

Reiser, Daniel. "Sarah Our Rebbe: R. Kalonymus Kalman Shapira's Feminine Spiritual Leadership in the Warsaw Ghetto." *Nashim: A Journal of Jewish Women's Studies and Gender Issues* 38 (Spring 2021): 7–24.

Rosen, Michael. *The Quest for Authenticity: The Thought of R' Simcha Bunim*. Jerusalem: Urim, 2008.

Rosenberg, Shimon Gershon (Shagar). *Faith Shattered and Restored: Judaism in the Postmodern Age*. Translated by Eli Leshem. Jerusalem· Maggid, 2017.

Sacks, Jonathan *Faith in the Future*. Macon GA: Mercer University Press, 1997.

Schachter-Shalomi, Zalman. *Jewish with Feeling: A Guide to Meaningful Jewish Practice*. New York: Riverhead Trade, 2006.

Schneerson, Menachem Mendel. *Likutei Sichot*. Vol. 2. New York: Vaad L'Hafotzas Sichos, 1998.

Schuck, David. "Eye See the End and It's the Beginning." In *Torah without End: Neo-Hasidic Teachings and Practices in Honor of Rabbi Jonathan Slater*, edited by Michael Strassfeld, 106–7. Teaneck NJ: Ben Yehuda Press, 2022.

Sefer HaHinuch. Jerusalem: Yafeh Nof, 2019.

Shapira, Kalonymus Kalmish. *B'nei Machshava Tovah*. Jerusalem: Vad Hasidei Piaseczner, 1989.

———. *Conscious Community: A Guide to Inner Work*. Translated and edited by Andrea Cohen-Kiener. Northvale NJ: Jason Aronson, 1996.

———. *Derekh haMelekh*. Jerusalem and Nanuet: Feldheim, 2011.

———. *Drashot M'Shanot Ha'Za'am*. Edited by Daniel Reiser. Jerusalem: Herzog Academic College and Yad VaShem, 2017.

———. *Experiencing the Divine: A Guide to Jewish Spiritual Practice and Community*. Translated by Yaakov David Shulman. Self-published, 2017.

———. *Sacred Fire: Torah from the Years of Fury 1939–1942*. Translated by J. Hershy Worch. Lanham MD: Rowman & Littlefield, 2002.

———. *Tzav V'Ziruz*. Jerusalem: Feldheim, 2001.

Shneur Zalman of Liadi. *Likkutei Amarim Tanya*. Brooklyn NY: Kehot Publication Society and Otzer HaHasidim, 2013.

Soloveitchik, Joseph B. *The Lonely Man of Faith*. New York: Doubleday, 2006.

Steinsaltz, Adin. *Opening the Tanya: Discovering the Moral and Mystical Teachings of a Classic Work of Kabbalah*. San Francisco: Jossey-Bass Publishing, 2003.

———. *Psalms with Commentary*. Jerusalem: Koren, 2016.

Stone, Ira F. *A Responsible Life: The Spiritual Path of Mussar*. New York: Aviv Press, 2006.

The Stone Chumash. Brooklyn NY: Mesorah, 1993.

Twerski, Abraham J. *Let Us Make Man: Self-Esteem through Jewishness*. Brooklyn NY: C.I.S., 1987.

Twersky, Manahum Nahum. *Me'or Eynayim*. Bnei Brak: Peer Mikdoshim, 2015.

Wiesel, Elie. *Messengers of God*. New York: Simon & Schuster, 1985.

Wineberg, Yosef. *Lessons in Tanya: The Tanya of R. Shneur Zalman of Liadi*. Translated by Levy Wineberg and Sholom B. Wineberg. Brooklyn NY: Kehot Publication Society, 1982.

www.ingramcontent.com/pod-product-compliance
Lightning Source LLC
Chambersburg PA
CBHW031602060326
40783CB00026B/4182